Jill Foster started out as an actress at the age of 12 and retired at 17. She has been a literary agent for 18 years and has run her own agency for 8 years, representing mostly television writers and actors. In 1970 she married Malcolm Hamer and they have a daughter, Polly.

Malcolm Hamer had a traditional education at Shrewsbury School and Trinity College, Cambridge, He worked in marketing for 10 years and in 1971 set up an agency to represent sportsmen. He is now a literary agent and specialises in non-fiction authors and television journalists.

The Peaudouce
Family Welcome Guide

JILL FOSTER AND MALCOLM HAMER

SPHERE BOOKS LIMITED
London and Sydney

First published in Great Britain in 1984 by Sphere Books Ltd
30-32 Gray's Inn Road, London WC1X 8JL
Copyright © 1984 Hamer Books Ltd.

0 7221 41890

Printed and bound in Great Britain by
Billings, Guildford and Worcester

To Polly, whose arrival ensured the conception of this Guide.

Our thanks to our tireless researcher, **Simon Moore,** who shouldered the burden of much of the initial research; and to **Sheila Devo, Ann Foster** and **Alison Sharpe** for their help and support.

Our thanks to J M Dent & Sons Ltd for permission to quote Dylan Thomas (pages 58 & 218); and to the Society of Authors, the literary representatives of the estate of A E Housman, and Jonathan Cape Ltd, Publishers of A E Houseman's 'Collected Poems', for permission to quote the lines on pages 109 & 208.

Contents

Introduction

When Polly was born to us – parents for the first time at the ripe old age of forty – we were prepared for some disruption to our comfortable lives, but not for the realisation that we could no longer, on a whim, bowl into any hotel, pub or restaurant that we fancied and be reasonably well looked after. Easy on a sunny day to sit in a pub garden, but what about the non-sunny days? (And we didn't want to inflict our brat on adults out to have a quiet drink.) No fun for Jill to fight a lamb chop or tackle a plate of spaghetti bolognaise with Polly balanced on her knee. These and other similar experiences led us to seek out places – particularly places where we could eat, drink and sleep – where the parents can relax and enjoy themselves because facilities are available for the children. So we wrote this guide.

The first thing that has to be said is that the standards in this country are appallingly low.

Of course there are exceptions – most of them in this book we hope – but mainly the food is poor, the service is sloppy and the buildings and decor shabby. Above all, parents who want some simple enjoyment are treated like second-class citizens.

The bare essentials we look for are these:

> HOTELS with cots, high chairs and a baby-listening service;
> PUBS with proper and legal children's or family rooms (the legal definition being rooms which do not serve alcohol);
> RESTAURANTS with high chairs and which offer a special menu and/or reduced portions for children.

Every establishment listed in the guide has those basic facilities and, where we could find it, more: for example we've found hotels with swimming pools, play areas, squash and tennis courts, access to golf courses, supervised crèches (nothing like enough of those); pubs with pleasant gardens and play areas; restaurants with somewhere for a mother to change and breast-feed a baby in comfort and privacy. Above all, we've tried to pick places we think you'll be glad to arrive at. We've had a couple of 'average' families in mind (two lots of friends actually) and imagined them travelling to places we've recommended. Then we've asked –

> Would they like to come here for a drink, for a meal or to stay?
> Will they feel welcome?
> Is the place good to look at?
> Are the staff pleasant?
> Can they park the car easily?
> Is it good value?
> What sort of food is served? and so on.

Attitude, atmosphere and comfort have been our over-riding concern.

1

THE ENTRIES

We have given basic simple information, with no confusing symbols –

Name of the town or village *and its county.*

Name of the establishment, and whether we recommend it as somewhere to stay (**H**) to drink (**P**) or to eat (**R**).

Company by which it is owned *if there is one.*

Address.

Phone number: *an exchange precedes the number only if it is different from the name of the town or village.*

Directions: *in the main we give a road reference and there is also a map reference. Occasionally we've had to resort to 'in the centre of the town' and, on rare occasions, suggest you ask a local (only when it's all too confusing to explain in print).*

Description: *in which we try to convey what the place is like and why it might be useful or interesting to you (for a short or long break, close to a main travel route, in an area of great beauty, fun, etc).*

Number of rooms: *family rooms, triple rooms, intercommunicating rooms, suites, etc. There's no specific definition of a family room and the purpose is to indicate which hotels have larger rooms for families, although most have other rooms which will take an extra bed or cot.*

Bed and Breakfast for two: *hotel prices are alarmingly high throughout the country, but unfortunately, modestly priced hotels rarely have the facilities which we consider necessary for families, let alone the ambience and extra comforts. We have taken the lowest price for a double or twin room including service and VAT, for one night. Many hotels include breakfast in the price as a matter of course; and many modern hotels have a bathroom with every room. Where there is a choice we have excluded breakfast (you can usually eat cheaper around the corner or just have tea and toast); and have used the price for a double room without a bathroom. We have put these prices into three categories:*

Cheap	up to £30
Moderate	£31–£45
Expensive	Over £45

Hotels are in any case extraordinarily expensive and one night stops the most expensive way of using them. Wherever possible it is wise to take advantage of the many 'breaks' which are offered – 2 day, 5 day, 7 day, weekend and off-peak breaks.

Terms for children are included in the description and are for children sharing with a parent or parents. We have quoted 1984 prices when they were available, and when they were not have made an educated guess (usually with the help of the hotel in question).

Open/Closed: not pubs as, with rare exceptions, they are open every day of the year.

Meal times and prices: *mostly we've quoted for weekdays as the variation at weekends is not great. The prices are table d'hôte unless otherwise indicated; à la carte (alc) prices are average for a three course meal, excluding wine but including VAT. Pub food prices are included in the description.*

Ale means *real ale and we name the variety on offer. Hotels and pubs often change their brands, of course, but the presence of real ale indicates to us a landlord whose heart is in the right place.*

Credit Cards: *we have listed the four major cards – Access, American Express, Barclaycard/Visa and Diners Club.*

Parking: *very important to know what is available especially with children, luggage, pots and pushchairs in tow. We indicate what is available but warn you that hotels are sometimes careless at directing visitors to their own car parks. We have sometimes excluded a place from the guide because the parking was too much of a battle.*

HOTELS

We have not included many hotels in large cities, even though they may provide the three basics of cot, high chair and baby-listening. Most of them provide little else and, anyway, we think that you would prefer to stay in a good hotel a few miles outside the city which is more likely to be attractive and to have additional facilities like a garden, swimming pool, squash courts or, simply, peaceful surroundings.

If you need a room or a meal in a big town, however, the large groups of hotels (THF, Best Western, Crest, Thistle, Prestige, Ladbroke, Inter, Queens Moat, etc) almost always provide the basic facilities with free or cut-price accommodation for your children if they share with you, and special menus or reduced portions for them.

Avoid single night stays if you possibly can: you receive the best value by taking advantage of the many 'breaks' which are offered by all the hotels – at weekends, during winter, for two or more nights during the week and, best of all, for longer periods.

You will see that we recommend some of the hotels as restaurants too. The bar snacks and buffet lunches at some of them are excellent value – you can eat very well for £2 to £3 per adult head. Often, too, they have coffee shops which are open all day where hungry and thirsty families can find a haven outside the normal mealtimes.

Inspect the rooms before you take them to avoid sleeping over a kitchen or boiler room. We experienced both, the first allowed sleep only between 1am and 6.30am and the other heated our room to tropical intensity. The hotels were aware of the problems but nevertheless let us the rooms at full price. In both cases we complained forcefully and to good effect.

Which brings us to the last point on hotels: the standards are generally very poor and will only get better if we protest. So, protest if things aren't to your satisfaction – and let us know how you fare.

3

PUBS

Good pubs which welcome families are hard to find. It's not too difficult to find a jovial host who doesn't mind his bars being overrun by children to the annoyance of adults hoping for a quiet drink. We are not interested in that sort of pub, and have only listed those with a comfortable and legal family or children's room. We ought to stress that a pub is the publican's 'house' and he can order anyone out if he wishes; that applies to badly-behaved children as well as badly-behaved adults. We have tended to smile on those landlords who have made it plain that the enjoyment of the many will not be spoiled by the bad manners of the few. Quite tough some of them – good.

The legal position is wonderfully dotty and for those who are interested the main points are: Children up to fourteen must not enter a bar during permitted licensing hours, but can at the discretion of the landlord frequent any room which does not serve alcohol, or a garden, corridor, etc. At fourteen they can enter a bar, again at the discretion of the landlord, as long as they stick to soft drinks. From sixteen to eighteen they can 'purchase and consume beer, cider, perry or porter' (not wine) as long as it accompanies a meal and as long as both are consumed in a room designated for eating purposes. Then they're adult and can stand their own round.

We've tried to put in pubs which we consider especially good, but in some barren areas of the country have included places which, though nothing special, we felt to be just about passable and better than nothing.

Our aim was to find pubs which are attractive at first sight, have a pleasant atmosphere, welcoming and cheerful staff, a reasonable range of food and, if possible, real ale. The most encouraging aspect was to see how many pubs serve a good range of well-prepared food at reasonable prices. They appear to be taking over the role of the family restaurant.

RESTAURANTS

We wanted to find restaurants which are welcoming and attractive and which offer the basic help to parents of high chairs and children's menus or portions. The search has been depressing: the choice poor, the cooking amateur and the prices astronomical. How do most of them stay in business? We believe the restaurants we've chosen have the right attitude and would like to hear how you fare.

We were concerned too for the mothers of small babies wishing to eat out (and God knows, no-one needs a break more than a mother of a small baby). She may not wish to expose her breast to the public gaze and not many customers want to gaze at a bare bosom while tucking into the boeuf Wellington. She may not be overjoyed either at having to attend to the other end of her infant on the lino floor of a small lavatory. We have indicated where something a bit better is available – sometimes a well-equipped and spacious ladies' lavatory, sometimes a private room offered by sympathetic owners. But it's often back to the car or on the floor, girls.

We had the impression that English cooking was improving and this research has been a real sock in the eye. There are so many pseudo-posh and over-priced restaurants – 'you must wear a jacket and tie, sir', £20 a head, and a trolley serving forty brandies – but they give you frozen vegetables and a clear flavour of Oxo in the sauce. They're con artists and we're mugs to put up with it. **Complain.**

The chains of 'fast food' restaurants which are springing up everywhere make some effort to welcome families with children. All of the following have high chairs, and some offer a children's menu:

Beefeater Steak Houses – a 'Mr Men' menu for the very young and a 'Junior Diner's' menu.
Berni Steak Houses – half portions are served.
Garfunkel's – all in London. A children's menu is available. Steaks, pizzas, pasta and, glory be, big salad bars.
Happy Eater – children's menu and play areas. Standard burger, bacon and egg places.
Huckleberry's – most in London. Children's menus. Burgers.
Little Chef – countrywide on main roads. Children's menus. Burgers and bacon and egg places.
McDonald's – Burgers.
Pizza Hut – Pizzas.

Two further matters for complaint:

Why is the signposting so appalling in British towns? – and particularly in town centres where, assuming you're lucky enough to find your way in, you certainly won't be able to find the right road out. Hoteliers, too, seem keen to make you work hard to trace them with tiny signs hidden, wherever possible, by a convenient branch. Why can't we adopt the French system of putting small hotel signs at junctions?

Why are nearly all the children's menus so appallingly unhealthy? Any parent who wants her child to have a healthy diet will be pushed to find much other than burgers and chips, sausage and chips, and chips and chips.

During our research we looked too at stores and supermarkets, railway stations, airports, stately homes, etc, and you'll find our conclusions at the back of the book. What the whole exercise has taught us is that parents and young children who are, after all, the major present and future customers, are getting a raw deal. We've begun to fight and hope you'll join us. Ask for help and if you don't get it . . . complain.

We have telephoned thousands of pubs, restaurants and hotels and have visited over 2,000 of them; at least one of us has visited every place in the book. Inevitably changes take place, chefs and publicans leave, properties change hands, policies change, and so on. If you like our choice, please let us know; and if you don't like our choice, please *let us know and, above all, if you happen upon anyone trying to improve the lot of parents out with their children, please let us know. (Suitable forms at the back of the book.)*

THE PEAUDOUCE AWARDS

We tried to pick out the 'best of the best' on the grounds that it might encourage other establishments to improve their standards.

When we broached the difficult task of selecting the outstanding hotel, pub and restaurant, we had in mind the obvious criteria: that the winners would offer outstanding facilities and an immediate appeal to families. But above all we looked for owners or tenants and staff who were particularly caring and hospitable and generally sympathetic to the needs of parents who were out and about with their children.

It is interesting to note that our initial short list of about thirty shows no establishments between Evesham and Cumbria, apart from two lone nominations in Shropshire and North Wales.

These are the winners, with two runners-up for each category:

HOTEL: Winner   ❁ PHILIPBURN HOUSE HOTEL, Selkirk, Selkirks.

Runners-up   ⚱ LODORE SWISS HOTEL, Borrowdale, Cumbria.

    ⚱ SAUNTON SANDS HOTEL, Saunton, Devon.

PUB: Winner   ♟ ♟ RING O' BELLS, Compton Martin, Avon.

Runners-up   ♟ THE FLEECE, Bretforton, Hereford & Worcs.

    ♟ WHITE HART, Fyfield, Oxon.

RESTAURANT: Winner   ♫ BESOM BARN, Longframlington, Northumberland.

Runners-up   ⑭ TY GWYN, Betws-y-coed, Gwynedd.

    ⑭ REFECTORY, Richmond, Surrey.

Abberley, Nr Worcester, Hereford & Worcs

map 3

H R *ELMS HOTEL* (Prestige) – phone Great Witley 666

On the A 443

A stately and delightful Queen Anne house in twelve acres of glorious gardens with fine lawns and mature trees (and a huge herb garden). The interior matches up; elegantly furnished with antiques and fine carpets. There is a hard tennis court, putting green and croquet lawn.

Children's accommodation costs £8 for a cot and £15 for an extra bed. Both the lunch and dinner menus are small and inventive: some typical starters – hot onion quiche, melon and strawberry cocktail, terrine of Evesham vegetables, hot quiche of crab and gruyère; and some main courses – curried pork fillet madras, lemon sole stuffed with leeks and watercress and poached in Champagne, fillets of Welsh lamb with pickled pears. Half portions are served in the restaurant and the attitude of the staff is to provide anything that their guests require: which is as it should be, but by no means all hotels take this view.

This really is a peaceful and relaxing spot with its view of distant Cotswold hills and is ideally placed as a base for touring the heart of England.

27 rooms, 1 family Expensive Open all year
Lunch 1-2pm – £8.50 Dinner 7.30-9pm – £15
Access/AmEx/Barclaycard P – own car park

Abbotsbury, Dorset

map 2

P *ILCHESTER ARMS*

On the B3157. This coastal road to the west of the village has some stunning views of the sea line up to and beyond Swyre (see entry there for The Bull).

A handsome, rambling, old stone pub in an attractive village not far from the Abbey and a famous swannery, which was probably started by monks in the 14th century. They bred swans for practical reasons – they ate them.

The children's room is at the side of the bar and is large and comfortable with a beamed ceiling.

Bar snacks are available at all times.

Ale – Devenish P – own car park

Aberaeron, Dyfed

map 3

R   ***THE HIVE ON THE QUAY*** – phone 570 445

A business-like, white-washed little caff that is part of the old wharf on the attractive Aberaeron harbour which is surrounded by colourful neat houses. The café shares the wharf with a Honey Bee Exhibition, Sea Aquarium and a craft shop. Lots of sandwiches and home-made cakes and scones are available all day. At lunch and dinner you can have soup and choose from a cold buffet which includes some unusual salads, and pies and quiches made with delicious wholemeal pastry. At dinner savoury pancakes (£2.20-£3.50) are added to the menu and a hot dish of the day. A marquee is set up during the summer.

There's an under 14s menu with salads for children at about £1.50.

It's back to the car if you wish to change or feed a baby – the ladies is bare breeze block – most uncomfortable.

Closed mid-September to March   Open 10.30am-5pm
Lunch 12-2pm   Dinner (Jul-Sep) 6-9pm   Licensed
No credit cards accepted   P – in the road

Aberdovey, Gwynedd

map 3

H   ***TREFEDDIAN HOTEL*** – phone 213

On the A493 west of the town.

A big cream-painted hotel in a wonderful position overlooking the golf links and, beyond, a vast expanse of beach and sea. There is a beautiful turfed garden in front of the hotel with a putting green. There are other excellent facilities here including a large and well-designed indoor heated pool with a separate paddling pool for children. It has a sun veranda beyond its sliding glass doors and the area is surveyed by closed circuit television – for safety reasons, not for any other esoteric purposes. There is also a hard tennis court, table tennis and pool in the games room, and, very unusual in Britain, an indoor badminton court. All this plus concessionary rates for guests at Aberdovey golf course, a wonderful links beloved of Bernard Darwin who wrote: 'About this one course in the world I am a hopeless and shameful sentimentalist and I glory in my shame.'

Cots are charged at £2.60 per day and an extra bed for a child is £19 per day, but this includes breakfast and dinner. There is a special children's menu available at lunchtime and for high teas.

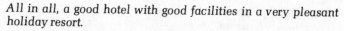

All in all, a good hotel with good facilities in a very pleasant holiday resort.

46 rooms, 3 sets of 3 adjoining rooms   Cheap
Closed mid-Oct to end Mar   Lunch 12.45-1.45pm – £5.50
Dinner 7.15-8.30pm –£8.50   Access only   P – own car park

Abergavenny, Gwent   map 2

H P R   *THE ANGEL* (THF), Cross Street – phone 7121

In the town centre.

A really fine old coaching inn, with a smartly white-painted Georgian façade, in this attractive market town in the heart of Wales. There are no extra facilities for families here because it is very much a town centre hotel, but the area has many attractions for tourists: nearby are the Brecon Beacons, the many Border castles and the lovely Wye and Usk valleys.

There is a pretty lounge in which to sit if you're just here for a drink and, on clement days, a courtyard by the bar. Bar snacks – salads and a dish of the day all at around £2 – are available at lunchtime, while the restaurant menu primarily concentrates on grills, steak and kidney pie, seafood pie, etc. You can find sustenance here at most times of the day as 'Hathaway's Kitchen' is open for breakfast, morning coffee, lunch, afternoon tea and dinner. Children have their own menu or can choose half portions from the main menu and are accommodated free up to the age of 5 or for a nominal £1 from 5 to 14.

29 rooms, 3 family   Moderate   Open all year
Lunch 12-2.15 (restaurant and bar)   Dinner 7-9.30pm –
£8.50 alc   Ale – Bass   Access/AmEx/Barclaycard/Diners
P – at rear, opposite public car park

Abingdon, Oxon   map 1

H R   *UPPER REACHES HOTEL* (THF), Thames Street – phone 22311

On the A415 Dorchester road out of Abingdon. It's right by the bridge where there's a large sign.

Appealing old stone hotel with a brick extension that fits in pretty well. It is located on an island – the Thames to one side and a mill stream to the other – and has a small garden by the stream and a patio by the river. Across the main road is the Old Gaol, a lovely building converted to a leisure centre with a swimming pool, badminton, snooker, table tennis and roller skating. The hotel's conference centre by the river is not so lovely however.

Children under 5 are accommodated free, with a token charge of £1 for children up to 14 sharing a single room with one adult or a twin room with two adults.

The restaurant has a special menu for children or will serve them half portions from the adult menu. The buffet lunch at no more than £2.25 has a hot dish of the day, a cold meat platter, etc, and the restaurant offers the usual run of prawn cocktail, paté, melon, steaks, scampi, veal and trout cooked in various ways.

20 rooms, 2 family Expensive Open all year
Lunch 12.30-2pm – £6 Dinner 7-9.30pm – £8.50
Access/AmEx/Barclaycard/Diners
P – own car park and moorings for boats too

Addingham, West Yorks   map 3

P   **THE FLEECE**

On the A65 at the east end of the village.

Virginia creeper covers the front of this lovely and well-run pub which has beautiful surrounding countryside.

The charming landlord has recently converted one of the large stone and oak rooms into a splendid dining and family room. Lots of stuffed birds and animals watch you eat and drink – even a moose over the fireplace. In the room are plenty of tables and chairs, a piano and a space invader machine.

Hot food is served from 12-2pm each day – steak and kidney pie, cottage pie, chilli con carne, lasagne for under £2 – and cold pie and pickles from 5.30-8pm.

Ale – Tetley   P – own car park

Adversane, Nr Billingshurst, West Sussex   map 1

R   **OLD HOUSE** – phone Billingshurst 2186

On the A29 one and a half miles south of Billingshurst.

A 14th century tea-room surrounded by a pretty and unfussy garden. You can buy anything from egg on toast to a large mixed grill – and you can purchase some antiques while you're waiting for your meal.

Half portions are served and there is a special children's menu.

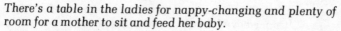

There's a table in the ladies for nappy-changing and plenty of room for a mother to sit and feed her baby.

Open 10am-5.30pm   Licensed
Access/Barclaycard   P – own car park

Alfriston, East Sussex map 1

An attractive and historic village whose main street boasts some splendid half-timbered houses and where we found two hotels which we think you'll like.

H   *DEANS PLACE HOTEL* – phone 870 248

On the B2108 at the edge of the village.

Part of this very attractive hotel was once a thatched Tudor manor house, and there have been various additions including some successful modern ones. There are lovely rambling gardens, bounded on one side by the river Cuckmere. An excellent outdoor heated swimming pool can be found in a partly walled garden. There is a croquet lawn, an old but serviceable badminton court, a tennis court and a huge games room where a short tennis court is set up.

Cots are charged at £1.50 per night and other reductions for older children can be negotiated.

High tea is served at 6pm and half portions are available in the restaurant. The menu changes each day and is mostly English cooking: Roast Beef and Yorkshire pud, steak and kidney pie, baked trout, grilled salmon steak, etc.

44 rooms, 3 family   Moderate   Closed Jan-mid Feb
Lunch 12.30-2pm – £4.50   Dinner 7-8.30pm – £7.50
No credit cards accepted   P – own car park

H R   *STAR INN* (THF), Nr Polegate – phone 870 495

In the centre of the village.

Archetypal 15th century English inn with heavily timbered façade and jutting oriel windows. It is reputed to be one of the oldest inns in the country and to have been a meeting place for local smugglers.

Free accommodation for children up to 5 and a nominal charge for children from 5 to 14 who share either a single room with one parent or a double with both.

The changing menus offer hot dishes and cold meats and salads. A typical lunch and dinner might be: lunch – kidney

11

and mushroom pasty followed by beef braised in Guinness or Cheddar baked lamb; dinner – hot shirred eggs with smoked salmon and cream sauce followed by baked trout filled with prawns, onions and mushrooms or poached suprême of trout filled with prawns, onions and mushrooms or poached suprême of chicken with asparagus spears and prawn sauce. Seasonal vegetables accompany the dishes. Children may eat from the special menu or half portions from the adult menu.

32 rooms, 16 family   Moderate   Open all year
Lunch 12.30-2pm – £7.50   Dinner 7-9pm – £9
Ale – Bass, Hall & Woodhouse
Access/AmEx/Barclaycard/Diners   P – own car park

Alswear, Devon   map 2

P   **BUTCHER'S ARMS**

On the A373.

Typical white-walled roadside country pub with low ceilings, oak beams and horse brasses. The quiet friendly landlord keeps the pub well.

There's a large pool room with juke box and space invaders off the bar or a bright stone-walled skittle alley where children can sit or play.

The restaurant is open in the evenings and hot and cold snacks and meals are available all week in the bar where an under-12s menu is also offered.

Ale – Ushers   P – on the opposite side of the road

Amberley, Nr Stroud, Glos   map 2

H P R   **AMBERLEY INN** – phone 2565

Off the A46 south of Stroud.

A delightful rambling Cotswold stone building close to Stroud and Minchinhampton and with a splendid view over the Woodchester Valley. It has a small quiet garden overlooked by the garden house extension: an old stone cottage. You can sit in the lounge with your children if you're there for a drink. At the back is the huge Minchinhampton Common – ideal for strollers, footballers, runners and liers-down. This is a good spot to stop for Cotswold tourers.

Accommodation is free for children up to 13 years. Snacks and grills are available at lunchtimes as they are for children at

6.30pm. Half portions are also served. The lunch à la carte is simple food – soup, fruit juice and steaks, scampi, chicken – served with chips and salad. The 'Speciality' menu is richer with a lot of sauces.

16 rooms, 2 family Cheap Open all year
Lunch 12.30-2pm – £5 alc Dinner 7.30-9.30pm – £7.50
Ale – Wadworth's, Hook Norton, Flowers
Access/AmEx/Barclaycard P – limited parking

Ambleside, Cumbria map 5

R **SHEILA'S COTTAGE,** The Slack – phone 33079

Hidden in an alley of the town's one-way system – keep looking to your right.

A bustling but cramped little stone tea shop which offers good food at reasonable prices. Coffee, pastries and cakes are served from 10.15 until 12 noon when the lunch menu comes into force until 2.30. Everything is freshly made – the soup, the fruit juices, the bread. There are several patés at about £2.25, meat dishes at about £3.50 and special Swiss dishes at under £3. A wide choice of puddings follows – all for under £1. The tea menu takes over at 2.30 with lots of cakes, muffins, and so on. During the afternoon as well a good selection of savoury snacks are served at under £3. They have a marvellous selection of good teas and other (non-alcoholic) drinks. At lunch you can take your own wine.

The reduction on dishes depends on the age and size of the child – only a nominal charge is made for very small children.

There is absolutely no space or privacy for attending to the changing or breast-feeding of a baby.

Wish we could find more restaurants like this – but bigger and with a mothers' room.

Closed Jan Open Mon to Sat 10.15am-5.30pm Unlicensed
No credit cards accepted
P – parking is difficult – find a public car park and walk

Amersham, Bucks map 1

A pretty little town with an attractive main street, in which are both our entries – nearly opposite each other.

H R **CROWN HOTEL** (THF), High Street – phone 21541

A Georgian front hides an Elizabethan building with splendid beams and panelling. It has a small patio at the rear in the hotel's cobbled courtyard.

None of the rooms will accommodate an extra bed, so you cannot take advantage here of the special THF rates for children. Some can take a cot though, so you could stay with a cot-sized infant for whom there will be no accommodation charge.

The table d'hôte menu at lunch offers two starters and two main courses with coffee – good simple fare like soup or deep-fried mushrooms, roast meat or mixed grill. Simple fare on the four course dinner menu too – Ogen melon, lemon sorbet and baked trout; or duck and port mousse, sorbet and rack of lamb are typical examples, served with fresh vegetables and followed by pudding or cheese. There's an à la carte menu serving similar food.

19 rooms, no family rooms – see text   Moderate   Open all year
Lunch 12.30-2.15pm – £5.25   Dinner 7-9.15pm –   £9.50
Ale – Morrell's   Access/AmEx/Barclaycard/Diners
P – the courtyard doubles as car park with space for 50 cars

R   ***WILLOW TREE RESTAURANT***, 1 Market Square – phone 7242

A pretty restaurant with a small patio, open for morning coffee and afternoon tea when the usual scones and pastries are served. The lunch menu changes every day but always reflects the friendly owners' refreshing resolve to offer good, wholesome and tasty food. No burgers and chips, no tired old cheesecake. There's always a home-made soup and main courses (£1.75-£3) which depend a lot on the weather, but here is some of the range from which the lunch menu will be made up – steak and kidney pie, moussaka, lamb chops in wine, shepherd's pie, lots of hot and cold quiches and pies, like corned beef pie and vegetarian pie, seafood platter, baked potatoes with various fillings, ploughman's and so on. A traditional roast beef lunch is served on Sundays. They specialise too in fresh-made puddings. They will serve children half portions or whatever variations of the menu are requested – they do keep some chips for emergencies, but they're rarely called for – who says children only like burgers and chips?

The sensible owners also provide unbreakable crockery for the children. They are happy, too, to help a mother needing to change or feed her baby. Aimed specifically at families, this is a very popular restaurant and you should book for lunch, particularly at the weekends. Take your own bottle – there's an off-licence next door.

Open 10am-5.30pm (6.30 on Sat and Sun), closed Christmas Day and New Year's Day
Price of main dish approximately £2.50   Unlicensed
No credit cards accepted   P – restricted, but car park nearby

Amesbury, Wilts

map 2

H P R *ANTROBUS ARMS HOTEL*, Church Street – phone 23163

In the town centre.

The façade of this 'county town', family-owned hotel is unremarkable Georgian but the interior is elegant and comfortable. A splendid entrance goes right through to the back of the hotel and looks out over a fine lawned garden with a spreading cedar tree, which is said to be over 400 years old. Both the spacious and attractive drawing room and the pretty restaurant have views of the garden which is floodlit at night. The bar, busy when we visited one lunchtime, is large and quite plush.

Children are welcome in the entrance hall, which has plenty of chairs at the garden end (and a sort of conservatory effect with its large windows) and in the lounge. There are some inexpensive bar meals to be had at lunchtimes including ploughman's, toasted sandwiches, cold meats and salads and a hot dish of the day from about 75p to £2.50. The table d'hôte lunch offers haddock mousse, trout, lamb cutlets, etc while the à la carte menu ranges from Scotland to Egypt via France: bouillabaise, snails, jumbo prawns, trout Cleopatra, sirloin highland fling and so on. The restaurant serves half portions for children.

Children's accommodation, cots or extra beds, costs £10 per night. If you fancy unravelling the secret of Stonehenge this hotel is very close to the site, and of course to many of the other attractions of this delightful part of England.

21 rooms,   1 family   Cheap   Open all year
Lunch 12.30-1.45pm – £6   Dinner 7-9.30pm – £10 alc
Ale – Bass, Wadworth's   Access/AmEx/Barclaycard/Diners
P – own car park

Ansty, Dorset

map 2

P   *THE FOX*

Well signposted in the minor minor roads near Milton Abbas.

A large rambling flint and brick pub well worth the detour you have to make to reach it. There are several bars, one of which is lined with coloured plates and another loaded with Toby jugs.

There is a large children's room with a rocking horse, pool table and games, and a small garden with benches and tables at the front.

A wide selection of food, amid which the cold table is very seductive, is available seven days a week.

Ale   Hall & Woodhouse and their own brew   P – own car park

Arduaine, by Oban, Strathclyde   map 5

H   *LOCH MELFORT HOTEL* – phone Kilmelford 233

On the A816.

The main part of the building would benefit from a lick of paint, and the extension at the side just stops short of being an eyesore. But the rooms are attractively furnished, and it is worth stopping here for the absolutely stunning view out over Loch Melfort which can be seen in detail from the powerful telescope in the scruffy Chart Room bar. There is a mass of bird life to be seen and next door are the Arduaine Gardens open to the public on certain days. Although there is no special entertainment for children, they will like the fields and rocks leading to the small beach where they can swim.

Cots are charged at £2 per night and extra beds at £5. There is a splendid range of bar foods at lunchtime including local giant prawns, salmon and trout, and half portions can be served in the restaurant.

26 rooms, 23 family   Moderate   Closed Oct-Easter
Lunch 12.30-2pm – about £5   Dinner 7.15-8.30pm – £11
Access only   P – own car park

Aston Clinton, Bucks   map 1

H   *THE BELL INN* – phone Aylesbury 630 252

On the A41 between Aylesbury and Tring.

A notable, elegant and expensive hotel housed in a Georgian inn and extended opposite into an old brewery. Here there are lovely walled gardens with a croquet lawn, and some of the ground floor rooms have their own tiny patios leading on to the gardens. A wonderful relief after travelling on the A41.

Accommodation for children up to 10 is £9 and from 10-16 £13, but you should note that for some strange reason these prices include a 'continental' breakfast and a service charge but no VAT. The restaurant does not offer special portions or prices for children which is why the Bell's restaurant does not qualify according to the criteria of this Guide. However, the hotel has a splendid reputation for its cuisine (and wines) and it would be

16

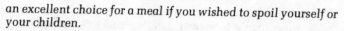

an excellent choice for a meal if you wished to spoil yourself or your children.

21 rooms, 2 sets of 4 connecting rooms   Expensive
Open all year   Lunch 12.30-2pm – £15 alc
Dinner 7.30-10pm – £20 alc
Access/Barclaycard   P – own car park

Auchterhouse, by Dundee, Tayside

map 6

H R   *THE OLD MANSION HOUSE* – phone 366/367

Follow the hotel sign from the A927 in the opposite direction to the village.

A delightful 16th century mansion house which is clearly greatly cherished. It has beautiful gardens and a courtyard where visitors and guests may eat outside one of the two bars. The interior is superb – stone walls and floors, antique furniture, huge open fires and an amazing Jacobean vaulted ceiling. Facilities include squash, grass tennis court, heated outdoor swimming pool, sauna and a croquet lawn. If parents wish to go out a member of staff will baby-sit.

The bar serves lunches of soups, salads, a hot dish of the day at £2.20 (superb haddock on our visit) and puddings. The chef will cook 'whatever they want' for children or they can eat at half price from the à la carte menu. There is no accommodation charge for children under 12 sharing with their parents.

An exceptional place to go to – whether for a quick drink or a longer stay.

6 rooms, 4 family, 2 suites   Moderate   Open all year
Lunch 12.30-2pm – £6.25 & alc
Dinner 7-9.30pm – main course from £7.50
Access/AmEx/Barclaycard/Diners   P – own car park

Aust, Avon

map 2

P   *BOARS HEAD*

Follow the A403 to Avonmouth (at Junction 21 of the M4 by the Severn Bridge) and turn left to Aust village.

Good-looking 17th century pub, smart and white-walled and only seconds from the M4, by the Severn Bridge.

There is a basic children's room with pool table, chairs and games machines and a pleasant grassy garden with climbing frame and picnic tables and benches.

The owners have an excellent range of food – and all so much nicer than a motorway caff. Bar snacks – toasted sandwiches, ploughman's, salads, etc – are available morning and evening except on Sundays. Their lunches, available from Monday to Friday, are really out of the ordinary. For a start there are something like thirty salads laid out – to accompany quiches, cold meats, salmon, seafood platter, game pie, turkey (smoked and plain), etc. The prices range from under £3 to just over £6, and since you are welcome to try all thirty salads if you can, they represent excellent value.

An excellent pub in a very useful spot for travellers up and down or across the country. There is a small camping site at the back of the pub.

Ale – Courage   P – own car park

Aylesbury, Bucks

map 1

H R   *BELL HOTEL* (THF), Market Square – phone 89835 and 82141

Right in the centre of the town.

A pretty 'county town' hotel with dormer windows atop the white façade. It is unfortunately marooned amidst racing traffic and 'No Parking' signs. If you have to stop in Aylesbury, however, it's fine for a meal or a brief stay because:

Accommodation is free for children up to 5 and a nominal charge of £1 is made for children from 5 to 14.

The restaurant serves plain English cooking – steak, fish, lamb, steak and kidney pie, spatchcock, etc, and a special children's menu and half portions are available in the restaurant.

22 rooms, 5 family   Moderate
Open all year   Lunch 12-2pm – £8 alc   Dinner 7-9.30pm – £8 alc
Ale – Charrington, Wethered
Access/AmEx/Barclaycard/Diners   P – multi-storey car park 200 yards from hotel

---

Ayr, Strathclyde

map 5

H   *BELLEISLE HOTEL* – phone 42331

On the A719 about two miles south of Ayr.

Not a place for peace and quiet as it's set in a popular public park – a splendid brass band plays each Sunday outside the front door. But it's worth a visit for its amazing ornate carvings and panelling – some of scenes from Robert Burns' poems – and its dining rooms copied from Versailles.

Although there's not a lot for children within the hotel, it's fine for a short stay. In the park is the pond, deer park, pets corner and two golf courses.

The charges for children sharing with parents are: up to 2 years £5.50, 2-4 years £6.50 and 5-11 years £9.50. High tea is served from 4-6 pm and bar food is available from 11am to 11pm. Children can order what they want from the restaurant or choose half portions from the adult menu.

16 rooms, 5 family   Moderate   Open all year
Lunch 12-2pm – about £3.75
Dinner 7.30-9.30pm (7.30-10pm Sat and Sun) – £7.50
Access/AmEx/Barclaycard/Diners   P – own car park

Bagshot, Surrey   map 1

H R   *PENNYHILL PARK HOTEL,* College Ride – phone 71774

Off the A30 at Bagshot, but beware – the hotel signs, on a busy road when one needs the maximum assistance, are hopelessly inadequate.

A truly elegant ivy-clad stone mansion in over 100 acres of gardens and grounds, with some magnificent mature trees. There is a great fund of facilities at the well-designed country club: a nine-hole golf course, a large heated outdoor swimming pool, three tennis courts, horse riding, trout fishing and clay pigeon shooting.

Half portions can be served in the restaurant, and there is a snack menu (pancakes, hamburgers, etc) in the Orangery – the country club restaurant – which is open from 10am to 10pm. The main restaurant is quite expensive andperhaps suffers from a surfeit of sauces with its fish and meat dishes – the full gamut of scampi, sole, salmon, trout, sweetbreads, chicken breast, duck, turnedos, etc, is served.

Children's accommodation is free when sharing – the hotel policy is to charge a flat rate for a double room, however many people occupy it.

40 rooms, 1 family   Expensive   Open all year
Lunch 12.30-2pm – £15 alc   Dinner 7.30-10.30pm – £15 alc
Access/AmEx/Barclaycard/Diners   P – own car park

Banbury, Oxon   map 1

H   *WHATELY HALL* (THF), Banbury Cross – phone 3451

At the Cross – the centre of the town.

A fine 17th century stone hotel in its own gardens close to Banbury Cross. The big garden of lawns and trees is slightly hemmed in by the hotel's modern extension and for pious souls there's a very ugly Baptist chapel. But quiet enough with plenty of tables and chairs on the lawned patio.

Children up to 5 are accommodated free and a charge of £1 is made for children from 5 to 14. There is a special children's menu and half portions are also served. As well as the restaurant, a grill room is open from 6.30pm to 10pm.

78 rooms, 17 family, 2 sets of adjoining rooms   Moderate
Open all year   Lunch 12.30-2pm – £6.25
Dinner 7-9.15 pm – £8.75   Ale – Hook Norton
Access/AmEx/Barclaycard/Diners
P – own car park

Bar Hill, nr Cambridge, Cambs

map 1

H   ***CUNARD CAMBRIDGESHIRE HOTEL*** – phone Crafts Hill 80555

On the A604 to Huntingdon – a fast road – look for signs to Bar Hill.

A modern, two-storey, rather motel-like building but not unpleasant in its overall aspect. For example, there are plenty of patios and lawns between the 'spokes' of the building. There are marvellous facilities: an excellent indoor heated swimming pool with a children's pool, three squash courts, two hard tennis courts, an eighteen-hole golf course and a play area with swings and a climbing frame.

Children up to 12 are accommodated free. There is a special children's menu served at 6pm and half portions are also available in the restaurant.

This is an excellent alternative to staying in Cambridge itself, which, sadly, has a traffic system designed to ensure total paralysis of the streets throughout the day.

100 rooms, 8 sets of adjoining rooms   Expensive
Open all year   Lunch 12.30-2pm – £8.50
Dinner 7-10pm – £8.50 Ale – Greene King
Access/AmEx/Barclaycard/Diners   P – own car park

Barnby Moor, Notts

map 4

H P R   *YE OLDE BELL* (THF) – phone Retford 705 121

On the A638.

This is a lovely hotel – white brick, leaded windows, ivy-covered – an oasis. There are several lounge areas where you can have a drink in peace and comfort and a very attractive wood-panelled restaurant. The bar serves a hot dish-of-the-day at £1.95 as well as the usual meat and salad buffet. The restaurant menus offer a good mix of reasonably plain fish and meat dishes – roast rack of lamb on a bed of apricot forcemeat, beef fillet in red wine and mushroom sauce, poached halibut in wine and dill sauce. Half portions are served to children in the bar and in the restaurant which also has a special menu for children.

In the large lawned garden are swings and a slide and tables where you can sit while the children play. Sunday is a good day to lunch here – 'Hungry Bear' entertains the children in a special play room while you linger over your meal. A baby could be breast-fed in the ladies' cloakroom.

Children under 5 stay free and 5-14 are charged at £1 per night. Queen Victoria must have been glad of the special rates when she stayed here – probably took the children to nearby Sherwood Forest too.

58 rooms, 1 family, 1 set of adjoining rooms   Moderate
Open all year   Lunch 12.30-2pm – £5.95 (Bar 12-2pm)
Dinner 7-9.45pm – £8.95   Ale – Webster's
Access/AmEx/Barclaycard/Diners   P – large car park

Barnstaple, Devon   map 2

H   *IMPERIAL HOTEL* (THF), *Taw Vale Parade – phone 5861*

On the A361 on the edge of the town – South Molton side.

A grand and beautifully cared for Edwardian hotel, iron balustraded and with a patio and small garden at the front. The restaurant claims views of the River Taw – well, if you stand on a table. . . . Across the River is the North Devon Leisure Centre which has many sports facilities including a swimming pool, a learner pool and squash courts and which are open from 9am to 10pm.

Accommodation is free for children up to 5 and a nominal charge of £1 is made for children up to 14. A special children's menu and half portions are available in the restaurant.

55 rooms, 3 family   Moderate   Open all year
Lunch – bar snacks only   Dinner 6.45-8.45pm – £8.25
Access/AmEx/Barclaycard/Diners
P – across the road at the back of the hotel

Barrington, Somerset   map 2

P   *ROYAL OAK*

Signposted from the B3168 and the A303 near Ilminster.

An attractive village pub built of mellow local stone in a particularly pretty film-set village. It has a beautiful little church, and indeed was voted the 'best kept village' in Somerset in 1983.

There is a pleasant enough large bar, and children can frequent the skittle alley, which is a bit scruffy. But the landlord really makes no pretensions about its being a specific children's room, and we have included the pub because we think you'll enjoy seeing the village and can stop here for a quick drink or meal. There are steaks at just over £4, fish and chips or salads at around £2, plus sandwiches – every day except Sunday lunchtime.

There is a small grassy garden with a few tables and chairs.

Ale – Golden Hill, Flowers, Hall & Woodhouse
P – own car park

Baslow, Derbys   map 3

H R   *CAVENDISH HOTEL* – phone 2311

On the A619.

A long low well-proportioned stone building which has been part of the Chatsworth Estate since 1830. It was rebuilt in the early 1970s and is furnished elegantly with many antiques from Chatsworth. The public rooms are attractive and all the bedrooms have views of Chatsworth. At the back of the hotel is a sloping lawn with croquet (some tricky lines here) and beyond green fields.

There is a good range of dishes in the restaurant, including game from the Estate and such things as fillet of beef braised in real ale. Children's portions can be arranged (at two-thirds of the adult price). There is also a children's menu at under £2 and the amiable staff will cook 'anything children like'. Cots and extra beds are charged at £5 per night.

13 rooms, 2 sets of adjoining rooms   Expensive
Open all year   Lunch 12.30-2pm – £8.95
Dinner 7-10pm – £8.95   Ale – Ruddles
AmEx/Barclaycard   P – own car park

Bassenthwaite, Nr Keswick, Cumbria

map 5

H   *ARMATHWAITE HALL HOTEL* – Bassenthwaite Lake 551

Off the A591 – don't go to Bassenthwaite village but follow the signs for the Lake. Turn off at the Castle Inn.

This is really a castle masquerading as a mansion. It is built of dark red stone with battlements on the top of one wing. It dates from the late 18th century and is set in 130 acres of parkland; its beautiful lawns flow down to Bassenthwaite Lake, where guests can fish (if they buy a permit). There are some wonderful rooms here: a huge lounge with a grand marble fireplace, splendid wood panelled ceiling and walls and leaded windows – all glassily surveyed by the stags' heads on the walls.

There are reasonable facilities here. As well as the fishing there is a hard tennis court, squash court and pitch and putt course, and a games room with table tennis and pool. A snooker table (for over-16s) is in a remarkable panelled room with walls covered with scores of original Punch cartoons.

Accommodation for children in cots is £3 per night, and £10 thereafter up to 12. Half portions can be served in the restaurant, but the under 10s must take high tea (anything they want) at 6pm. They are not permitted in the restaurant in the evening.

Sir Hugh Walpole knew Armathwaite Hall:

'Speaking of Romance, is there anything more romantic than Armathwaite Hall with its lovely habit of drawing Bassen-thwaite in a sheet of silver or orange to its very doors? With the trees that guard it and the history that inhabits it, and the lake that stretches before it, it is a house of perfect and irresistible atmosphere.'

37 rooms, 3 family   Moderate   Closed Jan 4 to Mar 9
Lunch 12.30-1.45pm – £6.50   Dinner 7.30-9.30pm – £9.75
Access/AmEx/Barclaycard/Diners   P – own car park

Bath, Avon

map 2

H P R   *FRANCIS HOTEL* (THF), Queen Square – phone 24257

In the middle of the town.

Solid stone Georgian building in the centre of the town and occupying the south side of the elegant Queen Square. Originally the hotel was six private houses built in the early 18th century.

Free accommodation for children under 5 and a nominal charge of £1 from 5 to 14. A children's menu and half portions are available in the restaurant, which concentrates on traditional dishes such as roast beef, veal Cordon Bleu, chicken chasseur, and various ways with trout, sole and plaice. There is a cold lunchtime buffet and a casserole of some kind.

There is plenty of room to park yourself if you are footsore from walking around beautiful Bath and excellent afternoon teas are served in the plush lounge at 4 pm.

90 rooms, 10 family   Expensive   Open all year
Lunch 12.30-2pm – £7.50   Dinner 7-9.15pm – £9
Ale – Bass, Flowers
Access/AmEx/Barclaycard/Diners   P – car park for 60 cars

H   ***LANSDOWN GROVE HOTEL*** (Best Western), Lansdown Road
      – phone 314 891

On the west side of the river and north of Royal Crescent.

A handsome ivy-clad Georgian hotel with a small but charming lawned garden. It is a few minutes from the centre of Bath, but is a useful alternative to the Francis Hotel.

There is free accommodation for children as long as they're staying for two or more nights, otherwise it's £5 for each extra bed. The restaurant serves half portions.

41 rooms, 3 triple rooms which will sleep 4   Moderate
Open all year Lunch (buffet) 12.30-2.30pm – £3.50
Dinner 7-9.30pm – £6.50 or £8
Access/AmEx/Barclaycard/Diners   P – own car park

R   ***HOLE IN THE WALL,*** 16 George Street – phone 25242

In the centre of the city.

This is one of the best known restaurants in Britain and has long had a reputation for cooking of a high standard. It is a smart and comfortable place and is well worth a visit if you are feeling rich.

A typical choice to start might be: watercress soup, fricassé of sole, fish soup, hors d'oeuvres (which, sensibly, may be a main course too), guinea fowl galantine or crab pancakes. The main courses may include venison and fruit pie, brill, carré d'agneau, veal tournedos and liver in lemon and honey sauce. There are special dishes available each day according to what is fresh and in season.

Half portions can be produced for children who, thank

goodness, are not offered chips here as a matter of routine. The owners will always help a mother if she has to change or feed her baby – there are rooms upstairs for example.

Closed Sundays & public holidays, 2 weeks at Christmas
Lunch 12-1.30pm – £12.50   Dinner 7-10pm – £15   Licensed
Access/AmEx/Barclaycard/Diners   P – street parking

Bawtry, South Yorks map 4

There's a dearth of places to eat, drink or stay in this area so we've included these two restaurants which are just about adequate. Go, if you can though, to the Olde Bell at Barnby Moor.

R   **THE CROWN HOTEL** (Anchor), Market Place – phone Doncaster 858 875

In the main street – the A638.

An ancient coaching inn, long and low-slung, white painted with shutters in the busy main street. It has a long history including a visit by Daniel Defoe.

A place for a quick stop since there is a special children's menu available as at most Anchor hotels. There is the usual lunchtime buffet of meat and salads (not that exciting) and one hot dish; and a full menu in the restaurant, mostly steaks, chops, duck, etc. Children can also order half portions from the main menu.

The restaurant manager was efficient and helpful but could not see some of his waitresses lurking in the lounge bar doorway puffing on their fags.

Open all year   Lunch 12.30-2pm – £2.50 (buffet)
Dinner 7-9.30pm – £5.75
Access/AmEx/Barclaycard/Diners   P – own car park

R   **DOWER HOUSE,** High Street – phone Doncaster 710 497

In the main street, the A638.

In this busy main street and at the entrance to a small shopping precinct is this restaurant. It is not very pretty from the outside but comfortable enough within and you can eat quite cheaply. Apart from light lunches – ploughman's, hors d'oeuvres from about £1.35 – there is a set lunch of three courses at £4 (smoked mackerel salad, anchovy egg mayonnaise, grilled plaice, ham with peaches, etc) The dinner menu is the same, between 7 and 8pm only, but at the still reasonable price of £5.25. There is also a much wider dinner menu at about £8 alc.

Half portions are available for children. There is a 'powder room' separate from the Ladies, where a mother could feed or change a baby in privacy if not in much comfort.

Closed Sun and Bank Holidays   Lunch 12-1.45pm – £4
Dinner 7-9.45 – £5.25 (7-8pm only) £8 alc   Licensed
Access/AmEx/Barclaycard/Diners   P – own car park

Beanacre, Nr Melksham, Wilts   map 2

R   *BEECHFIELD HOUSE* – phone Melksham 703 700

On the A350 north of Melksham.

This is a gem of a building, beautifully maintained. The Victorian Bath stonework, with elaborate carvings over the windows and doorway, is very striking and the house is set in beautiful gardens with spreading trees. An air of great elegance, both inside the building and outside, welcomes you.

Lunch might consist of a Wiltshire game terrine or garden pumpkin soup, and seafood ragout or breast of pigeon. The dishes range wider in the evenings and at Sunday lunch with the accent on fish and game – ballotine of duck, Cornish brill, Wye salmon, Cotswold lamb, Bromham duck, ragout of Wiltshire hare and chestnuts, etc.

Half portions are served for children and the 'Ladies Cloakroom' is large – room to change a baby and a chair to sit on for breast-feeding.

The famous village of Lacock is nearby – and after a meal at the Beechfield, the two mile walk would probably do you good – or perhaps a seventeen mile walk to Longleat.

Closed on public holidays   Lunch 12.30-2pm – £6.50
Dinner 7-9.30pm – £13 alc   Licensed
Access/AmEx/Barclaycard/Diners   P – own car park

Beeley, Derbys   map 3

P   *DEVONSHIRE ARMS*

On the B6012, off the A6, north of Matlock.

A smashing pub in a small village not far from Chatsworth House. It is built of stone and inside there are heavy beams, partly paved floors and rough stone walls. There is a children's room up some stairs to the right of the bar and it has a tiled floor with plenty of tables and chairs. On the other side of the bar is the dining room where children may also sit.

There is a fine range of bar snacks, available every day except Saturday evenings. For example pizzas, paté, beefburgers, steak pie at under £2, and at just over £2 fried chicken, gammon and egg, haddock and country casserole. There is also a self-service cold buffet, a chef's special dish and a special children's menu. There is a restaurant here, closed on Sunday evenings and all day Monday.

Ale – Theakston's   P – own car park

Berwick Station, East Sussex
map 1

P   ***BERWICK INN***

On the B2109 about one mile from Berwick – near Alfriston and signposted to the south off the A27 to Berwick Station.

A big rambling white-washed pub next door to the station. The great attraction is a large playground with swings, paddling pool and Wendy house.

The children's room is in a pleasant conservatory room off the main bar and there is also a children's bar in the garden with space invader machines.

The owners serve a special children's menu – fish fingers, burgers, etc, at around £1 – and a good range of food seven days a week. You can eat scampi, fish, steak, mixed grills, salads, etc, at prices from £2 to just over £6 for the steaks.

Ale – Charrington, Courage, Hall & Woodhouse
P – own car park

Betws Garmon, Nr Caernarfon, Gwynedd
map 3

H   ***PLAS-Y-COED*** – Waunfawr 284

On the A4085 between Beddgelert and Carnarvon.

This hotel does not qualify for inclusion in the Guide because it has no baby-listening service. So why are we bending the rules? Because it's a friendly hotel in an area of great beauty where we had extraordinary difficulty in finding anywhere for parents to stay where they would be reasonably comfortable and where they would be made welcome. There's a fortune to be made in this area of Wales for an hotelier who keeps his place clean and bright and who is prepared to smile at visitors. The cheerful proprietors here did smile and were extremely helpful. The hotel is small enough for a baby to be heard by one of them if it cries in its room.

Originally a fishing lodge, the hotel is in Snowdonia National Park in its own wooded and hilly grounds. It is well situated for families exploring this part of Wales and it isn't too far to sandy beaches and to many towns of historic interest.

There's a discount of 25% for children up to 12 years sharing their parents' room and high tea will be served to them on request.

There's bar and dining room food and children can have bar snacks or eat half price from the adult menu. Meals are simple with an emphasis on local fish – 'All the salmon in the freezer I saw alive' said one of the owners.

7 rooms, 3 family   Cheap   Open all year
Lunch 12-2pm   Dinner 7-9pm – £4.50
Ale – Gwynedd Breweries
No credit cards accepted   P – own car park

Betws-y-coed, Gwynedd   map 3

Two places for you at Betws which is at the edge of the beautiful Snowdonia region of Wales and a very good spot for a tourist base.

H   *CRAIG-Y-DDERWEN HOTEL* – phone 293

Cross the Waterloo Bridge from Betws and look for the hotel sign off the A5.

A country house hotel standing in its own lovely gardens by the River Conwy. It has a slightly run-down air, but is in a beautiful part of Wales and a good place for them as enjoys shootin' and fishin'. The hotel has fishing rights on two lakes – one about two miles away, the other four. Within the hotel and grounds is croquet, badminton, table tennis, a games room with bikes, trikes, table football and table skittles. Pony-trekking and canoeing can be arranged and there's lots to do and see in this tourist area. Free golf is available to hotel guests.

Cots and extra beds cost £2 and the family rooms are let at set prices – for 3 £30-36, for 4 £34-41. Children can choose from the bar snacks menu, the usual ploughman's, pizza, chicken, scampi and chips, which cost up to £2 and 85p for children, or can eat from the adult menus at two-thirds of the price. The à la carte and table d'hôte menus offer a good mix of fish, game, meat and casserole-type meals.

22 rooms, 6 family   Cheap   Closed Christmas and Boxing Days
Lunch 12-1.30pm – £8.50 alc   Dinner 7-8.30pm – £7.50
Access/Barclaycard/Diners   P – own car park

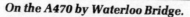

P R   *TY GWYN HOTEL – phone 383*

On the A470 by Waterloo Bridge.

A very handsome low-built stone pub, partly 17th century, in this renowned tourist area in the Snowdonia region. The interior is superb, with antique furniture scattered about, and this includes the entrance hall where children may sit. It is on the small side but has comfortable armchairs, highly polished oak furniture and old prints on the walls. The bar is most appealing with its low-beamed ceiling and slate fireplace.

Bar snacks are available every day, morning and evening, and include sandwiches and salads, and hot dishes from £1 to £2.50. The restaurant is formed from two rooms, with low ceilings and is a lovely sight with antique chairs, tables, china and paintings. There is quite a big menu with lots of fish: for example smoked mackerel and salmon and grilled trout as starters, and many other fish dishes as main courses up to £6. You can eat steaks and duck at around the same price and there is a big choice of salads at under £4.

Children, apart from the snack menu, can order smaller portions; and a mother who needs to change or breast-feed a baby can use one of the well-equipped bathrooms.

It is a gem of a place, busy and friendly in a wonderful tourist area and might have been nominated as one of the best pubs; but we decided that it should be a runner-up in the restaurant category. Once again it was the charming and welcoming attitude of the owner which left a lasting impression.

Open all year. Lunch 12-3pm – £8   Dinner 7-10pm – £8
Ale – Marston's
Access/AmEx/Barclaycard/Diners   P – own car park

Beverley, Humberside   map 4

H P R   *THE BEVERLEY ARMS* (THF) – phone 869 241

Just drive to the centre of town – getting in is easy, getting out more difficult since the south part of the A164 seems to have been erased by the town planners.

The front is Georgian – a typical nice town hotel – but the hotel is in fact over 300 years old – Dick Turpin appeared before magistrates here. Its licensed coffee shop, The Ridings Buttery, is exceptionally pretty; it overlooks the patio, has bamboo chairs, partly white brick walls, trellis and a 'garden' effect.

A good choice of food is served all day ranging from light snacks

29

– sandwiches, burgers, salads, omelettes – to full meals – chicken, plaice, liver, gammon – and lots of pastries and puddings. The restaurant menu is simple and the dinner menu has some interesting starters including Brown Windsor soup (we thought it existed only in Terence Rattigan plays). Main courses include steak, pork, chicken, and venison pie. The 'speciality' menu when we visited was trout – potted trout, trout terrine, trout Montmartre and so on.

Accommodation is free for children up to 5 and from 5 to 14 is £1 if they share their parents' room. They can eat half portions or choose from the special children's menu.

Beverley is a superb town with two exceptional churches and this is a good hotel for a short stay.

61 rooms, 2 family   Moderate   Open all year
Ridings Buttery 10am-7pm (Sun 10am-6pm)
Lunch 12-2.15 main course around £3
Dinner 7.30-9.45 – £8.75   Ale – Theakston's
Access/AmEx/Barclaycard/Diners   P – 70 spaces at the back

Biddenden, Kent   map 1

P   ***THREE CHIMNEYS***

On the A262 about one mile from the village of Biddenden.

A real gem of a country pub not far from Sissinghurst Gardens. Inside are a series of wood-beamed rooms and behind the bar the beers sit on their stillages in serried ranks.

The children's room is splendidly in keeping and leads out to a large and lovely lawned garden with benches and chairs.

A good range of hot and cold food, far from run-of-the-mill, (eg pigeon casserole) is available all week.

Ale – Adnam's, Felinfoel, Harvey's, Whitbread
P – own ample car park

Bilbrook, Nr Minehead, Somerset   map 2

H R   ***THE DRAGON HOUSE*** – phone Washford 40215

On the A39 about five miles west of Minehead.

A beautiful 17th century stone house with deep roofs set in over two acres of appealing gardens. It was once a smuggler's haunt and then changed character as a Methodist preaching house.

The rooms inside are superb: a galleried hall and a beamed lounge with a fine fireplace taking pride of place. There is some lovely old furniture and a generally welcoming atmosphere.

There is a separate and very pretty room where children may eat, and they can choose half portions from the main menu or have their own special meal. At lunchtimes there are various snacks on offer plus grilled meals – steak, trout, ham, egg and chips, etc – at prices up to £6. The set menu in the evenings offers good, plain cooking based on soups, patés and plenty of fish and meat dishes.

Cots are charged at £5 per night, and an extra bed £10.

Apart from the lovely gardens, there is a delightful paved courtyard in which to down a pint on summer days.

There are plenty of diversions nearby, and the hotel will arrange fishing or rough shooting or riding.

11 rooms, 1 triple   Moderate   Closed Nov
Lunch 12-2pm – £6   Dinner 7.15-9pm – £9.50
Ale – Hall & Woodhouse
Access/AmEx/Barclaycard/Diners   P – own car park

Billesley, Nr Stratford-upon-Avon, Warwicks   map 3

H   *BILLESLEY MANOR* (Celebrated Hotels) – *phone Stratford-upon-Avon 763 737*

Just off the A422 about three miles out of Stratford towards Worcester. Watch for the badly-placed sign.

This is a magnificent stone manor house of Tudor vintage. It stands in eleven acres of rolling walled gardens in which there is a pitch and putt course, two hard tennis courts, croquet and a weird and wonderful display of topiary. The terrace at the rear overlooks the gardens and at the side an extension has recently been built in the same style and succeeds as well as one might hope. There is also a lovely indoor swimming pool.

Children's accommodation charges are £5 for a cot and £15 for an extra bed. Half portions are served in the restaurant, which has a very large and comprehensive menu.

A splendidly peaceful place to stay with excellent facilities – and quite close to Stratford.

28 rooms, 1 family   Expensive   Open all year
Lunch 12.30-1.30pm – £9   Dinner 7.30-9.30pm – £15
Access/AmEx/Barclaycard   P – own car park

Binfield, Berks   map 1

Alexander Pope was living in Binfield when he wrote 'The Rape of the Lock'. A mini pub-crawl for you, with a choice of two excellent pubs:

31

P   **STAG AND HOUNDS,** Forest Road

On the B3034 on the east side of the village.

A splendid old pub, part of which dates from the 14th century. It's a long, smartly painted, building with a large grassy garden with bench tables at the front and another garden at the back. Inside are low ceilings, fine fireplaces and an abundance of horse brasses.

Children are welcome in the pub on any evenings, or at lunchtimes at the weekend (not lunchtimes from Monday to Friday). They are spoiled for choice because there are three rooms which they can use – all are small, very attractive rooms with low beams and plenty of tables and chairs.

There is a fair selection of pub food: at lunchtimes pizzas, sausage and chips, sandwiches and a range of salads from £2 to £3. In the evening the choice is smaller: sandwiches, plough-man's, pizzas and moussaka were on the menu when we visited.

It's a fine pub, and outside are the remains of an old elm which marks what was once the centre of Windsor Great Forest. In those days the building was probably a hunting lodge.

Ale – Courage   P – own car park

P   **VICTORIA ARMS,** Terrace Road North

Off the B3034, north-west of Bracknell.

A pretty well-tended village pub with an unusual design inside – the bar is in the middle of the room and there is a feeling of spaciousness as a result.

The bar looks out over a large and pretty lawned garden with plenty of bench tables. Here, under the main building, is an excellent children's room. It is well-heated in winter and is designed with children specifically in mind with its murals, mini-furniture and toys.

A good range of food is served six days a week (not Sunday). From 12 till 2 the dishes cost no more than £2 and include lamb and apple pie, lasagne, jacket potatoes with various fillings, burgers, sausages, etc. There is more choice, at slightly higher prices in the evening from 7 to 9.30 – rump steak at under £4, scampi, chicken and chips, pizzas, kebabs in pitta bread, paté and so on.

The enterprising landlord runs barbecues on summer evenings when weather permits.

Ale – Fuller's   P – own car park

Birmingham, West Midlands

map 3

H   *THE ALBANY HOTEL* (THF), Smallbrook, Queensway – phone
021 643 8171

In the centre of the city.

If, heaven forfend, you have to stay in the centre of Birmingham,
this hotel – large, modern and designed by an architect using a
Lego set – is a possibility. Packed with a business clientele, it
offers excellent facilities in its leisure centre including four
squash courts, a heated pool, a snooker room and a
well-equipped (and supervised) gym with static bikes, lots of
weights, etc.

In the Carvery you will find a cold buffet and help-yourself
roasts, and a wider range of dishes in the Four Seasons.
Children have their own special menu or half portions from the
main menus; and are accommodated free up to 5 years or for a
nominal £1 between 5 and 14.

250 rooms, 6 family   Expensive   Open all year
Lunch – Four Seasons Mon-Fri 12-2.30 – £7;
Carvery 12-2.30pm – £7.95 3 courses
Dinner – Four Seasons Mon-Fri 7.30-11pm – £7.25;
Carvery 6-10pm – £7.95
Ale – Davenport's
Access/AmEx/Barclaycard/Diners   P – own car park

Bishops Lydeard, Somerset

map 2

P   *BELL INN*

Off the A358.

A fine sandstone pub by an ancient church. The beamed
interior has walls of rough hewn stone. There is a lovely garden
at the front and a little patio with a rock pool at the side.

Children can use a room at the back of the pub or one of the two
skittle alleys.

Food is served every day from 12 to 2 pm and from 6pm to
9.45pm (slightly shorter hours on Sundays). There is a good
range of hot and cold pub food from sandwiches at under £1 to a
rump steak and vegetables at under £4; and in between such
dishes as chicken and mushroom pie, steak and kidney pie,
ploughman's, chicken kiev, plaice, scampi, etc.

Ale – Usher's   P – own car park

Blackboys, East Sussex   map 1

P   *BLACKBOYS INN*

Situated on B2192 at the southern end of the village on the Heathfield-Lewes road.

A lovely Tudor pub with a brick and black boarded façade. It has a huge back garden with apple trees, a goat, chickens and rabbits; and a duck pond at the front.

There's a separate children's room at the side – large and a bit barracky but with climbing frames and games.

The restaurant serves such things as chicken kiev, veal escalopes, porterhouse steaks and lobster, and the snack menu concentrates on traditional pub food at under £2 – baked potatoes, sausage and chips, hot pies, sandwiches, ploughman's, etc.

Ale – Harvey's   P – ample parking

Blakeney, Norfolk   map 4

H   *BLAKENEY HOTEL* (Best Western), The Quay – phone Cley 740 797

On the A149.

A fine building of flint and brick in a marvellous situation overlooking the harbour, for small craft only now, but in medieval times a noted port. The area is a paradise for naturalists and ornithologists; and for golfers too, with Hunstanton, Brancaster and Sheringham close by.

There is a lawned garden shaded by tall trees, and an indoor heated swimming pool which becomes outdoor in the summer – the transparent roof can be rolled off. There is also a games room with a pool table and table tennis, and some swings for children in the garden.

Children under 12 are accommodated free, and, as well as half portions in the restaurant, high teas are served at 6pm. The five rooms in the Granary, on the ground floor and with a patio each, are ideal for families, as are the three rooms in the Garden Cottage.

54 rooms, 17 family   Moderate   Open all year
Lunch bar snacks 12-2.15pm   Dinner 7-9.30pm – £8.20
Ale – Bass, Greene King
Access/AmEx/Barclaycard/Diners   P – own car park

Blanchland, Nr Consett, Co. Durham map 5

H   *LORD CREWE ARMS HOTEL* – phone 251

On the B6306.

A gem of a North-Eastern village in the Derwent Valley and a great centre for grouse shooting on the beautiful Blanchland moors. The hotel, built in the middle of the 13th century, was once the home of the Abbot of Blanchland. Naturally, it has a ghost. The interior has stone flags and walls, fine fireplaces and oak beams. There is a good sized grassy garden which looks away to the open country, and with a dove aviary at one side.

Accommodation is free for children up to the age of 12, and children's portions are available ('anything they require') in the restaurant. The restaurant is sometimes open for lunch, and bar snacks are always available.

A good place to stop if you are touring in this magnificent countryside.

17 rooms, 1 family   Moderate   Open all year
Dinner 7-9.15pm – £7.95   Ale – Vaux Samson
Access/AmEx/Barclaycard/Diners
P – on the street or in the village

Bledlow, Bucks map 1

P   *LIONS OF BLEDLOW*

Off the B4009 near Chinnor.

A lovely old rambling pub near the Chilterns. There is lots of oak panelling plus a huge log fire. There are a few tables outside at the front and a sheltered garden at the rear.

The children's room, a little gaunt, is off the main bar.

A good range of bar food – sandwiches and hot meals – is available every day except Sunday evenings. These include paté and salad, fisherman's platter, various pies (steak and kidney, etc), canneloni, lasagne, etc, at prices up to £2.

Ale – Young's, Wadworth's   P – own car park

Bodfari, Clwyd map 3

P   *DINORBEN ARMS*

Follow the signs to Tremeirchion from the A541 – it's right by the village church.

A truly amazing black and white pub built on a hill. It has several bars with low oak-beamed ceilings, oak furniture, stained glass and wonderful wood carvings throughout. The dining room has a splendid jug collection suspended from its beams. There is a pretty covered terrace and many other terraces on different levels.

The children's room – the 'Garden Room' – is in the same fine style and there is also a grassy enclosed play area for them, with a swing, a little away from the pub.

At lunchtime (12-2.30pm) French rolls with lots of different fillings are served – single 80p, double £1.50 – together with a smorgasbord buffet at £4.75 for adults and £2.90 for children. The evening menu (6-10.15pm) is vast – start and finish by choosing from the well-displayed Starters and Sweets Bar and from main courses as varied as chicken curry, roast pheasant, Hungarian goulash, scallops en brochette – need I go on?

A very enterprising landlord has done a first class job in building up a pub that offers everything. Except, possibly, peace. We visited out of hours, but would guess it fairly heaves during the season.

P – masses of parking space

Bolney, West Sussex   map 1

R   **BOLNEY STAGE**, London Road – phone 312

On the A23.

A splendid 15th century tile-fronted pub with a beamed interior and a patio at the front and side. It has a sizeable restaurant with a view over a garden and offers a varied menu – normally fourteen starters and fourteen main courses. There is a fairly conventional range of starters – soups, roll mop herring, tuna fish salad, whitebait, etc – and main courses such as fish pie, plaice, cod, duck, chicken kiev and steak and kidney pie and pudding.

Half portions are served to children, but there are no facilities to change or breast-feed a baby.

It's a good stopping off point near the Sussex coast.

Closed Sun dinner/Monday   Lunch 12.30-2pm — £8
Dinner 7.30-10pm – £8
Ale – Young's, Harvey's, Courage, Martlet
Access/AmEx/Barclaycard   P – own large car park

Borrowdale, Nr Keswick, Cumbria

map 5

H   *LODORE SWISS HOTEL – phone 285*

On the B5289 off A66/A591

The dining room and lounge of the Lodore Swiss are slightly reminiscent of Majorcan package tours, but otherwise this hotel has everything you could want. A big dry-stone building it is set in beautiful surroundings by Derwentwater in the heart of the Lake District. Its amenities include indoor and outdoor swimming pools and children's paddling pool, tennis, squash, exercise rooms, free weekday golf at nearby Keswick (the hotel sponsored a hole), sauna, solarium and massage. And you can enjoy all these at your leisure as there are two trained nannies on duty in the nursery every day from 8.30am to 6pm. It's a large bright L-shaped nursery with toys, games, books and a vintage rocking horse. Seven infants were having breakfast there when we visited – very happy and not a peep out of them. Children under 6 are not allowed in the dining room and good menus (which include fresh vegetables, not just chips) are offered in the nursery – breakfast, lunch and supper – so you can eat in peace too. There's lots else to do – films, television, enclosed playground with sandpit, wendy house, etc, trampoline, games room with table tennis and games machines. There are splendid laundry facilities and a good shop within the hotel.

The food is varied and interesting – treat yourself to the chef's Menu Surprise at £35 for two if you're feeling rich – and sandwiches, open sandwiches and pastries are available all day.

Accommodation prices for children sharing with parents are: up to 12 months £8, 1-2 years £11, 3 years £15, 4 and 5 years £18 – prices include all nursery meals. Any extra bed thereafter is £6 b and b.

We picked this hotel as a runner-up in its category for its superb all-round facilities. It exudes an air of friendly efficiency and is in a wonderful part of Britain.

72 rooms, 14 family   Expensive   Closed 4 Nov to 29 Mar
Lunch 1-2pm £6.50   Dinner 7-9pm £9
AmEx only   P – own car park

Botley, Hants

map 1

R   *COBBETTS*, 14 The Square – phone 2068

On the A3051 a couple of miles west of Southampton.

This is an attractive restaurant both inside and out, with its 16th century façade and attractively decorated interior. The high chair is in the same wheelback style as the other chairs.

The emphasis, despite the restaurant's name, is on French cooking and the short and manageable menu might contain salmon marinated in dill and basil, sweetbreads in a pastry case, salade paysanne and frogs' legs; and main courses like pigeon flamed in cassis, grilled lobster and poitrine de canard.

The owners are very helpful towards parents with children, and, apart from offering half portions, will lend an upstairs room to a mother who needs to feed or change a baby. But they do not encourage the presence of very young children in the restaurant during the evening.

Closed Sat lunch, Mon lunch, Sun and public hols
Lunch 12-2pm – £7.50   Dinner 7.30-9.45pm – £12 alc
Licensed   Access only   P – 15 spaces only

Bournemouth, Dorset   map 2

H   *LADBROKE SAVOY HOTEL,* West Cliff – phone 294 241

Follow the signs from the centre of the town to West Cliff.

Huge old mellow brick seaside hotel with some balconied rooms set on a cliff top. The lawned gardens lead down to a wide sandy beach and have a good swimming pool with paddling pool and refreshment bar. Below the sun terrace are new rooms – pity they look like the fronts of suburban betting shops.

There is no charge for children to the age of 14 sharing their parents' accommodation. The restaurant has a special children's menu and half portions too are served. During May to September a children's hostess (nanny to you and me) is on duty from 11am-9pm every day organising the children in all manner of activities. A great bonus for parents in search of psychological retrenchment.

88 rooms, 21 family   Expensive   Open all year
Lunch buffet only 12.30-2pm   Dinner 7-8.45pm – £8.50
Access/AmEx/Barclaycard/Diners   P – own car park

H   *ROYAL BATH HOTEL* (De Vere), Bath Road – phone 25555

Smack at the centre of the sea front.

An imposing Victorian edifice: it is the grandest of grand luxury hotels with a long white façade and vast and elegant public rooms. It has three acres of beautifully kept formal gardens in which is a large heated pool with a patio and a refreshment bar.

Indoors there is a huge games room with table tennis, a pool table, space invaders and other toys. There is a resident nanny from 9am to 5.30pm during the summer season and baby-sitting can also be arranged with prior notice.

The restaurant has a special children's menu and serves half portions. During July and August children under 15 are accommodated free: at other times children under 5 are charged at one-third of the adult rate.

As an alternative, across the road is another de Vere hotel, the Marsham Court.

133 rooms, 70 family   Expensive   Open all year
Lunch 12-2.30pm – £7.50   Dinner 7-9.30pm – £10
AmEx/Barclaycard/Diners   P – own car park

Bowness-on-Windermere, Cumbria   map 5

H   *BELSFIELD HOTEL* (THF) – phone Windermere 2448

Above the Lake in the centre of the town. The entrance is at the back of the hotel.

Imposing hotel above Lake Windermere in its own six acres of grounds and with grand public rooms. Try to get a bedroom overlooking the lake. It has a lot to offer parents with children – primarily the fact that the light, bright nursery has a nanny available 'all the time' (we couldn't pin them down to nursery hours – they insist that if you want a nanny, you shall have one). There is also a play area with a swingbridge, tunnel-thro-a-dolphin and other equipment, a covered swimming pool, a putting green, table tennis, and curling. A short walk across the road takes you to the Lake.

Accommodation is free for children up to 5 and a nominal charge of £1 is made for children aged from 5 to 14. Tea is served in the nursery at 5.30 and children have their own special menu or can choose half portions from the adult menu. Lunch is bar snacks only and has a good choice of food at reasonable prices – salad, smorgasbord, sea food kebab, burgers.

71 rooms, 7 family, 6 suites, 2 sets of adjoining rooms
Moderate   Open all year   Bar lunch 12-2pm – £2-4
Dinner 7-9.15pm – £9.50
Access/AmEx/Barclaycard/Diners   P – own car park

H   *THE OLD ENGLAND HOTEL* (THF) – phone Windermere 2444

By the lakeside in the centre of town.

A grand old Victorian hotel by the shores of the Lake. It has some very elegant public rooms, spacious and high-ceilinged, and decorated in the most fetching style. The pretty lawned garden by the Lake has a sizeable heated swimming pool, and a games room is set up during the season (it had become a temporary office when we visited). Guests here can also use the facilities at the Belsfield over the road – see above.

There are lots of family rooms here – 4 quadruple, 6 triple and the 26 rooms in the Lake Wing all take an extra bed. The charges and food for children, are, like the Belsfield, the usual THF bargain – free for under-5s, £1 for 5s to 14s, with special menu or half price. Lunch consists of buffet or bar snacks – meat salads, sandwiches – and there is a barbecue during the summer.

82 rooms+ (see text)   Expensive   Open all year
Lunch 12.30-2.30pm – from £2   Dinner 7-9.15pm – £9.50
Ale – Tetley
Access/AmEx/Barclaycard/Diners   P – own car park

Box Hill, Nr Dorking, Surrey   map 1

H R   *BURFORD BRIDGE HOTEL* (THF) – phone Dorking 884 561

On the A24 on the north side of Dorking.

A rambling two-storey building in lovely gardens at the foot of famous Box Hill. It has naval and literary associations – Lord Nelson was a regular visitor with Lady Hamilton and Keats is said to have written part of 'Endymion' here. There's a large heated outdoor swimming pool and a patio where one can eat.

The unobtrusive extension at the rear has 22 rooms – all family rooms. Children under 5 have free accommodation with a nominal charge of £1 made for 5s to 14s. A special children's menu is available and half portions are served.

There is a lunchtime buffet of cold meats and salads at under £4 and a substantial ploughman's at £2.25. The restaurant menu has some interesting dishes such as sea bass and salmon terrine, 'symphony of seafoods' (with Elgar sauce?), a Covent Garden tart (wonder what that is?) and we detected on the list a 'Maigret of duckling'. There is also an excellent afternoon tea at around £5 and it is served between 4 and 5.30 pm.

52 rooms, 25 family   Expensive   Open all year
Lunch 12.30-2.30pm – £7   Dinner 7.30-9.30pm – £11.75
Access/AmEx/Barclaycard/Diners   P – own car park

Bramber, West Sussex map 1

R *OLD TOLLGATE RESTAURANT* – phone Steyning 813 362

Just off the A283 as you enter village.

A busy restaurant in a very pretty village, which was one of William the Conqueror's regional capitals. The National Butterfly Museum is here.

It's a bright and appealing place, with paved floors, wood panelling and beams, and wallpaper with a red brick pattern. It sounds frightful – but it works. There are two long rooms: the bar, where snacks can be ordered, and the dining room, and they look out to a long, lawned garden with a few tables and chairs.

The menu is uncomplicated – either two or three courses – with a good choice of fish, roasts and casseroles and a wide variety of salads. They will serve half portions, or any size of portion, to children and charge accordingly.

The 'Ladies' has adequate room to deal with a baby's needs.

Closed Sun evenings Lunch 12.30-1.45pm
Dinner 7.15-10pm – £5.95 or £7.95 Licensed
Access/AmEx/Barclaycard/Diners P – adequate space

Brandon, Nr Coventry, Warwicks map 1

H R *BRANDON HALL HOTEL* (THF) – phone Coventry 542 571

On the A428, east of Coventry.

Quite attractive cream-painted country house in lovely wooded and lawned grounds. The dark red brick extension for some reason fits in well, as does the separate squash centre with its six courts. There is a patio by the bar, a pitch and putt golf area and an outdoor play area for children with a slide, swings and climbing frame. Quite a peaceful haven between the Midlands motorways.

Children up to 5 are accommodated free; and there is a nominal charge of £1 up to 14.

The restaurant offers a special children's menu and half portions. The main menu is comprehensive and British in conception. Lemon sole and fresh trout are offered in various styles, and there are old favourites such as roast turkey, roast saddle of lamb, steak, mushroom and oyster pie, ribs of beef and so on. The bar food at lunchtimes ranges in price up to £2.50, and includes hot beef rolls, a casserole, omelettes, smoked mackerel and plaice and chips.

68 rooms, 4 sets of adjoining rooms   Cheap   Open all year
Lunch 12-2pm – £5.95   Dinner 7-9.30pm – £7.25
Access/AmEx/Barclaycard/Diners   P – own car park

Bray, Nr Maidenhead, Berks   map 1

H R   *MONKEY ISLAND HOTEL* – phone Maidenhead 23400

From the centre of Bray there are some rather small signposts to Monkey Island.

A very interesting hotel on, as its name tells you, an island. The hotel has a rather Doric mien with its pillars, and indeed was built as a temple by the 3rd Duke of Marlborough in the early 18th century. The restaurant and bar is a separate building and was once a fishing lodge. Surrounded by the Thames and lovely sweeping lawns, one's peace is only impinged upon by the distant hum of M4 traffic and the not unpleasant chug of boats.

The menu is quite extensive and offers the normal hotel fare – smoked trout, patés and prawn cocktail to begin, and to follow sole, halibut, and trout, steaks or lamb cutlets.

Cots are available at no extra cost, and an extra bed costs half the single rate. Children's portions are offered in the restaurant at reduced prices.

25 rooms, 1 family   Expensive   Open all year
Lunch 12.30-2pm – £11.50   Dinner 7.30-10pm – £11.50
Access/AmEx/Barclaycard/Diners   P – own car park

Bretforton, Hereford & Worcs   map 2

P   *THE FLEECE*   ♟

In the centre of the village off the B4035 east of Evesham.

A magnificent medieval pub, which was a farmhouse until the middle of the 19th century and is now owned by the National Trust. It is wonderfully furnished throughout its four paved and beamed rooms with old oak tables, a dresser, grandfather clock and high-backed settles – a real classic.

Children are welcome in a room next to the food servery and there is a huge garden.

There is an excellent range of food which is available every day, mornings and evenings, from Easter to October 1. You can eat sandwiches, paté and salads, plaice, sausages, scampi, steaks, gammon, ploughman's, etc – at prices from 60p to £5. In the winter, no food is offered on Monday and

Tuesday evenings.

This is one of the two runners-up for our 'best pub' award. It is one of the most attractive pubs in England and with a splendid room where parents may take their children. With its friendly atmosphere the pub had to be singled out for special praise.

Ale – Donnington, Hook Norton, Marston's
P – in village square

Brighton, East Sussex   map 1

H   *HOTEL CURZON* (THF), Cavendish Place – phone 25788

In a cul-de-sac at the Hove end of the main promenade.

We could not leave Brighton out, with its many attractions and splendid atmosphere, and this charming Georgian building houses a comfortable hotel just west of the pier. It's not as big as its THF sister hotel down the road, the Dudley, which you might bear in mind as an alternative.

You are close to the centre of the town here, and there are the usual THF terms for children – free accommodation to the age of 5, and £1 a night from 5 to 14.

A buffet lunch is in operation from Monday to Saturday from 12.15pm to 2pm, and this includes cold meats and salads, sandwiches and hot dishes such as turkey à la king, boeuf bourguignon – at prices around £2. Children have their own menu or can eat half price from the main menu.

46 rooms, 2 family   Moderate   Open all year   Ale – Webster's
Access/AmEx/Barclaycard/Diners   P – 16 spaces

Broadway, Hereford & Worcs   map 2

Broadway is one of the most glorious of English villages and is in the Cotswolds – an area of great beauty and historical interest.

H   *DORMY HOUSE HOTEL*, Willersley Hill – phone 852 711

Just outside Broadway on the A44 to Stow-on-the-Wold. There is a sign half way up a steep hill.

A handsome 17th century stone building, once a farmhouse, ivy-clad, delightfully situated on top of a hill above Broadway and right next door to the golf course. Many of the outhouses have been converted to rooms and there are little quiet grassy courtyards to be found, and a patio by the bar. Inside there is plenty of wood panelling and a lovely stone walled dining room with lots of quiet alcoves.

43

Accommodation for children is more or less free – no charge for cots and £5 charged for an extra bed, but this includes breakfast. The restaurant will serve 'whatever is required' to children or half portions.

50 rooms, 40 family   Expensive   Open all year
Lunch 12.30-1.45pm – £8.50   Dinner 7.30-9.30pm – £11
Access/AmEx/Barclaycard/Diners   P – own car park

R   ***HUNTER'S LODGE,*** High Street – phone 853 247

A most appealing building, Cotswold stone and ivy – archetypal Broadway. It has a big grassy garden at the back with plenty of tables for summer days.

There is a pleasant sitting room and pretty dining room where adults as well as children may have half portions of anything. How sensible. There is plenty of choice on the menu with richer dishes in the evening: for example côte de porc au Roquefort, carré d'agneau à la diable and so on.

The friendly but firm owner does not welcome children under 8 in the evening – she takes the view that adults should be able to enjoy their evening out undisturbed. Hear, hear!

The Ladies is spacious enough to cope with a baby.

Closed Sun evenings and Mon, 3 weeks in Jan
Lunch 12.30-2pm – £8 alc   Dinner 7.30-10pm – £14 alc
Licensed   Access/AmEx/Barclaycard/Diners   P – own car park

H R   ***LYGON ARMS*** (Prestige) – phone 852 255

In the main street.

This famous inn has a tradition of excellence and dates from the time of Henry VIII. It is built from Cotswold stone and looks warm and welcoming with its high gables and tall chimneys. It has fourteen acres of grounds and a lovely lawned and flower-bedecked garden about 200 yards long. There is also a hard tennis court.

Some imagination is put into the table d'hôte menus: parsnip and apricot soup and boiled leg of lamb with onions for lunch for example, and fish salad in herb dressing and mignon of veal and prune for dinner. The restaurant will serve half portions to children and offers them their own special menu.

An extra bed in the parents' room costs £10 and a cot £7.50

67 rooms, 5 family   Expensive   Open all year
Lunch 12.30-2pm – £7.25   Dinner 7.30-9.15pm – £13
Access/AmEx/Barclaycard/Diners   P – own car park

Brockenhurst, New Forest, Hants

H P R *CAREY'S MANOR*, Lyndhurst Road – phone Lymington 23551

On the A337 just north of the village.

Lovely old ivy-clad mansion of tall chimneys. Part of it dates from the reign of Charles II who used it as a hunting lodge. The new wing is a bit motel-like, but does not spoil the overall effect. There are several acres of pleasant, partly-walled garden.

In the grounds is the hotel's own pub – the 'Jugged Hare'. It's modern but with an excellent conservatory, which is used as a children's room and with lots of tables and bentwood chairs. It has its own patio and garden and offers a big range of food seven days a week – lots of cold meats, salads and hot dishes of the day.

£6 is charged for an extra bed and £3 for a cot. A children's menu is available at dinner in the restaurant and half portions are also served. The menu here has the usual items – patés, soups, duck, moussaka, roasts, etc – but also some less usual dishes, for example fillet of brill, monkfish and jugged hare.

57 rooms, 37 family   Moderate   Open all year
Lunch 12.30-2pm – £6   Dinner 7-10pm – £9
Ale – Wadworth's, Strong's, Flowers
Access/AmEx/Barclaycard   P – own car park

H   *LADBROKE BALMER LAWN HOTEL* – phone Lymington 23116

On the A337 just north of the village.

A balconied Georgian hotel which is set well back from the main road and overlooks the village cricket ground. Odd-looking but not unpleasant building – perhaps they should lop off a floor to achieve better proportions. It has an exercise room with wall bars and a rowing machine – and a games room: table tennis, pool table, space invader and table football. In the gardens are two squash courts, a tennis court and a heated swimming pool with a refreshment bar.

Children are accommodated free up to the age of 14; £7.50 if they occupy a separate room. A special menu is available for children as well as half portions.

60 rooms, 29 family   Moderate   Open all year
Lunch 12.30-1.45pm – £6.50   Dinner 7-9pm – £7.50
Access/AmEx/Barclaycard/Diners   P – own car park

45

Brodie, by Forres, Grampian

map 6

R   *BRODIE COUNTRYFARE* – phone 339

On the A96 east of Nairn.

A basic café/coffee bar with a plain interior and pine benches and tables. There is a good range of salads at 30p each, several hot dishes each day at about £1.50, good puddings and fresh rolls. Good value.

There is a table in the 'Ladies' where a baby can be changed but no privacy for breast-feeding.

Next door are craft and farm produce shops.

Closed at Christmas and first 2 weeks of Jan
Open 9.30am-5.30pm (Sun 10am-6.30pm)
No credit cards accepted   P – own car park

Bromley Cross, Nr Bolton, Gt Manchester

map 3

H R   *LAST DROP HOTEL* – phone Bolton 591 131

Signposted off the A666 just north of Bolton.

A marvellous little integrated village, amazingly well done from what were originally old stone farm buildings and with new additions which marry in very well. Complete complex of hotel, bistro, pub, tea shop (with highchairs) and shops including an art gallery. Lots of gardens and views to the hills. Why do we have doubts? Because: it looks as if the Disney Corporation built it; apart from the garden, there's nothing specifically for children; and it's situated in the Lancashire industrial heartland. Okay for a stopover or a meal.

A charge of £6 is made for each child up to 12 years and the restaurant serves half portions from the menu and table d'hôte for children at £2.60 at lunchtimes. The set lunch is very good value with plenty of choice of main course – roast beef or pork, grilled gammon, kidneys turbigo, plaice, etc. The evening menu is comprehensive and has such local dishes as black pudding and Southport shrimps, as well as smoked salmon and snails; there are lots of fish and steak dishes, veal and duck.

69 rooms, 28 triples   Moderate   Open all year
Lunch 12-2pm – £4.95   Dinner 7-10pm – £10 alc
Access/AmEx/Barclaycard/Diners   P – own car park

Buckden, Cambs

map 1

H   *LION HOTEL,* Great North Road – phone Huntingdon 810 313

Turn off the A1 to the village – the Lion is in the centre.

Very smartly renovated white painted old coaching inn with deep tiled roofs and overhanging windows in a small and pretty village. It is very close to a lovely old manor house of mainly 17th century origin. Unusually, this hotel which was once owned by THF, was bought back by the present owners. Buffet lunches are served at around £3 and the restaurant has standard hotel fare.

Cots are free and £1 is charged for an extra bed for a child of up to 14. Half portions are served to children in the restaurant.

12 rooms, 4 family   Cheap   Open all year
Lunch 12.30-2.15pm – £4   Dinner 7-9.15pm – £10 alc
Access/AmEx/Barclaycard/Diners   P – own car park

Buckingham, Bucks

map 1

H P R   *WHITE HART HOTEL* (THF), Market Square – phone 815 151

In the middle of the town.

This is an archetypal county town hotel, with a Georgian façade. It is small, well looked after and comfortable, and has a spacious lounge area where families can sit. When we visited it was crowded with parents and children who were about to have lunch, for which one can choose amongst grills, steak and kidney pie, seafood pie, etc. Alternatively the bar meal menu offers a ploughman's, sandwiches, a hot dish of the day, steak and kidney pie, or cold meat and salad at prices up to £2.75.

Children up to 5 are accommodated free and a charge of £1 is made for children from 5 to 14. The restaurant has a special children's menu and serves half portions from the main menu.

A pleasant welcoming place to stop in an interesting old market town.

19 rooms, 2 family   Moderate   Open all year
Lunch 12.30-2.15pm – £8 alc   Dinner 7-9.30pm – £8.25
Ale – Hook Norton, Courage
Access/AmEx/Barclaycard/Diners
P – own car park

Burley, Hants

map 2

H P R *BURLEY MANOR HOTEL* – phone 3314

Close to the centre of the village.

This is a rather appealing building, of mid-19th century vintage, in patterned brick with elongated chimneys, square stone windows and turrets and topped by dormer windows. It is surrounded by open country and has a huge lawned garden.

There is an excellent outdoor heated swimming pool, table tennis and riding stables in the grounds. Also in the grounds is a big white-painted pub/restaurant called Charcoals which serves a range of charcoal grilled meals from 12-2pm and 6.30-10pm. There is a small room for families to use at one side and a lawned garden with bench tables by the stables – we hope the loud music doesn't frighten the horses. They will serve half portions, as will the hotel restaurant which has a wider repertoire of dishes. High teas are also served from 6.30 to 7.30pm.

No charge is made for the accommodation of children up to the age of 15.

22 rooms, 4 family   Moderate   Open all year
Lunch in Charcoal's only except Sundays.
Dinner 7.30-10pm – £8.45   Ale – Strong's (in Charcoals)
Access/AmEx/Barclaycard/Diners   P – own car park

H *MOORHILL HOUSE HOTEL* – phone 3285

At the Queen's Head in the centre of the village go up the hill and turn right at the Cricket ground – there is a hotel sign.

A solid looking and well cared for Victorian building in the heart of the New Forest above the busy village of Burley. The hotel, tiled around the top half of its façade, is at the end of a long drive in three acres of lawns surrounded by towering trees.

There are some useful facilities indoors, including a heated pool, a sauna and a whirlpool – all together in a small, new 'leisure complex'.

The amiable owner stressed that they are keen to welcome families: 'we don't get upset if a child drops a glass', and when we visited was preparing, with genuine enthusiasm, to greet for the weekend families with about twenty children between them.

There is no charge for cots; and thereafter children up to 12 years are charged at half the adult rate.

23 rooms, 7 family   Moderate   Open all year
Access/AmEx/Barclaycard   P – own car park

P   *QUEEN'S HEAD*

Off the A31.

This is a big rambling pub, in brick and with an appealing tiled façade, in a busy tourist village. Inside there are a number of small and interesting rooms, most of them with paved stone floors. There are low beams and wooden settles, an intricately carved fireplace in one room, and in another a wood-burning stove.

There is a small, but reasonably comfortable, children's room and a narrow patio which runs the length of the front of the pub and has a few tables and chairs. There is a range of snacks, sandwiches and salads at lunchtimes, but in the evening only baps with various fillings.

In summer waggon rides start from the pub car park.

Ale – Flowers, Strong's   P – own car park

Byworth, West Sussex   map 1

P   *BLACK HORSE*

Close to Petworth – look for the sign off the A283.

A great old pub, medieval, with a stone and brick front. There is a small terrace at the back, and the garden rambles, slightly but charmingly unkempt in steps down to wooded countryside. There are a couple of willow trees in the garden. The interior has not been messed about, and at the rear of the pub there are rooms which are primarily intended for eating and where children may go.

There is a good array of food available seven days a week, but beware of 'last orders' which is at 1.45pm and 9.45pm (and slightly earlier on Sundays). Apart from basic pub food such as shepherd's pie, sausages and hamburgers, there are more interesting items such as barbecued spare ribs and lambs kidneys in sherry (both under £2) and chicken Alexandre and chicken Milanese (both under £3).

The pub is only a mile or so from that interesting town Petworth and Petworth House with its magnificent collection of paintings by Turner, Van Dyck, Holbein, Rembrandt, Gainsborough, et alia, and is a good place to repair to after the rigours of sightseeing.

Ale – Young's   P – difficult: on street only

49

Caersws, Powys
map 3

H R *MAESMAWR HALL HOTEL* – phone 255

On the A489 just east of Caersws.

After turning into the drive you catch your first glimpse, through the trees, of this glorious example of Elizabethan architecture. Built in 1535, it's a real gem with its black and white façade and leaded windows. You enter through a wide oak door and, avoiding the accusing eye of the stag's head on the wall, can admire the carved oak panelling, superb fireplaces and beamed ceilings. All this and set in spacious and peaceful lawned grounds.

This is a haven for fishermen, as the Severn runs through the grounds and the hotel can offer three-and-a-half miles of salmon and trout fishing, plus some salmon pools near Newtown and coarse fishing during winter. The hotel can also arrange pony-trekking nearby.

There is a full lunch menu and a good choice of bar snacks too – steak, chicken, scampi, omelettes, ploughman's from about £1 up to £5. The restaurant itself offers plain dishes such as sole meunière, Welsh lamb, pork chops, sauté of chicken, etc. Children's dishes (at around £1.50) can be arranged: fish fingers, beans on toast, and things with chips.

Cots are charged at £4 per night; an extra bed costs 50% of the adult rate for a child up to 10 years; and there is a 25% reduction from 10 to 14 years.

20 rooms, 5 family   Moderate   Open all year
Lunch 12.30-2pm – £4.75   Dinner 7.30-9pm – £6.75
Access/AmEx/Barclaycard/Diners   P – own car park

Callander, Central
map 5

H R *ROMAN CAMP HOTEL* – phone 30003

Look for the sign in the town.

A quiet secluded collection of pretty pink-walled buildings form this hotel and restaurant which comes as a delightful surprise, as its entrance between two cottages is not immediately promising. Peace is the watchword and they want to keep it that way – so, only well-behaved children need apply. (There were some young children playing very happily in the grounds when we visited.) The rooms are superbly elegant with their oak panels, original fireplaces and ornate ceilings. Some rooms look over the River Teith and some over the beautiful lawned and wooded gardens – twenty acres of them. Residents may fish free on the hotel's stretch of the river, and nearby are many other sporting and recreational facilities.

The manageable lunch menu offers a few choices for each course and includes fresh salmon, poulet poché Ali Baba and roast beef. In the evening you might be tempted by Cullen Skink (smoked haddock soup to Sassenachs), entrecôte Helder, or medallions de cerf Baden Baden (venison). There are several other interesting dishes such as cherry and red wine soup and fresh pike.

They charge £7.50 for children aged 3 to 14 sharing their parents' room and £3.50 for children under 3. At 6.30 high teas are served for residents only and half portions are given to children on request.

11 rooms, 2 family, 2 suites   Moderate
Closed mid-Dec to end Jan   Lunch 12.30-2pm – £8.50
Dinner 7-9pm – £11.50
No credit cards accepted   P – own car park

Cambridge, Cambs
map 1

H R   *GARDEN HOUSE HOTEL* (Prestige), Granta Place, off Mill Lane – phone 63421

Off Trumpington Street – a main road.

This is a superbly designed modern building in mellow brick, with deep slate roofs. The balconies, cleverly emphasised with dark wooden rails, look over the terrace and the lawns down to the river. The hotel is in one of the prettiest parts of Cambridge, by the mill. Some misguided person tried their best to ruin it all by erecting a monstrosity called 'the University Centre' – only four storeys, thank goodness, but obviously designed in bits of Lego.

The public rooms are comfortable enough, and the restaurant has the great merit of overlooking the garden and the river. The menus go comprehensively through the card of soups, fish, steaks, roasts, etc. Children's portions are available.

Cots cost £5.50 a night and an extra bed £8.50 per night.

This is a smart, if rather expensive hotel, in an unrivalled position in this superb and interesting town. If you fancy your skills as a waterman, punts can be hired outside the hotel.

117 rooms, 3 triples, 3 sets of adjoining rooms   Expensive
Open all year   Lunch 12.30-2pm – £8.45
Dinner 7-9.30pm – £7-11
Access/AmEx/Barclaycard/Diners   P – own car park

H **POST HOUSE HOTEL** (THF), Lakeview, Bridge Road, Imping-
ton – phone Histon 7000

North of the city at the junction of the A45 and the B1049.

A brand new Post House, designed and built to a very high
standard. The building is of dark brick with the occasional use
of black wood facings on the façade – very effective. The interior
is spacious and airy with lots of wooden pillars and beams
throughout the entrance hall and bar.

There are splendid facilities for families: a leisure centre with a
large and very smart swimming pool and a small, well-designed
gymnasium with static bikes and weight-training equipment,
and qualified instructors to ensure that you fight the flab
sensibly. The pool looks out to a terrace and a garden, and there
is a play area here with swings, a slide, a climbing frame and a
little open-sided hut. The biggest bonus, however, is the
'hospitality hostess' (nanny to you and me) who is on duty from
three to five hours (depending on demand) every Friday,
Saturday and Sunday.

The coffee shop is open every day from 10.30 to 7 with its day
menu – club sandwiches, bacon and eggs, omelettes, burgers,
fish and chips, mixed grill, etc, at prices from about £2 to £7.
Children can order half portions or tuck into their own special
menu. The Carvery takes over at 7pm – roast beef, steaks, duck,
etc.

Accommodation for children under 5 is free, and for 5s to 14s is
£1 a night. A special menu is available for children or they can
eat half portions from the adult menus.

This hotel has a lot to offer, and presents a good alternative to
staying in the centre of traffic-clogged Cambridge.

120 rooms, all family, including 11 sets adjoining   Expensive
Open all year   Coffee Shop – 10.30am-7pm
Dinner 7-10.30pm – £12.95   Ale – Greene King, Tolly
Access/AmEx/Barclaycard/Diners   P – own car park

R **HOBBS PAVILION**, Park Terrace – phone 67480

Right on Parker's Piece.

It really is the old pavilion by Parker's Piece, where Jack Hobbs
learned his cricket, and romantics can imagine him donning his
pads where they sit and sup. It's still plain and simple – a high
ceilinged room with pine tables, pine dresser, old advertising
plates and a few watercolours on the wall.

During the day you can eat wholemeal rolls, cakes, cheese,
scones and choose between several types of tea. Lunch from 12

until the lunch food runs out encompasses quiche, pizzas, smoked turkey and chicken, pastrami, prawns, smoked mussels with salads at £2 to £3 a time. You can have alcohol from 10.30am to 3pm with your food.

Smaller portions can be ordered for children and there is a small terrace and the whole of Parker's Piece on which to romp. No facilities for attending to a baby are available – the only lavatories are the public ones by the pavilion.

Open Tue-Sat 10.30am-5pm, Fri & Sat 6.30-10pm.
Closed Sun & Mon, public holidays, 1st 2 weeks Aug, Christmas week   Lunch £5 Dinner £8   Licensed
No credit cards accepted   P – not easy – street parking only

---

Canterbury, Kent   map 1

H   *CHAUCER HOTEL* (THF), Ivy Lane – phone 64427

In the centre of town, close to the Cathedral.

A large, comfortable hotel, partly rebuilt after the war, in the centre of the town and within walking distance of the famous Cathedral – hence its inclusion.

Accommodation free for children up to 5 with a charge of £1 from 5 to 14.

The buffet lunches are good value – salads and dishes of the day such as steak and kidney pie, beef stroganoff, or chicken curry – and the dinner menu, as well as roasts, might have Whitstable oysters Mornay to offer. There is a special children's menu in the dining room and half portions are also offered.

51 rooms, 4 family   Moderate   Open all year
Lunch 12.30-2.30pm – £3 alc   Dinner 7-9.30pm – £7.95
AmEx/Barclaycard/Diners   P – own car park

Cartmel, Cumbria   map 3

P   *KING'S ARMS*, Market Place

In the village centre by the huge and superbly preserved medieval Priory.

A great pub with a cosy interior and beams adorned with a large collection of bank notes. It doesn't have a garden but there are a few tables and chairs outside on the charming square. It gets very busy in the season.

The comfortable oak-beamed children's room is long and bright with plenty of benches and tables and one video game.

Hot and cold lunchtime snacks are available all week, with sandwiches from 75p to £1.40, salads at £1.75 to £3.25 and quiches and pies at £1.50.

Ale – Hartleys
P – restricted parking on the square and in side streets

Cartmel Fell, Cumbria

map 3

P   ***MASON'S ARMS***

On a minor road between the A592 and the A5074 and between Newby Bridge and Kendal.

A great old pub, smartly painted in white, and sitting high above the Winster Valley. You can sit on the small patio at the front and gaze, or relax inside this very 'pubby' pub with slate floors, low beams and a splendid old fire place. There are some interesting paintings and samplers on the walls.

The children's room is in keeping – small, white painted, beamed and charming.

There is a catholic range of dishes available each day: sandwiches at about £1, lasagne, moussaka and pies and vegetables at under £2.50, and assorted salads at about £3. Unusually for a pub there is a choice of a few vegetarian dishes and this is indicative of the interest shown in the food.

Ale – Thwaites   P – at front and rear

Castle Combe, Nr Chippenham, Wilts

map 2

H   ***THE MANOR HOUSE*** (Best Western) – phone 782 206

There is a sign in the centre of the village opposite the White Hart.

This is a delightfully interesting stone building, started in the 15th century and added to over the next two centuries or so. It sprawls, with triangular roofs and elaborate curly chimneys, in twenty-six acres of lawned grounds. Looking down on the hotel is a splendid Italian garden, complete with stone cherubs.

There are good facilities here: an outdoor heated swimming pool next to a hard tennis court; and trout fishing in the River Bybrook.

Accommodation is free for children up to 16 years; there is a children's menu in the evening and half portions can be served in the restaurant. Afternoon teas also.

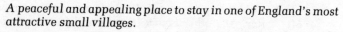

A peaceful and appealing place to stay in one of England's most attractive small villages.

34 rooms, 13 family   Expensive   Open all year
Lunch 12.30-2pm – £7   Dinner 7.30-9pm – £12.50
Access/AmEx/Barclaycard/Diners   P – own car park

P   *WHITE HART*

A lovely spruce white-painted pub in the main street of this classic English village, and opposite the church.

Inside the bar it has a big open fireplace and the children's room is spacious, with low beams and plenty of tables and chairs.

There is a good range of pub foods on offer seven days a week: a cold buffet, soups, hot snacks, toasted sandwiches, pizzas and the like, at prices up to £2.

Ale – Eldridge Pope, Theakston's, Hall & Woodhouse, Wadworth's   P – difficult

---

Castle Hedingham, Essex   map 1

P   *BELL, 10 St James Street*

On the B1058.

A splendid pub in an attractive village with a notable Norman Castle. Inside the pub is a lovely and large brick-walled and black oak-beamed bar, which is furnished most appealingly rather like someone's sitting room.

There is a smallish but adequate children's room with space invaders, etc, a small patio and a big, grassy and rambling garden.

A varied range of food, including especially crusty baps, is on offer except on Monday evenings.

Ale – Greene King   P – own car park

Cenarth, Dyfed   map 2

P   *THE WHITE HART*

In the village – on the A484 west of Newcastle Emlyn.

A little village pub of 16th century vintage and the yellowed cream paint on the stone façade is getting on a bit too. The interior is scruffy but charming. For example one of the two rooms which children can use is minute with a low ceiling and a

black kettle sitting by its open fire – shades of 'How Green Was My Valley'; the other is just like a small front parlour with well-worn easy chairs.

Food is available every day and a local salmon was being cut into steaks when we visited. The local fish dishes and grills cost up to £6 and there is a range of snacks, some home-made and Welsh in origin such as pastai catrin and tarten cenin.

I cannot say that we had a friendly reception – please let us know how you fare.

Ale – Buckley's   P – own car park

Chagford, Devon   map 2

H   ***MILL END HOTEL,*** Sandy Park – phone 2282

On the A382 – not in Chagford.

An attractive roadside hotel with a pretty interior and with a river running amid the grounds where guests can fish. it has a secluded walled garden at the front and a more grassy one at the back by a stream.

Children are accommodated free to the age of 17.

The dining room has a varied range of table d'hôte menus and they are very accommodating over children's food. There are plenty of snacks available at lunchtimes, or, if you order in advance, a table d'hôte lunch will be provided. The dinner menu offers a small but interesting choice, eg salmis of duckling, beef and Burgundy pie, etc. They discourage children under 5 in the dining room in the evening but will serve supper at about 6pm.

It's a lovely part of the country – on the edge of Dartmoor – and its other claim to fame is that Evelyn Waugh wrote Brideshead Revisited while staying in the village in 1944.

15 rooms, 2 family   Moderate   Closed 10 days at Christmas
Lunch 12.30-2pm – £6.50   Dinner 7.30-9pm – £10
Access/AmEx/Barclaycard   P – own car park

Chailey, East Sussex   map 1

P   ***FIVE BELLS***

On the A275.

A lovely, sprawling 17th century pub by the roadside but surrounded by open country.

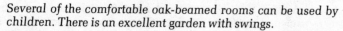

Several of the comfortable oak-beamed rooms can be used by children. There is an excellent garden with swings.

Food is available every day except Sunday and, as the landlord succinctly put it, includes 'anything from cheese to a T-bone steak' – at prices from about £1 to £6.

Ale – Whitbread   P – own car park

Chapel-le-Dale, North Yorks map 3

P   *OLD HILL INN*

On the B6255.

Along a Roman road which runs arrow-like between brooding rock-scarred fells you will find this remote 17th century inn, built of stone and oak. To call it unspoiled would be an understatement – perhaps eccentric is the best description. The main bar has stone walls and a big fireplace and an extraordinary array of oddments on the walls and in the bar. There are a couple of cartwheels set into walls to form an alcove; a few fox's heads; a sheep's head mounted above the bar; a juke box; many prints; some games machines; and an Irish dog-carrier. On the other side of the pub is a smaller bar with a pool table and a huge television screen, and beyond that a low-ceilinged dining room with rough wooden tables.

Children can use the small covered-in veranda, and there is a patch of garden with bench tables. But you are surrounded by wonderful countryside anyway – it's a very popular area with walkers.

Food is available seven days a week, and you can have pies, pasties, chicken and chips, sandwiches, curry and chips, etc, at no more than £2 a time.

Apart from the ever-present Theakston's the other beer varies – but is always a strong one.

An unique pub in a wonderful part of the countryside – well worth a visit.

Ale – Theakston   P – own car park

Charlwood, Nr Horley, Surrey map 1

H   *RUSS HILL HOTEL* – phone Norwood Hill 862 171

One mile from the village of Charlwood which is close to the junction of the A23 and A217 near to Gatwick Airport. Look for the sign to Russ Hill in the village.

57

A long low white-painted hotel in eight acres of attractive lawned gardens with lovely trees. The original façade is half hidden, unfortunately, by an ugly modern extension. There is a good-sized heated indoor swimming pool and tennis court. An alternative place to stay if you have an early flight from Gatwick.

Children in cots are accommodated free, and half portions are available for children in the restaurant.

80 rooms, 5 family   Moderate   Open all year
Lunch 12.30-2pm – £6   Dinner 7-10pm – £6.25
Access/AmEx/Barclaycard/Diners   P – own car park

Charmouth, Dorset   map 2

H   ***FERNHILL HOTEL*** – phone 60492

This is an eye-catching hotel, white painted with black shutters, on a hill on the A35 and easily visible from the road.

Although a long way from Dylan Thomas' Fern Hill, his description of 'daft and happy hills' suits the West Dorset ones. The hotel has fifteen acres of rolling grounds where there are plenty of facilities: a heated outdoor swimming pool and paddling pool, a squash court and a climbing frame. By the pool is a large games room with table tennis, a slide, a swing and a rocking horse. The local golf club at Lyme Regis offers guests a reduced green fee.

A complicated sliding scale of charges is made for the children.

There are bar meals only at lunchtimes, but a fair selection, hot and cold, and a special children's menu is also available for lunch and for high tea. Very young children are not encouraged in the restaurant.

There are also thirty-five self-catering apartments in the grounds which are run by a different company but which share all the same amenities.

15 rooms, 6 family   Cheap
Closed early Nov to mid Mar   Lunch 12-2pm
Dinner 7.30-8.45pm – £7.95
Barclaycard only   P – own car park

Chedington, Dorset   map 2

P   ***WINYARDS GAP INN***

On the A356 on the way to Dorchester four miles from Crewkerne.

Nice old whitewashed pub with a large garden with a slide and climbing frame and a wonderful view of the countryside.

The children's room is large, bright and airy and doubles as a function room and skittle alley.

There is a very wide menu of hot and cold dishes, seven days a week, and this includes a special children's menu.

Ale – Bass, Eldridge Pope   P – own car park

Cheriton Bishop, Nr Exeter, Devon   map 2

P   *THE OLD THATCH*

On the A30.

A well-run pub with a low-ceilinged long bar divided by a stone fireplace open to both sides.

The family room, off the main bar, is also the dining room. 'Well behaved children . . . are permitted in the family room at lunch time and until 8.30pm in the evenings. Parents are asked to supervise their children so that no annoyance is caused to other customers' it says on the pub door. (Shame about the ill-tuned radio which caused us annoyance on one visit.) There are some seats outside, but no proper garden (they plan one during 1984).

There is food available every day, at lunchtimes from 12 to 1.45pm, and in the evenings from 6 to 9.30pm. The dining room serves dishes around the £2 mark such as fried scampi, curry, steak and kidney pie. The bar food consists of soup, paté, chicken, plaice and the usual salads and sandwiches.

Ale – Ushers, Founders   P – across the road

Chester, Cheshire   map 3

Chester is a town with a long history and much of it is still evident in its buildings. For several hundred years it was a Roman city and their walls still survive; there is a Roman amphitheatre site; and 'The Rows' – a two storey row of shops with balconies, probably built in the 15th century.

H   *CHESTER GROSVENOR* (Prestige), Eastgate Street – phone 24024

In the city centre.

A big, quite grand and rather expensive city hotel. There are no extra facilities here for children or families – no garden or play areas – but if you are feeling flush it is a good place to stop right in the centre of this historic city.

At least the children are accommodated free up to the age of 12, and the hotel itself is elegant and stately and, side-stepping the scrums of American tourists, you can enjoy its style.

The buffet lunch includes a soup of the day, and cold buffet or a choice of hot dishes, and the dinner menu includes such as Arbroath smokies, darne of salmon, as well as steak, chicken, etc. Half portions are available for children.

101 rooms, 3 family   Expensive   Open all year
Lunch 12-2pm – £6.25   Dinner 7-9.45pm – £9.50
Ale – Sam Smith's
Access/AmEx/Barclaycard/Diners   P – NCP at rear of hotel

H   ***MOLLINGTON BANASTRE*** (Best Western), Parkgate Road – phone 851 471

On the A540 Chester to Hoylake Road.

This is something of a businessman's hotel, but might be useful if you are touring and want to look at Chester. The core of the hotel is a Victorian mansion which is now almost totally hidden by a series of modern brick extensions. There is plenty of lawned garden and a gravel terrace to lounge on and a small play area with some swings.

The hotel runs a cold buffet at lunchtimes – they call it a smorgasbord – at £3.50, and there is a pub attached to the hotel with Marston's bitter, a terrace at the front, but no children's room. It also does snack meals – salads, cold buffet and a couple of dishes of the day at around £2.

Children up to 14 are accommodated free; high teas are available from 6 to 7pm; and half portions can be served.

50 rooms, 8 family   Moderate   Open all year
Lunch 12.30-2pm – alc or smorgasbord – £3.50
Dinner 7-9.30pm – £8.50
Ale – Marston's – in the 'Good Intent'
Access/AmEx/Barclaycard   P – own car park

H R   ***QUEEN HOTEL*** (THF), City Road – phone 28341

By the station.

For the sightseer this hotel, opposite the railway station, might offer a good place to stop. It's a great big Victorian pile with quite a pretty garden with lawns and trees. It is rather overshadowed by a big office building on one side, but pleasant enough to sit in with a drink or a snack.

The entrance hall is very grand. The staircase with its iron balustrade winds up towards a glass roof. Bar snacks are available at lunchtimes, for example salads or a dish of the day at around £2. The evening menu offers a good array of meat dishes plus smoked local trout, Cheshire mushrooms, etc. Children have their own menu or can choose half portions from the main menu. Their accommodation is free up to 5, and from 5 to 14 there is a nominal £1 charge.

91 rooms, 11 family   Moderate   Open all year
Buffet lunch 12.30-2pm   Dinner 6.30-9.30pm – £7.65
Access/AmEx/Barclaycard/Diners   P – own car park

Chesterton, Oxon   map 1

R   *WOODS* – phone Bicester 41444

On the A4095 three miles south west of Bicester.

The restaurant is housed in a very attractive Cotswold stone barn with a nice stretch of lawn down to a brook, and by the bar a smaller lawn with a few tables and chairs. Inside the dining room is on two levels, with some tables in a gallery, and a big stone fireplace on the ground level. The bar, with its paved floor, is below the gallery.

There are some interesting dishes on the menu: for example savoury cheese peach with curry mayonnaise, stuffed breast of chicken in puff pastry with a sherry and mushroom sauce, as well as steaks, fresh salmon, etc. The half portions are intended for smaller children: the owners were not too keen on a recent sixteen-year-old guest with a gargantuan appetite and a taste for good claret being palmed on to the half portion menu. Incidentally, there is also a single choice, three-course menu available at lunchtimes for £5.75.

The owners, with four children of their own, understand the problems of parents out and about with children, and permit the use of their house, which adjoins the restaurant, for mothers who may need to change or feed a baby. They also encourage the children to use the reasonably spacious garden.

Closed Sun evenings   Lunch 12-2pm – £11.50
Dinner 7-10pm – £11.50   Ale – Hook Norton
Access/AmEx/Barclaycard/Diners   P – own car park

Chichester, West Sussex   map 1

This splendid town is well worth a visit; it is one of the oldest in Britain, although within the city walls the buildings are primarily 18th century. The Cathedral, Norman in structure, has had an exciting history – it burned down twice and its spire collapsed in 1861. The town also holds its famous Arts Festival in July.

H R **DOLPHIN AND ANCHOR HOTEL** (THF), West Street – phone 785 121

Opposite the Cathedral and alongside the 15th century Market Cross.

Two old inns were combined to form this attractive long-fronted hotel. The Dolphin was a thriving inn during the 17th century, although the present façade has an 18th century look in keeping with the rest of the central part of the town.

Accommodation is free for children up to the age of 14 when sharing a room with their parents.

As well as the restaurant, there is a coffee shop, open throughout the day and in both special menus are available for children as well as half portions. The Buttery serves the usual range of grills, sandwiches, burgers and salads (prices from £1 to £6) and the restaurant a conventional choice of roasts, fish dishes, etc.

54 rooms, 6 family   Moderate   Open all year
Lunch 12.30-2.30pm – £6.50 Dinner 7.30-10pm – £8.50
Access/AmEx/Barclaycard/Diners
P – 40 spaces

P **SHIP HOTEL,** North Street

In the centre of the town.

A handsome Georgian building which is in need of some external care and attention. Inside it is comfortable and spacious with a large lounge where parents can take their children.

The lunchtime food includes meat and salads, quiche, smoked trout, game pie, etc. and the prices are around £2 or just over.

Ale – Hall & Woodhouse, King & Barnes   P – own car park

Chiddingfold, Surrey   map 1

P R **THE CROWN** – phone Wormley 2255

On the A283.

A superb 14th century pub of huge oaken beams in a delightful village with a charming church of similar age close by.

It's a big rambling pub with some splendid rooms and amongst them is the high-beamed family room in the middle of the building. It has a stove and old church pews on which to sit.

You can eat in the bistro or the restaurant, but the latter is closed on Mondays. The bistro offers some good meals at reasonable prices – for example, stilton and walnut paté, oak smoked mackerel, duck and cherry pie, sole, giant prawns, etc, or a cold buffet. A three-course meal would cost around £7. The bistro is also open for breakfasts and teas. The main restaurant concentrates on grills, and dishes such as rack of lamb, medallions of venison, marinated pigeon breasts, etc. The enterprising owners have occasional food festivals – seafood or game, for example.

Half portions are available for children, and mothers can use the Ladies or a small room – the Tudor Room – if it's free.

Restaurant closed all day Mon   Lunch 12-2.30pm – £12
Dinner 7-9.30pm – £12   Ale – Young's, Hall & Woodhouse
AmEx/Diners   P – own car park

Chipperfield, Herts   map 1

H   *TWO BREWERS INN* (THF), The Common – phone King's Langley 65266

Between the A413 and A41.

A haven of peace between King's Langley and Amersham. An elegant white-painted, low-slung 17th century building facing a huge common with its village cricket pitch and with a lovely flint church to one side. All redolent of England as it ought to be.

There is no charge for children under 5 sharing their parents' accommodation and from 5 to 14 a charge of £1. The restaurant offers a special children's menu and half portions.

There is a buffet lunch every day at around £2 per dish – meats and salads and a hot dish – and the restaurant menus usually offer a roast of the day, a fish dish, and a 'chef's special' – steak and kidney pie for instance.

20 rooms, 2 sets adjoining   Moderate   Open all year
Lunch 12.30-2pm – £6.50   Dinner 7-9.45pm – £8.95
Ale — Greene King
Access/AmEx/Barclaycard/Diners   P – own car park

Chipping Norton, Oxon   map 2

H P   *WHITE HART HOTEL* (THF), High Street – phone 2572

In the centre of town facing the square.

A typical THF county town hotel – a rather attractive 18th century stone front hides a 14th century interior. There's a small patio/courtyard at the rear where barbecues are served in the summer.

There is no accommodation charge for children under 5 and from 5 to 14 years of age there is a token charge of £1.

At lunchtime there are bar snacks and the special children's menu and in the evening the restaurant will also provide half portions for children.

22 rooms, 3 family   Moderate
Open all year 12-2pm buffet lunches
Dinner 7-9pm – £7.95   Ale – Hook Norton
Access/AmEx/Barclaycard/Diners
P – car park for 6 cars only, but public car park opposite

Chobham, Surrey   map 1

P   ***WHITE HART*****, High Street**

Large rambling old pub in the main street next to the village church and its grassy graveyard.

Airy children's room, with tables and chairs, up the stairs by the bar.

Big range of snacks, salads, hot dishes, etc, available only at lunchtime seven days a week.

Ale – Courage   P – own car park

Chollerford, Northumberland   map 5

H   ***GEORGE HOTEL*** *(Swallow)* – phone Humshaugh 611

On the B6318 Chollerford roundabout.

A nice old stone building, ivy-clad, by the banks of the North Tyne River on which guests can fish. The extension is quite well done and the gardens running along the river are a mass of flowers in summer. At the end of the garden is an excellent indoor heated swimming pool with some exercise equipment, and a sun patio. There is a large grassy play area here, with swings, a slide, see-saw and putting green.

Accommodation is free for children up to 12 years. There is a special children's menu and half portions are also available in the restaurant.

A pretty spot and very close to Hadrian's famous Wall. Indeed the B6138, a Roman road which runs from here to Newcastle, is a magnificent example of Roman road-building. Pity they weren't around to build our motorways.

54 rooms, 3 family   Moderate   Open all year
Lunch 12.30-2pm – £6   Dinner 7-9pm – £8
Access/AmEx/Barclaycard/Diners   P – own car park

Cirencester, Glos   map 2

H   ***STRATTON HOUSE HOTEL,*** Gloucester Road – phone 61761

Just outside Cirencester on the A417.

Cotswold stone – part four-square Georgian and part very attractive 17th century. There is an execrable one-storey stone extension at the side which should tone in with the rest in about 150 years. OK for a touring stop-over. The pretty walled garden with a croquet lawn and a paved terrace is ideal for a relaxing drink.

Accommodation free for children up to 10; up to 15 a charge of £10 is made.

A good range of food on the menus, and children's portions are always available.

31 rooms, 2 family   Moderate
Open all year   Lunch 12.30-1.45pm – £5.95
Dinner 7.30-9.45pm – £7.50   Ale – Arkell's
Access/AmEx/Barclaycard/Diners   P – own car park

Claines, Hereford & Worcs   map 3

P   ***THE MUG HOUSE***

Just off the A449 north of Worcester.

Cross a path alongside a ploughed field and you will come to this excellent village pub. It is small and has been very well restored with wooden beams and brick, although a glass panel on the front shows the old make-up of the façade. The pub is situated between a charming village church and the 'big house'. There is an attractive and snug room with a beamed ceiling, tiled floor and several tables and chairs and children are welcome in there. There is a garden which seems to merge into surrounding fields, and on the lawn rows and rows of garden benches.

The food, not served on Sundays, is absolutely basic – rolls, sausage rolls, and in winter hot pies.

Ale – Banks   P – on the roadside

Clanfield, Oxon

map 2

Two pubs to visit in this attractive Oxfordshire village, both on the A 4095.

P ***CLANFIELD TAVERN***

A glorious Cotswold stone pub, which has a small, pretty room off the main bar which parents with children may use at lunchtimes.

The landlord will provide changing mats for mothers to use in the ladies' cloakroom.

There is a nice choice of bar snacks, available at all times, such as taramasalata, venison pie, sweet and sour pork, Burgundy beef and trout, as well as sandwiches, ploughman's, etc. The prices are around the £2.50 mark.

Ale – Arkell's, Hook Norton, Morland   P – own car park

P ***THE PLOUGH***

A superb Elizabethan stone building (of 1560 vintage) opposite the village green and with a pretty front lawn.

An elegant small lounge with antique furniture off the bar can be used by well-behaved children with their (well-behaved) parents.

Bar snacks, hot and cold, are served every day. You can have sandwiches (including smoked salmon), paté and hot dishes of the day such as steak and kidney pie, prawn omelette and beef bourguignon, with a maximum price of £2.50.

Ale – Flowers, Wadworth's   P – own car park

Clifton, Lancs

map 3

P ***THE WINDMILL INN***

Off the A 583 Preston to Blackpool road.

This is a smashing pub in a part of the country not exactly crammed with hostelries with facilities for families. One end of it is a converted windmill and this can be sighted from the main road. The rest of the pub is a very charming long low building of deep-red brick. There is a lawned garden with plenty of bench tables.

There are three areas on a higher level above the main bar where children may take their adults. The main eating area here has a high beamed ceiling and there is a variety of food available. At

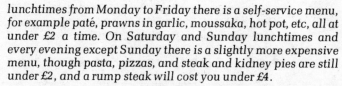

lunchtimes from Monday to Friday there is a self-service menu, for example paté, prawns in garlic, moussaka, hot pot, etc, all at under £2 a time. On Saturday and Sunday lunchtimes and every evening except Sunday there is a slightly more expensive menu, though pasta, pizzas, and steak and kidney pies are still under £2, and a rump steak will cost you under £4.

Ale – Mitchell's   P – own car park

Clifton Hampden, Nr Abingdon, Oxon   map 1
P   *BARLEY MOW*

Off the A415.

An old thatched white-painted building probably built in the 13th century. It is described in Three Men in a Boat – 'It is, without exception, I should say, the quaintest, most old-world inn up the river. It stands on the right of the bridge, quite away from the village. Its low-pitched gables and thatched roof and latticed windows give it quite a story-book appearance, while inside it is even still more once-upon-a-timeyfied.'

Well, to more prosaic matters. . . . The children's room, like the lounge bar, is oak-beamed and panelled and leads on to a lawned garden with tables and chairs.

Bar snacks, hot and cold, are available every day.

Ale – Usher's   P – opposite

Coatham Mundeville, Nr Darlington, Co. Durham   map 5
H   *HALL GARTH HOTEL* – phone Aycliffe 313 333

On the A167, the turning to Darlington, very close to the A1(M).

Lovely stone ivy-clad house with a separate pub. The pretty dining room is open from Monday to Saturday and is flexible in feeding children. Or you may prefer to eat at the pub where children's portions are 80p. No children's room in the pub, alas, but there are ample lawns, a terrace and beer garden. There's a good play area with swings, slides and a roundabout, a putting green and an outdoor swimming pool.

There's a charge of £5 for a child sharing its parents' accommodation. Although there's no direct baby-listening system, they offer to check regularly and are willing to arrange a baby-sitter, so we're including them in the guide as a hotel – also because it's an attractive place and because of the amenities offered.

The Peaudouce Family Welcome Guide

19 rooms   Moderate   Closed 10 days at Christmas
Lunch 12.30-1.30pm – £5.95
Dinner 7.30-9.15pm – 3 courses £10.25
Ale – McEwans
AmEx/Barclaycard/Diners   P – own car park

Cobham, Surrey

map 1

H   ***LADBROKE SEVEN HILLS HOTEL,*** Seven Hills Road – phone 4471

Just off the A3, close to where it meets the A245, and close to the M25.

About twenty miles from London, this is a sprawling modern hotel (with an older building which houses the restaurant) which overall is rather attractive amid its tree-strewn grassy gardens. There is a patio at the rear overlooking a heated outdoor swimming pool; two excellent hard tennis courts and squash courts.

Accommodation is free for children up to 14; and there is a special children's menu and half portions available in the restaurant.

92 rooms, 1 family   Expensive   Open all year
Lunch 12.30-2pm – £7.50   Dinner 7-10pm – £8.50
Access/AmEx/Barclaycard/Diners   P – own car park

Compton Martin, Avon

map 2

P   ***RING O'BELLS***

On the A368.
A long low sprawling spacious pub, almost shiningly white in its smartness, and set against a backdrop of heavily wooded gentle hills. There is a super garden, large and grassy, with lots of split-log tables and benches scattered among the trees. There is a slide and some swings.

Inside there is lots of space in the bars, and one of the best looking and best organised children's rooms we have found so far; its stone walls topped by a high vaulted ceiling and with a good array of wooden tables and chairs. The children can tuck into their 'kiddies specials', available every day – beefburger or fish fingers with crispy fries and noodles at around £1. The main menu is very extensive indeed – and here are just a few selections: paté or taramasalata at under £2; lasagne at under £3; baked fish crumble at £3.50; a big range of salads (crab, ham, prawn, salmon, etc) at between £4 and £5; steaks, etc.

68

This pub, so smart and appealing, offers everything a family could wish for – an exceptionally wide choice of food, including a children's menu, good beer, a splendid garden, a superb children's room and friendly and helpful staff. It is an outstanding pub in every way and takes the top prize for best family pub of the year.

Ale – Butcombe, Marston's   P – own car park

Comrie, Tayside   map 5

R   *TULLYBANNOCHER FARM FOOD BAR* – phone 70827

Just west of Comrie on the A85.

One of the excellent café/restaurants which are linked to craft shops of which we found several in Scotland. This is a large log cabin, timbered inside and out, and with an attractive array of wooden tables and benches inside. There are three shops: craft, knitwear and garden. The area is surrounded by a big grassy garden with picnic tables and benches. A lovely spot.

The accent is on simple food, well-prepared and at reasonable prices: for example chicken and salad at £2.70, fresh salmon and salad at £4. The salads are particularly good and good value; there are lots of pastries and a children's meal of burger, beans and baked potato at 80p.

The loo is clean if not comfortable for seeing to an infant.

Closed Oct-Mar   Open 10am-6pm every day   Licensed
No credit cards accepted   P – own car park

Congleton, Cheshire   map 3

R   *MOODY HALL,* Moody Street – phone 77364

A restaurant in a big Georgian town house not far from the town centre. It has a rather barracky, but not unpleasant, dining room with French windows on to a lawn which has an old climbing frame to one side.

There is a heavy reliance on steak, chops and scampi – mostly with chips. But the owners do a 'kiddies' menu at £1 – chicken, fish fingers, etc, with, of course, chips. Recommended because there is a dearth of restaurants in this area which are prepared to cope with children.

The owners, with several children of their own, are very helpful to mothers and will make space available upstairs for breast-feeding and changing.

Closed Mon/public holidays/Sat lunch/Sun dinner
Lunch 12-2.30pm – £3 alc   Dinner 7.30-10pm – £7.50
Licensed   Access/AmEx/Barclaycard/Diners   P – own car park

Conwy, Gwynedd   map 3

H   *THE CASTLE* (THF), High Street – phone 2324

---

*Follow the one-way system and keep looking to your right –
you'll spot the THF sign.*

A very interesting building with a façade of ornate red brick on a
darker stone. It looks Jacobean but was built on to the hotel in
the late 18th century. The 18th century interior has some
splendid paintings on Shakespearian themes, both on the walls
and direct on to door and wall panels, by the Victorian artist,
Dawson Watson.

The usual THF rates apply to children's accommodation – free
to the age of 5, then £1 up to 14. They have their special menu
also and can order half portions from the main menu.

There are bar snacks at lunchtimes from £1 up to about £3: such
things as smoked mackerel, plaice and chips, mixed grill,
various salads and a dish of the day. The dinner menu is similar
with starters such as smoked mackerel, plaice, roasts and
salads.

A pleasant place to stop in this historic town with its famous
castle.

26 rooms, 6 triples   Moderate   Open all year
Lunch 12-2pm   Dinner 7-9.30pm – £7.50
Access/AmEx/Barclaycard/Diners   P – own car park

Cookham, Berks   map 1

R   *THE FERRY* – phone Bourne End 25123

On the A4094.

A big and busy pub by the side of the Thames. The restaurant is
upstairs overlooking the river and mostly serves steaks and
salads. There is a patio by the side of the river, and during the
summer season a charcoal grill is put to use. Shame about the
slightly intrusive music.

An eight ounce fillet will cost you just over £6, and there are
burgers, scampi and chicken kiev. Children are very much
catered for, and that includes their own special menu.

The 'Ladies' is ample for a mother looking after a baby – it's one of the biggest rooms in the building.

Lunch 12-2.30pm – £5   Dinner 7-10.30pm – £5
Ale – Marston's, Ruddles, Young's
Access/AmEx/Barclaycard/Diners   P – own car park

Corse Lawn, Glos   map 2

R   ***CORSE LAWN HOUSE HOTEL*** – phone Tirley 479

On the B4211 south west of Tewkesbury.

A big brick house built as an inn in 1745, and a fine example of the Queen Anne style. It is surrounded by green fields on a quiet road and has a large pond at the front wherein it is said the coaches were washed. There is a big grassy garden too.

All the food is fresh and freshly cooked: and supporting evidence was to hand when we visited the restaurant at 6pm and spotted a sous-chef on his hands and knees in the kitchen garden snipping at the vegetables.

The menu ranges wide and there is an interesting selection of bar food as well. Children are served 'whatever they require', but must not disturb the other guests, as the amiable owner rightly emphasised.

Mothers will find ample facilities to tend to their very small children.

Closed Mon all day and Sun evenings
Lunch 12.30-2pm – £8.50   Dinner 7-10pm – £11.75   Licensed
Access/AmEx/Barclaycard/Diners   P – ample car park

Cottesmore, Nr Oakham, Leics   map 4

P   ***SUN INN***

On the B668 about 3 miles north east of Oakham.

A smart attractive white-washed stone pub with a thatched roof and set back from the main street of this pretty village. There is a small patio with a few tables at the back of the pub, where the thatch ends and a steeply pitched roof of stone tiles takes over. There are also some tables and chairs and benches at the front of the pub.

There is a small children's room at the back of the pub – it's almost a conservatory – with nice wicker tables and chairs.

*There is a good range of pub food – chicken, steak, sausages, etc,
with chips – available every day except Sunday.*

Ale – Everard's   P – on street

Crantock, Cornwall   map 2

P   ***OLD ALBION***

In village off A30, close to Newquay

*An ancient thatched pub by a church (and opposite a modern
monstrosity which also boasts a 'family room').*

*The lovely oak-beamed children's room was the original 16th
century pub and also serves as the food bar. Small beer garden.*

*Hot and cold food is available all week (pasties only during the
winter).*

Ale – Courage   P – own car park

Crawley, West Sussex   map 1

H R   ***GEORGE HOTEL*** (THF), High Street – phone 24215

In the centre of the town.

*An ancient inn with a half-timbered and tiled façade; behind
are some modern additions. The town is not that appealing, but
this well-run hotel is a possibility if you have to stay near
Gatwick Airport.*

*Accommodation for children is free up to 5 years with a
nominal charge of £1 from 5 to 14.*

*The Coffee Shop, open from 10am to 10.30pm, has the usual
choice of steaks, sole, gammon, burgers, omelettes and salads at
prices from £1 to about £6. The restaurant menu is also fairly
standard – roasts, steak and kidney pie, trout, veal provençale,
etc.*

75 rooms, 15 family   Moderate   Open all year
Lunch 12.30-2.15pm – £5.50   Dinner 7-9.30pm – £6.75
Access/AmEx/Barclaycard/Diners   P – own car park

Criccieth, Gwynedd   map 3

R   ***MOELWYN RESTAURANT,*** Mona Terrace – phone 2500

By the sea front off the A497.

The owners have skilfully made the most of this Victorian building, creeper-clad and in a fine position on the sea front with views of Cardigan Bay and the hills. The dining room is smartly decorated with red patterned wallpaper and pink tablecloths.

Children are catered for with various dishes with chips, a roast and vegetables at prices up to £1.50, and half portions from the à la carte menu. The lunch menu has dishes up to just over £2, and they include quiche, pizza, mackerel, plaice and sea clams. The dinner menu also features lots of local fish and steaks, escalopes, etc. Cream teas are served from 3.30 to 5pm.

The owners would always make a room available to mothers who need to take care of either end of a baby.

Open all year/closed Mon-Thur during Nov-Mar
Lunch 12-2pm   Dinner 7-9.30 – £7.95   Licensed
Access/Barclaycard   P – public car park in square just outside

---

Cuckfield, West Sussex   map 1

P   *KING'S HEAD*, South Street

A spacious old pub in the main street of this pretty village.

The large children's room – called 'The Zoo' – is well-furnished, and has a pool table and a log fire. There is a small walled garden at the rear.

A good range of food, eg moussaka, lasagne, pies, sandwiches and salads, is available at all times.

Ale – Harvey's, King & Barnes
P – restricted, but public car park nearby

Dartington, Devon   map 2

R   *CRANKS HEALTH FOOD RESTAURANT*, Shinners Bridge –
        phone Totnes 862 388

Look out for the Dartington Cider Press Centre on the A 384.

Within the Centre is the clean, efficient self-service restaurant with an array of Cranks healthy salads, pizzas, quiches and puddings. An excellent patio with sun shades and tables and chairs – and of course an old cider press. Also in the complex are a craft shop, glass shop, farm foods, toys, pottery, etc.

Take a look at the magnificent Dartington Hall while you are here.

There are chairs in the ladies' lavatory where a mother can attend to her baby.

Closed – Sunday/Christmas/New Year's Day/Good Friday
Meals served all day Monday-Saturday 10am-5pm
Dishes start at £1   Licensed
No credit cards accepted   P – in the complex

Dawlish, Devon

map 2

H   *RADFORDS* – phone 863 322

Get a map from the hotel – it is in the wilds and there are few signposts.

The basis is a pretty pink-washed thatched building with modern accretions. Children are very well catered for: huge games room with pool, table tennis, space invaders, etc, and entertainment of various kinds is organised for them every day. Large grassy garden, patio and good play area with swings, slide, etc. There's a separate indoor pool with a children's pool and jacuzzi. A great place to go with small children, but not if you are seeking peace and quiet. Parents can escape in the evening, however, as there's a resident baby-sitter from 7.30pm to 11.30pm.

There is half price accommodation for children sharing their parents' room.

24 rooms all family rooms   Cheap
Closed Nov-March
No credit cards accepted   P – own car park

Dedham, Essex

map 1

Pretty villages are something of a rarity in these parts, but here's one and it boasts two good pubs. The painter, Constable, used to go to school in Dedham, and there is a museum here of Sir Alfred Munnings' work (open on certain days in summer).

P   *MARLBOROUGH HEAD*

It is a lovely old timbered inn with a spacious bar with splendid exposed beams – a busy place where hot and cold food is ordered from an exceptionally wide-ranging menu (available seven days a week).

The children's room is the hallway and is roomy and comfortable. There is also a large walled garden at the rear.

Ale – Ind Coope   P – own small car park and street parking

74

P   *SUN*

Opposite an impressive church, this is a sprawling pub dating from Tudor times with two large bars and a children's room which is big but appears to be something of an afterthought stuck as it is between the bar and the restaurant. But there is a very pleasant and large walled garden at the rear with plenty of tables and chairs.

The food, available at all opening times, offers less choice than the Marlborough Head (about 100 yards away) to which it is an alternative.

Ale – Tolly   P – own car park

Dinnington, Somerset   map 2

P   *ROSE AND CROWN*

Off the A356, north of Crewkerne, near its junction with the A303.

An ordinary looking village pub, built of honey-coloured stone; when we visited it one lunchtime its customers were primarily local. We include it because the landlord has made great efforts to appeal to families. There is a new children's room at the back; it's a bit sparse but has table football and space invaders. And children can eat with their adults in a room just to the side of the main bar. There is food seven days a week: pasties, sandwiches at just over 50p, and how about lasagne or a vindaloo curry for under £1.50. The latter should test the Peaudouce nappies.

There is a big lawned garden at the back with benches and tables, a slide, a climbing frame and, wonder of wonders, an old tractor for children to play on. And more garden attractions are planned for next year. Watch this space.

Ale – Bass, Courage, Tisbury   P – own car park

Dolgellau, Gwynedd   map 3

H P   *GOLDEN LION ROYAL HOTEL* – phone 422 579

Follow the A470 to the town centre and there it is.

Dolgellau is well situated for tourists and, although the reception we had was sloppy and raucous, we assume that visitors will be better treated. We can't vouch for how quiet a stay you'll have and would like to hear from you. A good reason for visiting is to see the two splendid bars which are red plush and packed with an amazing collection of militaria – not to be missed if you're in this part of Wales. Next door is a shopping precinct.

The food prices are good – lunchtime main courses in the restaurant are under £3 (omelettes, roast, ham & eggs, plaice) with much the same food in the bar at under £2.50 and you can eat in one of the two lounges. One lounge is very welcoming with a huge rough stone fireplace. Dinner in the restaurant is plain meat and fish fare. Whichever meal you take half portions are offered for the children and their suppers can be served to them in their rooms between 6 and 7pm at £3.50.

Accommodation for children sharing with parents is 25% of the room price.

I think we can fairly call this cheap and cheerful.

22 rooms, 4 family   Cheap   Closed at Christmas
Lunch 1-2pm – £5 (bar snacks 12.15-2pm)
Dinner 7-9pm – £8.50
Access/AmEx/Barclaycard/Diners
P – own car park — go right at the hotel, turn left and left again

Dorchester, Dorset   map 2

H P   *THE KING'S ARMS HOTEL* (Best Western), 30 High East Street – phone 65353

In the town centre.

A fine old coaching inn with literary and historical associations: some scenes in Thomas Hardy's novel The Mayor of Casterbridge were set here; and Lord Nelson's captain, Hardy, was a frequent visitor.

'The building before whose doors they had pitched their music stands was the chief hotel in Casterbridge – namely the King's Arms. A spacious bow-window projected into the street over the main portico, and from the open sashes came the babble of voices, the jingle of glasses, and the drawing of cords.'

It hasn't changed.

There is plenty of choice on the lunchtime buffet menu amongst quiches, jacket potatoes, pizzas, cottage pies and dishes of the day from £1 to no more than £3. The restaurant menu sticks to plainish British dishes – trout, salmon, scampi, veal, steaks, lamb cutlets, beef casserole, etc.

Accommodation is free for children of 12 and under, and half portions are available in the restaurant. There is a comfortable room off the main bar where children may sit.

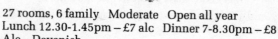

27 rooms, 6 family   Moderate   Open all year
Lunch 12.30-1.45pm – £7 alc   Dinner 7-8.30pm – £8
Ale – Devenish
Access/AmEx/Barclaycard   P – own car park

Dorking, Surrey   map 1

H   ***WHITE HORSE HOTEL*** (THF), High Street – phone 881 138

In the town centre.

A charming old coaching hotel with a modern extension (passable) at the rear. Some parts of this attractive hotel date back to 1500 and it was first in use as an inn in the mid-18th century. Charles Dickens is said to have written part of The Pickwick Papers here.

Accommodation is free for children up to 5; a nominal charge of £1 up to 14.

A special children's menu and half portions are available in the restaurant. Bar snacks are served at lunchtimes (but not on Sundays) and include salads and a dish of the day at about £2.50. In the restaurant you can opt for a two-course meal – with rump steak it costs £8.50 – or the à la carte.

There is a good-sized heated outdoor swimming pool at the back of the hotel.

70 rooms, 18 family   Moderate   Open all year
Lunch 12.30-2.30pm – £10 alc   Dinner 7-9.30pm – £10 alc
Access/AmEx/Barclaycard/Diners   P – own car park

Dovedale, Nr Ashbourne, Derbys   map 3

Dovedale, in an area of great natural beauty in the Peak District National Park, is thought to be the model for Eagle Valley in George Eliot's Adam Bede. It's a wonderful spot, overawed by the peak of Thorpe Cloud and in great walking and fishing country. You'll find the Izaak Walton and Peveril of the Peak on a minor road off the A515, north of Ashbourne.

H   ***IZAAK WALTON HOTEL*** (Best Western) – phone Thorpe Cloud 261

The original part of the building, a 17th century stone farmhouse, is handsome but the hotel is rather a hotch potch of additions with the inevitable grey pebble-dash, some of it mercifully hidden by ivy. But the hotel has a lovely stretch of lawned gardens and is surrounded by gentle peaks. As befits this eponymous hotel there is a three-mile stretch of trout fishing available.

77

Cots and extra beds cost £5 per night and half portions are available in the restaurant.

27 rooms, 3 family rooms, 1 set adjoining   Moderate
Open all year   Lunch 12.30-1.45pm – £6.50
Dinner 7-9.15pm – £8.50   Ale – Ind Coope Burton
Access/AmEx/Barclaycard/Diners   P – own car park

H R   ***PEVERIL OF THE PEAK HOTEL*** (THF) – phone Thorpe Cloud
333

The core of the building was possibly once a rectory and has a certain charm but the additions (more cream pebble-dash) are not pretty and rather motel-like. Even the reclaimed stone outhouses have the nasty pebble-dash on the top storey. But the hotel has a delightful garden, packed with flowers and a hard tennis court at the side.

Buffet lunches only here – for example a ploughman's at under £2 and a chef's casserole at around £3. You will find such things as game soup, fisherman's pancake, devilled whitebait, roast beef, casserole of lambs kidneys and poached haddock Duglere on the dinner menu.

The special children's menu is available at meal times and half portions can also be chosen from the main restaurant menu. Accommodation is free for children up to 5; with a £1 nominal charge up to 14.

41 rooms, 6 family   Moderate   Open all year
Lunch 12-2pm – £3 alc   Dinner 6.30-9.15pm – £7.95
Access/AmEx/Barclaycard/Diners   P – own car park

Dover, Kent   map 1

H   ***HOLIDAY INN,*** Townwall Street – phone 203 270

In the town centre.

The normal Holiday Inn set-up in an unremarkable modern building. It has a comfortable interior, efficient staff and a heated indoor swimming pool. A dependable place to stay prior to, or after, a Channel crossing. Good economic sense too if your children are with you as accommodation is free for them up to the age of 19. Four of you could share a room with two double beds for around £50.

There is a Coffee Shop menu on the go all day from 6.30am to 11.30pm and a buffet lunch of salads and dishes of the day. The fuller à la carte menu is available at lunchtimes and for dinner.

83 rooms, 6 family   Moderate   Open all year
Bar lunch 12-2pm buffet £5.95
Dinner 7.30-10.30pm – £10 alc
Access/AmEx/Barclaycard/Diners   P — limited parking

Dunblane, Central
map 5

H   *STAKIS DUNBLANE HYDRO* – phone 822 551

On the A9.

This building sits above the A9 over Dunblane and resembles a vast Victorian municipal hospital. It does, though, have several good facilities for families. For example they have a really good and very large heated indoor swimming pool, a games room with table tennis and pool table, two tennis courts, a putting green and a small outdoor play area with swings and log climbing frames. There is also an indoor play room, rather Spartan and dungeonesque, with some toys.

Children up to 5 are accommodated free and up to 14 for £7 per day and that includes dinner and breakfast. High teas are served for children from 6-6.30pm.

126 rooms, 12 family   Moderate   Open all year
Access/AmEx/Barclaycard/Diners   P – own car park

Dunkirk, Nr Badminton, Avon
map 2

H   *PETTY FRANCE HOTEL* – phone Didmarton 361

On the A46 a couple of miles north of junction 18 of the M4.

A handsome Georgian hotel with a slightly battered exterior. There are four acres of superb walled gardens in which you and the children can wander at will, and there's a swing. Some rooms across the car park, converted from the old stables, are particularly charming.

Snacks are available at lunchtimes – sandwiches, soups, prawns, etc – and the main menu ranges comprehensively through trout, sole, roast beef, pork, veal, rabbit casserole, etc. The table d'hôte menu at £10, incidentally, includes half a bottle of house wine.

Children up to 3 are accommodated free, £6 from 3 to 14 years.

17 rooms, 1 suite of 2 adjoining rooms   Moderate
Open all year   Lunch 12-1.45pm – £10   Dinner 7-9.45pm – £10
Ale – Flowers
Access/AmEx/Barclaycard/Diners   P – own car park

Dunster, Somerset

map 2

H R   *THE LUTTRELL ARMS* (THF) – phone 555

In the main street.

A building of lovely mellow stone, magnificent inside and out, dating from the 15th century and with some rooms with their original 16th century moulded plaster decorations. An open walkway leads past an exquisite courtyard to extensive tranquil gardens which look out on Dunster Castle and its parkland.

Accommodation is free for children up to 5 with a nominal charge of £1 from 5 to 14.

There is a limited lunch menu from Monday to Saturday – for example French onion soup and the hot dish of the day which will cost you less than £4. There are some good-sounding dishes in the evening – stuffed loin of pork with gooseberry sauce, drunken bullock, beef in Guinness, etc. A set lunch is served each Sunday. The restaurant offers a children's menu and half portions.

21 rooms, 2 family   Moderate   Open all year
Buffet lunches 12.30-2pm   Dinner 7.30-9.30 – £6.95
Access/AmEx/Barclaycard/Diners
P – two public car parks opposite

East Horsley, Surrey

map 1

H   *THATCHERS HOTEL* (Best Western), Epsom Road – phone 4291

On the A246 between Leatherhead and Guildford.

The hotel is in two parts – the front is an attractive black and white beamed building with wooden stairs and a balcony. Unfortunately the building at the back is fake black and white beamed both inside and out. The ceiling beams, when tapped give a most satisfactory hollow timbre.

The reason for including it is that twenty-two of the rooms, all family sized, are grouped around an excellent outdoor heated swimming pool with a large patio.

Accommodation is free for children up to 12 and half portions are served in the restaurant whose wines, by the way, are appallingly over-priced – a bottle of ordinary Beaujolais is nearly £7.

30 rooms, 22 family   Expensive   Open all year
Lunch 12-2pm – £3.50 (buffet)   Dinner 7-9pm – £8.75
Access/AmEx/Barclaycard/Diners   P – own car park

80

East Ilsley, Berks

map 1

P *CROWN & HORNS*

Off the A34.

A pretty pub in a quiet, lovely village in 'horsey' country.

The children's room has plenty of tables and chairs, a space invader machine and a television set. The old stable yard with a paved floor and chestnut trees has tables and chairs for summer days.

It's well worth a short detour from the busy A34 – if only to check the range of real ales, which are frequently changed to suit the customers' tastes. There is a variety of bar snacks to suit your tastes also – steak and kidney pie, Cornish pasties, curry and rice, chicken and ham pie, salads, sandwiches and ploughman's – nothing over £2.

Ale – Fuller's, Wadworth's, Morland's, Arkell's, etc.
P – own car park

East Lambrook, Somerset

map 2

P *ROSE AND CROWN*

In a maze of minor roads off the B3168 north east of Ilminster.

A most appealing village pub built from mellow honey-coloured stone and hidden away in the Somerset countryside. The lounge bar is small and attractive with its beamed ceiling and huge open fireplace below a massive black beam. It has some handsome pieces of furniture. Children are welcome in the skittle alley at the back, and this is clean and bright, white washed and beamed with plenty of tables and chairs. The garden is splendid, with lots of lawn, flowers, shrubberies and bench tables scattered about.

The friendly landlady offers basic pub food – sandwiches, pasties and ploughman's lunches – at Sunday lunchtimes ploughman's only because 'the pub is full of people wanting a drink'. It's certainly worth seeking out if you fancy a drink with the children.

Ale – Eldridge Pope, Hall's, Ind Coope Burton   P – own car park

East Preston, West Sussex

map 1

R *OLD FORGE,* The Street – phone Rustington 2040

Off the A259.

An attractive ivy-clad building with a wide-ranging menu of English and French cuisine. There is a pleasant ambience to this restaurant, helped by the welcoming attitude of the owners.

The lunch menu has a reasonable choice, and, at under £5, represents good value. Whitebait or moules marinière, followed by roast leg of lamb or kidneys à la créme, and finished off with Cabinet pudding seems to us a bargain. The evening menu ranges much wider and you might fancy frogs' legs, or hot Sussex smokies; a choice of fish – salmon, trout, sole; or one of the many types of steak or veal escalopes. Half portions are available for children.

The 'ladies' is spacious and a baby can be changed in comfort.

Closed Sunday dinner/Monday   Lunch 12-2pm – £4.50
Dinner 7-10pm – £10 alc   Licensed
Access/AmEx/Barclaycard/Diners   P – own car park

Eastbourne, East Sussex   map 1

H   **GRAND HOTEL** (de Vere), King Edward's Parade – phone 22611

Very imposing seafront hotel in the 'Grand' tradition with balconies and an ornate Victorian façade. It has a spacious and comfortable interior and its gardens look out over the promenade to the sea. Outside is a heated outdoor swimming pool and indoors a children's playroom.

Accommodation is free for children up to 15 during the summer; in the winter free up to 5 and 50% off up to 12.

A special children's menu is available in the restaurant (at £3.25) and half portions can also be served.

If you fancy a traditional seaside break. . . .

178 rooms, 30 family   Expensive   Open all year
Lunch 12.45-2.30pm – £10   Dinner 7-9.30pm – £12
Access/AmEx/Barclaycard/Diners   P – own car park

Eddleston, Nr Peebles, Borders   map 5

R   **CRINGLETIE HOUSE HOTEL** – phone 233

One-and-a-half miles from Eddleston towards Peebles on the A703.

This is a most appealing and distinguished sandstone country house, rather Gothic with its high windows, half towers and tall chimneys. It is set in twenty-eight acres of lovely gardens against a background of soft rolling hills. The two dining rooms are elegant, well-proportioned and beautifully furnished.

The menu is primarily traditional British (or should we say Scottish), for example poached fresh salmon with fennel Hollandaise, roast duckling with cranberry and Dubonnet sauce, sirloin of beef with Meaux mustard sauce, etc. Reduced portions are served to children. You can eat à la carte from about £4. Teas are also available from 3.30 to 4.30 pm.

The Ladies has a separate area with a dressing table and a stool where a baby could be fed and changed in reasonable comfort.

Closed Jan and Feb   Lunch 1-1.45pm – £7
Dinner 7.30-8.30pm – £11
No credit cards accepted   P – own car park

Elterwater, Nr Ambleside, Cumbria   map 5

P   *BRITANNIA*

Off the B5343 just west of Ambleside.

A nice village pub. Low and white painted with space to sit outside at several tables and a small raised patio with a couple of bench tables. It has a rather splendid sign showing the schooner 'Britannia' under full sail.

Children can sit in the hallway where there are a few tables and chairs or in the dining room where, incidentally, a restaurant with a high chair opens in the evening.

There is a range of snacks available every day – up to 1.45pm at lunchtime and up to 9pm. Sandwiches, burgers, sausages and chips, flans and pies at under £2 and local trout at £3. What a bargain.

Ale – Bass, Tetley   P – on the road: plenty of room

Eskdale Green, Cumbria   map 5

P   *BOWER HOUSE*

On a minor road east of the A595.

This is a fine pub in stunning countryside. The easy route to it is from the A595, but you can approach it (but probably not in the depths of winter) from Ambleside via Wrynose Bottom and the utterly magnificent and daunting Hard Knott Pass. The pub has several delightful rooms including a low-beamed bar where you can tackle the snacks every lunchtime or up to 7pm in the evening (not Sunday evenings). It's basic pub food including Cumberland sausage.

Children can use an attractive and comfortably furnished lounge, and the garden with its sheltered lawn is particularly pretty.

An alternative choice is the King George IV just down the road. It has a clean white-painted pool room where children may go and food is served every day.

Ale – Hartley's, Younger's   P – own car park

Everleigh, Wilts map 2

P   **THE CROWN**

On the A342, north-west of Andover.

A large, smart white-washed pub on the edge of Salisbury Plain. It has a lovely grassy walled garden with plenty of trees, and the children can play here in safety.

There is a small but light children's room which overlooks the garden.

Hot food (grills, etc), salads and snacks are available at all times except Sunday evenings when no hot meals are served.

Ale – Wadworth's   P – own car park

Exeter, Devon map 2

H   **BUCKERELL LODGE HOTEL** (Crest), Topsham Road – phone 52451

B3182 Exeter to Exmouth road. From Junction 30 of the M5 the hotel is on the south side of the city – follow the 'City Centre' signs from the A379.

A refurbished Regency building with a new extension. The extension fits in very well, indicative of the care that has been taken. Better to pause here and not take a car into the city – a chimp could have made a more competent job of the road-signing.

Children under 14 are accommodated free and an extra bed for over-14s is £10 – children can have their own room if one is available.

In addition to the restaurant, which offers a special children's menu, the Crest Pantry provides a range of hot and cold dishes from 12 till 2pm. You can eat paté, soup, plaice and chips, or the chef's special for just over £2.

54 rooms, 2 family, 4 sets adjoining   Moderate   Ale – Bass
Access/AmEx/Barclaycard/Diners   P – own car park

Exmouth, Devon

map 2

H   *IMPERIAL HOTEL* (THF), The Esplanade – phone 74761

On the seafront.

An imposing white mansion in four acres of gardens and facing Lyme Bay. There is an open air swimming pool, two splendid tennis courts, mini-golf and curling. Many facilities for children including a paddling pool, climbing frame, video shows, garden games and a Wild West play area. Indoors there's a spacious games room with table tennis, space invader, playpen, darts and a huge blackboard.

There is no accommodation charge for children under 5 and only £1 for children from 5 to 14.

There is a splendid 'palm court' dining room. Although only snacks are available at lunchtimes (full lunch on Sundays) there are special children's menus and half portions. There is a children's tea party each day at 5.30.

65 rooms, 11 family   Expensive
Open all year   Lunch – snacks only   Dinner 7-9pm – £6.50
Ale – Bass
Access/AmEx/Barclaycard/Diners   P – own car park

Falmouth, Cornwall

map 2

H   *PENMERE MANOR* (Best Westen), Mongleath Road – phone 314 545

Easy to miss as the signs are badly placed. Get a clear map from the hotel.

Very attractive white-painted Georgian country house, with a just passable extension, in five acres of splendid gardens and woodland. The heated swimming pool is in a lovely walled grassy garden. There is a spacious three-roomed cellar games area, with tables tennis and pool. Squash and tennis are free at Falmouth Club.

Accommodation is free for children of 12 and under sharing with their parents, except during the high season, and half portions are served in the dining room.

29 rooms, 7 family   Moderate   Open all year
Lunch 12.30-1.30 snacks only   Dinner 7-8.30pm – £7
Access/AmEx/Barclaycard/Diners   P — own car park

Fawley, Nr Henley-on-Thames, Bucks

map 1

R   *THE WALNUT TREE* –phone Turville Heath 360

Off the A423 and B480, north of Henley-on-Thames.

A large, mainly brick-built pub in a lovely wooded setting, beside a country lane and a few miles from Henley. It has a large garden where meals can be eaten when it's warm enough.

There is a menu with a wide choice, both in the restaurant and at the bar, where there are half portions and snacks for children. There are several patés always available, smoked prawns, lasagne, salmon trout, chicken kiev, swordfish, crab mornay and steaks, as well as home-made pies and hamburgers. The prices vary from about £1 to the most expensive dish – steak – at just under £7.

The friendly owners will make a room available for a mother to change or feed her baby.

Lunch 12-2pm – £7.50   Dinner 7-9pm – £7.50
Ale – Brakspear's
Access/Barclaycard   P – own car park

Ferndown, Dorset

map 2

H   *DORMY HOTEL* (de Vere), New Road – phone 872 121

Just off the A347 Bournemouth Road.

A well-appointed hotel in twelve acres of beautiful gardens with lily ponds, rock pools and waterfalls. Outdoors is a swimming pool, with poolside bar, and grass tennis court, and Ferndown golf course is next door to the hotel.

Children sharing with parents have free accommodation up to the age of 5 and a 50% reduction to 12. A member of staff will baby-sit by arrangement

91 rooms, 30 family   Expensive   Open all year
Lunch 12-2.30 – £6.50   Dinner 7-9.30pm – £8   Ale – Bass
Access/AmEx/Barclaycard/Diners   P – own car park

Fingest, Nr Henley-on-Thames, Bucks

map 1

P   *CHEQUERS INN*

Off B482, north of Henley-on-Thames.

A fine flint and brick pub with deep tiled roofs opposite a part-Norman church. It has a big garden with tables and chairs.

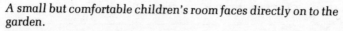

A small but comfortable children's room faces directly on to the garden.

Bar food is served from 12-2pm and in the evenings – but not on Sunday. And – beware – lunchtime food stops on the dot of 2 o'clock no matter how hungry you are!

Ale – Brakspear's   P – car park at back of pub

Flichity, Inverness-shire map 6

P R   *GROUSE AND TROUT* – phone Farr 314

On the B851 between Farr and Crochy.

This bar and restaurant is well worth the trip down a winding road south of Inverness. Beautiful stone buildings, low and deep-roofed, once a farm, form an open square, within which is a most attractive walled garden with tables and chairs. You can contemplate the low hills from here and perhaps listen to the plop of tennis balls on the adjacent court.

At lunchtimes there are snacks at reasonable prices – toasted sandwiches at 50p, a poacher's platter at £1.55, and cold meat salads at £2.50. The dinner menu includes trout, chicken and steaks. Children may have half portions of a lot of the dishes.

The interior is well-designed and there is a comfortable sitting area where you can take the children. The 'Ladies' is fine for breast-feeding and nappy-changing.

Be sure to check that the restaurant is open before you set off as it's a favourite spot for weddings and other private celebrations.

Closed Jan and Sun dinner   Lunch 12-2.30pm
Dinner 7.30-9.30 – £10 alc   Licensed
Access/AmEx/Barclaycard/Diners   P – own car park

Folkestone, Kent map 1

H   *BURLINGTON HOTEL,* Earls Avenue – phone 55301

Just off The Leas, Folkestone's promenade.

A striking Victorian brick building with a view of the sea and with a pretty and secluded lawned garden and terrace. An hotel which is useful as a stop-over before a Channel crossing.

Children under 14 are accommodated free and have their breakfast free.

55 rooms, 3 family   Moderate   Open all year
Access/AmEx/Barclaycard/Diners   P – car park for ten cars

H   *CLIFTON HOTEL* (THF), The Leas – phone 41231

On the main promenade, near the bandstand.

Big and imposing seafront hotel with good views of the sea from most rooms. There is a large and pleasant garden (Council owned) at the rear of the hotel.

Accommodation is free for children up to the age of 5; a nominal charge of £1 up to 14.

A special children's menu is available and half portions are also served.

62 rooms, 2 family   Cheap   Open all year
Lunch 12.30-2pm – £6 alc   Dinner 6.45-9pm – £6.95
Ale – Bass
Access/AmEx/Barclaycard/Diners   P – car park opposite

Fonthill Bishop, Wilts   map 2

P   *KING'S ARMS*

On the B3089, west of Salisbury.

A pretty renovated pub with white shutters. There is a pleasant well-furnished bar with darts and bar-skittles off to one side.

An attractive children's room with tables and chairs leads out to a lawned garden with benches, tables and sun-shades.

A wide range of food is available every day including a hot dish of the day like roast chicken or pork or chilli con carne at just over £2, and trout or a rump steak at just over £4.

Ale – Wadworth's   P – own car park

Forton, Lancs   map 3

P   *NEW HOLLY HOTEL*

On the A6.

A big, busy and noisy roadside pub with a dining-cum-pool room for children. There is a field at the back where children can play. It's a useful stopping off point close to Junction 33 of the M6, and there is a wide choice of food available seven days a week. Your choice ranges from a sandwich at under £1 to a sirloin steak at £4 and in between are toasted sandwiches, prawn cocktails, curries, chicken, scampi and lots of grilled fish, including salmon, plaice and halibut.

Ale – Thwaites   P – own car park

Framfield, East Sussex map 1

R   *COACH HOUSE,* The Street – phone 636

Off the B2102.

A nice-looking tile fronted 17th century restaurant which is very spacious inside and which has a delightful bonus in the large lawned garden – an outdoor swimming pool where you can sharpen up your appetite on summer days.

There's an extensive range of dishes on offer, most of which can be served in children's portions. The lunch is pretty good value with such things as devilled mushrooms, lamb's liver and a pudding available. The same goes for the set dinner at £5.50 – chicken liver paté, marinated trout and a pudding for example.

There's plenty of space in the Ladies for changing and feeding a baby.

Closed – Monday/Sunday dinner/Tuesday lunch
Lunch 12.15-1.45pm – £5   Dinner 7-9pm – £5.50 (£10 alc)
Licensed   Access/Diners   P – own car park

Fyfield, Oxon map 1

P   *WHITE HART*

Off the A420, seven miles from Abingdon.

A splendid pub, built in the 15th century, and now owned by an Oxford College.

The main room has a high ceiling with stone windows and is overlooked by a pretty gallery in which children may sit. There's an embarrassment of riches here for parents because there is a second room on the ground floor, spacious and well-furnished, where children are welcome. There is a lawn at the back of the pub.

There is a catholic selection of snacks – frogs' legs are sometimes on the menu as well as chilli con carne, king prawns, game casserole, steak and kidney pie, sandwiches, ploughman's, etc. Half portions will be served to children. An equally catholic array of real ale barrels faces you at the bar.

A most impressive pub both in its approach to food and to beer. It is run by a friendly and efficient staff and has outstanding facilities for families. Hence its nomination as a runner-up in the pub category.

Ale – Morland, Wadworth's, Bass, Theakston's, etc.
P – own car park

Gargrave, Nr Skipton, North Yorks

map 3

P *ANCHOR INN*

On the A65 west of the village.

A handsome stone roadside pub – big and busy. It dates back to the 16th century and was once used to stable the canal horses. Children can sit in the very large function room at the back of the pub or might prefer the spacious and nice-looking dining room which overlooks the garden. They have a special menu and there is a good choice of dishes on the main menu – for example, liver and onions, chilli con carne, chicken and chips all at around £2; and trout, steaks, etc, at higher prices. These are available every day.

In addition the big garden, flanked by the canal (well populated by holiday barges) has a remarkable array of swings, roundabouts, slides, climbing frames and other playthings. Happily abandon the little darlings and get on with your Theakston's.

Ale – Theakston's   P – own car park

Gatwick, West Sussex

map 1

H *POST HOUSE HOTEL* (THF), Povey Cross Road – phone Horley 71621

At the junction of the A23 and A217.

Modern brick-built Post House about half a mile from the Airport to which there is a regular courtesy bus. The hotel is set in six acres of grounds with a pleasant outdoor heated swimming pool at the rear with tables and chairs. This is a good bet if you have an early flight from Gatwick.

There are many family rooms at economic rates and children up to the age of 5 are accommodated free with a nominal charge of £1 made for children up to 14.

149 rooms, 15 family   Expensive
Open all year   Ale – Webster's
Access/AmEx/Barclaycard/Diners   P – own car park

Gisburn, Nr Clitheroe, Lancs

map 3

H *STIRK HOUSE HOTEL* – phone 581

Off the A59.

The hotel is set in lovely open country not too far from the Yorkshire Dales. The original building, an ivy-covered stone manor house of 16th century vintage, is very attractive. The two extensions are not: a single storey grey elongated prefab and a two-storey motel block. Housed in a separate building is a medium-sized swimming pool and two squash courts, plus table football and space invaders. From Monday to Friday free golf can be had at Skipton Golf Club, and at half price over the weekends.

The lunch menu is reasonably priced and children can order whatever they require in the way of sausages, fish fingers and other snacks. The evening menu is quite extensive and goes through the gamut of meats plus trout, omelettes, etc.

Cots are charged at £2.50 a night and older children up to the age of 11 are charged at half the single rate.

An hotel in a good spot on the Lancashire/Yorkshire border. So close your eyes to the two execrable annexes.

52 rooms, 3 family   Moderate   Open all year
Lunch 12.30-1.45pm – £5 alc   Dinner 7.15-9.45pm – £7.95
Access/AmEx/Barclaycard/Diners   P – own car park

Gleneagles, Nr Auchterarder, Tayside   maps 5

H   *GLENEAGLES HOTEL* – Auchterarder 2231

On the A823 – clearly signposted.

The famous Gleneagles – a massive and expensive hotel in 610 acres – offers pretty well everything you could want except peace and tranquility. The hotel is justly famous for its golf facilities – four courses including the renowned King's and Queen's, which are popular and busy. The superbly designed modern Country Club has a large swimming pool, children's pool, jacuzzi, outdoor Canadian tub and fitness area. There are also saunas, communal Turkish baths, massage rooms, squash courts, tennis courts, children's playground. The Club has its own bar open from 11am to 10pm serving all-day meals with silly names: 'Par 3', 'The Chip Shot' and with 'Tee Time' between 4 and 6pm Monday-Saturday. Here and in the three hotel restaurants half portions of many dishes are offered to children. Baby-sitting can be arranged at short notice. Is it unkind to describe it as an up-market and costly Butlins?

Children under 14 sharing with parents are accommodated free.

206 rooms, 13 family, 1 suite   Expensive   Open all year

Lunch 12.45-2.30pm – £12.50   Dinner 7.30-9.45pm – £15.50
Access/AmEx/Barclaycard/Diners
P – own car park

Glyn Ceiriog, nr Chirk, Clwyd   map 3

H P R *THE GOLDEN PHEASANT HOTEL* – phone 281

On the B4500, west of Chirk.

This is an exceptionally pretty country inn which is unexpected
as you go through a housing estate to reach it. Behind, though, is
the beautiful Ceiriog Valley. The hotel has its own small garden
and two tiled patios. Inside it is very welcoming, with two
splendid bars – a gun room with open range and another bar full
of stuffed birds. There's a stuffed peacock to greet you in the
'cottagy' dining room and a live mynah bird by the front door.
The lounge, where children may sit, looks out to the hills.

At lunchtime you eat from the bar 'Bistro' menu – which offers a
good mix of simple dishes such as Ceiriog trout, pizza, curry
and rice, spaghetti bolognese, plaice and chips. In the evening
the dining room serves simple dishes like grilled Welsh lamb
and other grilled meats and some fish dishes, together with a
special each day which might be a roast or a more elaborate
game dish. There is also a gourmet menu (eg fresh mussel soup
and partridge à la Vigneronne) which changes nightly.

Cots cost £1.50 per night, and beds for older children cost £5.50
up to the age of 12 and this charge includes breakfast and high
tea.

19 rooms, 6 family   Moderate   Open all year
Lunch 12-1.30pm – £3 alc   Dinner 7.30-9pm – £9 alc
Access/AmEx   P – own car park

Gosforth, Nr Newcastle upon Tyne, Tyne & Wear   map 5

H *GOSFORTH PARK HOTEL* (Thistle) – phone 364 111

Follow the Gosforth Park signs from the A6125 north of
Newcastle.

A huge modern hotel by Gosforth race course which you would
not visit in order to admire the architecture. It is a functional
building but efficiently run by cheerful staff and well-placed for
a stop-over when travelling up and down the country. There are
splendid facilities to revive the travel-weary: a leisure centre
with indoor heated swimming pool, sauna and fitness room;
two squash courts; a 'trim trail' (a route for running or walking

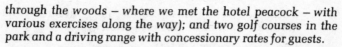

through the woods – where we met the hotel peacock – with various exercises along the way); and two golf courses in the park and a driving range with concessionary rates for guests.

Accommodation is free for children up to 14. There is a children's menu in the Vineyard restaurant as well as half portions. A variety of salads are served here as well as grills. There is another restaurant, more expensive, and where the food is rather rich.

178 rooms, 24 family rooms Expensive Open all year
The Vineyard 11.30am-11.30pm – £6.75 dinner
Access/AmEx/Barclaycard/Diners P – own car park

Grantham, Lincs   map 4

H P R *THE ANGEL AND ROYAL* (THF), High Street – phone 5816

In the centre of town.

Said to be one of the oldest inns in England, parts of the building date back to the 12th century when it may have been a manorial hall. King John held court here, and both Edward III and Richard III were visitors. The hotel now has a fine stone front (probably 15th century) and an archway leads to a long stone patio between two wings of the building. There are tables and chairs here and wooden stocks – handy for recalcitrant children.

The children are accommodated free to 5 years, and for £1 up to 14 years. There is the special Munch Bunch menu and half portions can be chosen from the main menu.

The bar snacks, available lunchtimes (12-2.15pm) and evenings (6.30-10pm), are good value – cold meats and salad, hot pie or a casserole with jacket potatoes cost around £2. A lunch in the restaurant is just over £5 for, say, soup, navarin of lamb and a hot pudding. The dinner menu is traditional roasts, chops and fish dishes.

A delightful place for a stop-over for a family on the move.

32 rooms Moderate
Open all year Lunch 12.30-2pm – £5.25 Dinner 7-10pm –
£7.50 (Sun £6.50) Ale – Sam Smith's, Ruddles
Access/AmEx/Barclaycard/Diners P – at the back – take the first
turn after the hotel from whichever direction you approach it

---

Grasmere, Cumbria   map 5

A justly famous village in stunningly attractive countryside, *where the Wordsworths lived for fourteen years. William and his wife are buried in Grasmere Churchyard.*

H P R *THE SWAN HOTEL* (THF) – phone 551

On the A591.

It's corny to quote Wordsworth when speaking of Grasmere, but he did say in The Waggoner 'Who does not know the famous Swan'. And it's worth knowing – a white roadside inn about 200 years old and with a well-tended air which gives it a very welcoming atmosphere. You have a choice of three lounges in which to sit, drink, talk and eat; bar food is served from 12 to 2pm: ploughman's for under £2, fisherman's pie for under £3 and a hot dish-of-the-day for £3.50. The dinner menu when we were there had some unusual offerings – pike dumplings and a vegetarian dish (still pretty rare) plus more usual meat and fish dishes.

Accommodation for children aged between 5 and 14 is £1 with no charge for younger ones. A special menu is offered for them or they can choose half portions.

This is a comfortable hotel for a stay or to stop a while and is surrounded by stunning Lake District scenery.

41 rooms, 4 family   Moderate   Open all year
Lunch 12-2pm – £7   Dinner 7-9.30pm – £10.50 (5 courses)
Access/AmEx/Barclaycard/Diners   P – own car park

H R *WORDSWORTH HOTEL* – phone 592

In the village centre off the A591.

This is a splendid hotel, a two-storey, rambling stone building, recently restored with great care and skill. Its entrance hall, so handsome with its padded courting seat, superb grandfather clock, and oil painting of the poet, sets the scene for the rest of the delightful public rooms.

The hotel has an exceptionally good indoor swimming pool, sparkling clean (no murky waters here), and its glass sliding doors open on to a wide patio and the spacious gardens.

The children are looked after with a high tea available from 5.30-6.30 – soups, melon, spaghetti, minute steaks, etc – at a cost of £3. Looked after but not indulged – under-12s must be out of the dining room by 7.45 at night so that the adults can play in peace. The children are accommodated for £12 (including breakfast) and cots cost £3.50 a night.

This is a great place to stay in one of the most famous villages in the beautiful Lake District.

35 rooms, 3 sets of adjoining rooms   Expensive
Open all year   Lunch 12.30-2pm – £11 alc   Bar snacks (eg cold buffet) 12.30-2.30pm – £3.25   Dinner 7-9pm – £11.50
Access/AmEx/Barclaycard/Diners   P – own car park

Great Bardfield, Essex map 1

R   *CORN DOLLY*, High Street – phone Great Dunmow 810 554

On the B1057, north of Great Dunmow.

A 16th century building in an attractive village. There is an airy oak-panelled dining room and an elegant upstairs drawing room overlooking the garden for post-prandial coffees. The emphasis is on English cooking of the home-made variety (although coq au vin occasionally slips in): liver and bacon casserole, Elizabethan beef pudding, rump steak, fillet of beef en croute, roast duck, etc. The owner stressed that 'there are no frozen vegetables in this restaurant.' It is open also for morning coffee and afternoon teas.

Half portions are available for children and a mother can change and feed her baby in the spacious and smart separate 'powder room' in the ladies' lavatory.

Closed – Monday/Tuesday/Sunday dinner
Lunch 12.30-2pm – £6.50   Dinner 7.30-9pm – £11 for 5 courses
Licensed   No credit cards accepted   P – street parking only

---

Great Dunmow, Essex map 1

H   *SARACEN'S HEAD HOTEL* (THF), High Street – phone 3901

In the town centre.

A country hotel with an 18th century façade which masks a much older building. It's a typical town THF hotel – extended to the rear – with a pleasant beamed interior.

There is quite a range of bar meals available at lunchtimes. Apart from ploughman's and toasted sandwiches, you can have a grill (lamb or bacon chops, for example) at under £4 or the 'Chef's Special' at just over £4; or plaice and chips, meat and salad, etc. The restaurant menu is fairly conventional hotel food – roasts, grills and fish dishes.

Children under 5 are accommodated free and from 5 to 14 a token charge of £1 is made. The dining room offers a special menu and half prices for children.

20 rooms, 3 suites, 1 set of adjoining rooms   Moderate
Open all year   Lunch 12.15-2.15pm – £4.25
Dinner 7-9.30pm – £8.50   Ale – Rayment
Access/AmEx/Barclaycard/Diners   P – own car park

Gullane, Lothian
map 5

H R   *GREYWALLS HOTEL* – phone 842 144

Off the A198 east of the town centre.

The walls are not grey – they are of soft pink stone from Rattlebags quarry as are the walls of the secluded gardens. The interior is as beautiful as the exterior – pale green archways lead to a long wide corridor, book-lined lounge, conservatory and other public rooms, all superbly furnished and decorated. Within the grounds is tennis and a sunken croquet lawn looking out over the renowned Muirfield Golf Club. It is the oldest golf club in the world (founded in 1744) and offers one of the finest tests of a golfer's ability. This is of course famous golfing country and although the hotel does not offer facilities specifically for children nearby are some good beaches – use the village car park – and parents would certainly find this an exceptional place to stay.

Cots or extra beds are charged at £10 and the dining room will serve special meals for children on request. There is a short lunch menu – a flan, a seafood pancake, or pitta sandwiches with beef, etc (or à la carte). The dinner menu sounds mouth-watering – such dishes as avacado and chicken in curry mayonnaise, fresh salmon soufflé, and rosettes of lamb.

It ain't cheap!

23 rooms, 1 suite in the South Lodge, separate from hotel
Expensive   Open all year   Lunch 12.30-2pm – £6.75
Dinner 7.30-9.30pm – £15.95
Access/AmEx/Barclaycard/Diners   P – own car park

Gwbert-on-Sea, Nr Cardigan, Dyfed
map 2

H   *THE CLIFF HOTEL* (Best Western) – phone Cardigan 613 241

On the B4548 north of Cardigan.

This is a real old hotch-potch of odd buildings – but close your eyes to the architecture and appreciate the excellent facilities and superb position in solitary splendour in thirty acres of headland overlooking Cardigan Bay. There is a nine-hole golf course alongside the hotel, a putting green, squash court, a games room with snooker tables (children must be supervised) and a table tennis table. The heated outdoor pool is a good size and sheltered by a wall. Fishermen are also catered for with free fishing on the famous River Teifi – as long as you buy a licence. Other nearby pastimes are sailing, riding, bird watching.

The Buttery is open from 12 to 2pm and 6.30 to 10pm and has a wide range of main dishes – pizzas, poultry dishes, grills, steaks and salads from £2 to £6 or so – as well as sandwiches and bangers and mash. There is a children's menu and all the dishes are under £1. The dinner menu in the restaurant concentrates on local fish and grills.

Children are accommodated free up to 14.

70 rooms, 3 sets of adjoining rooms   Moderate
Open all year   Lunch 12-2pm   Dinner (restaurant) 7-9pm –
£7.25   Dinner (Buttery) 6.30-10pm   Ale – Felinfoel
Access/AmEx/Barclaycard/Diners   P – own car park

Hackness, Nr Scarborough, N. Yorks   map 4

H   *HACKNESS GRANGE HOTEL* (Best Western) – phone
Scarborough 69966

Off the A170 a few miles East of Scarborough.

A stone building of two storeys, built in the mid-19th century. It looks handsome and classical behind a lake (man-made but very effective) and framed by gentle hills. Its annexe, in the same stone, marries in very well. There are beautiful grounds, with smooth lawns, and all within the North York Moors National Park. They have some good facilities: an indoor heated swimming pool of reasonable size and with glass doors opening on to the garden: a hard tennis court; a pitch and putt course; and several miles of trout fishing on the Derwent.

It is a pleasant spot, with lots of space to roam, but expensive, if you only stop for one night. Our advice is to seek one of the many bargain breaks here and then it makes economic sense.

Cots are charged at £5 per night; under 5s cost one-third of the single rate; and thereafter up to 12 half of the adult rate. Half portions are available in the restaurant and high teas (for residents only) from 5.30.

27 rooms, 7 family   Moderate   Open all year
Lunch 12.30-1.30pm – £7 alc   Dinner 7-9pm – £10.75
Access/AmEx/Barclaycard/Diners   P – own car park

Hallow, Hereford & Worcs

map 3

P   *THE CROWN*

On the A443.

Big, friendly, welcoming roadside pub. There is a delightful, oak-beamed area available for children, with a log fire and next to the main bar, and a splendid large garden with tables and benches.

You can eat food here on any day of the week, and up to about 10pm. A good range of pub meals is on offer – scampi, curry, flans, chicken and chips and a dish of the day, at prices up to £3. The children's meals – things and chips – cost £1 a time.

Ale – Wm Younger   P – own car park

Hamble, Hants

map 1

R   *BETH'S*, The Quay – phone 4314

Go through Hamble till you see the sea.

A very charming two storey brick house in the Queen Anne style right by the sea in this pretty yachting village. The interior is equally charming and there is a shortish but interesting menu with, naturally, several fish dishes: for example home cured salmon, bourride de poissons and fresh lobster. The prices quoted below are for two courses. Half portions are served for . children.

There is a paved garden at the rear on various levels with plenty of bench tables where, on summer days, barbecued dishes are served. No credit cards are accepted for the garden food, nor is there anywhere convenient for changing or feeding a baby.

Closed Sun evenings and Nov-May
Lunch 12.30-2pm – £6.75   Dinner 7-10pm – £7.75   Licensed
Access/AmEx/Barclaycard/Diners
P – public car park across the road

Harrogate, N. Yorks

map 3

H   *HOTEL MAJESTIC* (THF), Ripon Road – phone 68972

Off the A61 near the centre of the city.

Shut your eyes as you approach . . . A vast and ugly Victorian pile built in 1900: a typical spa hotel. But inside it is truly 'majestic' with its Wembley arena of a dining room, and an amazing long lounge with marble pillars, frescoes and flying *staircase. Fit for an early Orson Welles film. The games room is worth a look too, not for its solitary table tennis table but for the extraordinary carved oak fireplace.*

We include this hotel because it has a hard tennis court, a squash court and a heated swimming pool covered by a sort of glass hangar. There is a stretch of lawned garden too.

Children are accommodated free to the age of 5 and for £1 from 5 to 14. They have their own menu and can order half portions from the main menu. The buffet serves salads, pizzas and a hot meal of the day.

160 rooms, 6 family   Expensive   Open all year
Lunch 12.45-2.15pm – £7   Dinner 6.45-9.15pm – £9
Access/AmEx/Barclaycard/Diners   P – own car park

Harwich, Essex   map 1

R   ***THE PIER AT HARWICH,*** The Quay – phone 3363

Apart from catching a boat, this restaurant is one of the few reasons for visiting Harwich, so if you find yourself in this neck of the woods and fancy an excellent meal, head for the Pier Hotel – follow the signs for 'the Quay' and there it is: an interesting old building which houses a fish restaurant and overlooks the sea. As well as the more elaborate dishes they have plainer food, eg fish pie and cod au gratin. The management have a welcoming attitude towards families out to eat and offer fish and chip portions for children at £2.50.

There is a large powder room where mothers can feed and change their offspring.

Closed – Christmas Day   Lunch 12.30-2pm – £12
Dinner 6.30-10pm – £12   Ale – Adnam's
Access/AmEx/Barclaycard/Diners   P – own car park

Haslemere, Surrey   map 1

H   ***LYTHE HILL HOTEL*** (Prestige), Petworth Road – phone 51251

On the B2131.

A mixture of styles, ancient and modern, which merge very well. They range from 14th century stone buildings to the black and white timber-framed Auberge de France restaurant which, in its separate location, overlooks the lake and the lovely sprawling grassy gardens (fourteen acres of them). There is a tennis court and guests can also fish in the lake. The set menus in the hotel restaurant (the 'Entente Cordiale') offer dishes such as ham and asparagus comets, blanquette of veal, roast duck, fillet of sole, etc. The Auberge de France serves much more elaborate and expensive meals – stick to the hotel restaurant.

Accommodation for children up to 14 is an extra £5 and half portions are served to them in the dining room.

34 rooms, 8 family   Moderate   Open all year
Lunch 12.15-2.30pm – £7.25 Dinner 7.15-9.45pm – £9.25
Access/AmEx/Barclaycard/Diners   P – own car park

Hastings, East Sussex   map 1

H R   **BEAUPORT PARK HOTEL,** Battle Road – phone 51222

On the A5100 between Battle and Hastings.

The hotel is a superb Georgian mansion in about thirty acres of parkland and with very attractive and spacious gardens. There is a very ugly extension at one side, fortunately partly hidden by trees. There are two grass tennis courts, a putting green, squash courts, a heated outdoor swimming pool and, next door, an eighteen-hole golf course (run by the local Council).

Accommodation is free for children up to about 14 years; half portions are available in the restaurant, which also has a special children's menu.

Both lunch and dinner menus offer a small and good selection of food at reasonable prices: a typical lunch might include cream of camembert and Champagne soup, baked eggs mornay, sautéed pork chop Niçoise, fried liver and onions; and dinner goes French with perhaps oeuf Marie Rose, caneton rôti cerise noir, sole grillée maître d'hotel, jambon grillé au nectarine, and both menus have a choice of cold meat dishes.

20 rooms, 5 family   Cheap   Open all year
Lunch 12.30-2pm – £6   Dinner 7.30-8.30pm – £7.95
Access/AmEx/Barclaycard/Diners   P – own car park

Hatherleigh, Devon   map 2

P   **GEORGE HOTEL**

On the A386 in the village (on a bend).

Splendid rambling 15th century coaching inn, superb inside and out. It has a croquet lawn, a swing and an outdoor swimming pool which non-residents may use.

The large family room off the main bar is well-furnished and oak-beamed.

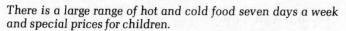

There is a large range of hot and cold food seven days a week and special prices for children.

Ale – Courage, Whitbread   P – own car park

Hawkshead, Cumbria map 5

Go straight to the public car park which is a few yards from the centre of this pretty tourist village where we found three pubs we liked:

P   *RED LION*

In our opinion the best of the three. It's a fine pub with oak beams and superb oak panelling. The children's room is good and can be seen from the main bar through a windowed wall. Outside is a small patio with tables and chairs.

The menu offers a good variety of food at very reasonable prices – for instance trout with vegetables and chips at £2.75, shepherd's pie with red cabbage and peas at £1.20. There are sandwiches from 60p, the usual chicken, steak, scampi pub dishes and each day a chef's special – Frogs' Legs Provençale with rice on one of our visits. Children are offered things with chips, peas and beans at 85p and the serving times are unusually generous: 11.30am-2.30pm and 6-9.30pm (Sundays 12-1.45pm and 7-9.30p,m).

Ale – Hartley's.

The other pubs are:

P   *THE QUEEN'S HEAD*

A black and white fronted building with an interior of beamed ceilings and panelled walls. The children's room is a small one off the main bar.

As well as sandwiches and salad, there's a good choice of hot food and half portions for children – plaice at £2.15, trout £2.40, lasagne and salad £2.50.

Ale – Hartley's

P   *THE SUN*

The Sun has a large and comfortable dining room where the children can sit and a small patio with tables and chairs. It too offers a good range of food.

A nice old pub but rougher and readier than the other two.

Ale – Bass

Hay-on-Wye, Powys

map 2

R   *THE GRANARY* – phone 820 790

In the centre of this exceptionally pretty tourist village which is a book-lover's paradise. Local colour is added by a noticeable number of young men looking like hippies left over from the 70s. Artists we guess. If you like street markets, visit on a Thursday.

Machinery and pulleys witness that this really was a granary and it has that bare but welcoming look you'd expect. There's a good choice of home-cooking – soup, ratatouille, lasagne, shepherd's pie, pork hot pot, salad, baked potatoes, etc, at prices up to £2.50 – available all day, to which is added in the evenings something like pork ragout and local fish. Home-made scones and cakes are on sale too. Children can have half portions of most dishes.

Real ale comes from the wine bar next door and upstairs is a gallery of local art.

There is absolutely nowhere to change or feed a baby.

Closed 4 days at Christmas
Open each day 9am-6pm, to 9pm during Easter and summer holidays   Ale – Hancocks
Access only   P – plenty of street parking except Market Day

Hayle, Cornwall

map 2

P   *BIRD IN HAND*

Follow the signs to Paradise Park.

Imposing stone pub and brewery which serves its own Paradise Bitter in addition to six other real ales which are always available from a running selection of thirty beers. Their brew is named after Paradise Park, which is next door, where there is a complex with a farm and bird sanctuary. The pub has a large grass garden.

In addition to the splendid pool room, children can play in a screened area with something like a dozen electronic games which is 'considered separate by the local magistrate'.

Food is always available but in winter limited to pasties and toasted sandwiches. There is a little more on offer in the summer, with salads and such things as plaice, sausages, etc, at a maximum of £2 a time. Children can have fish fingers, beans and chips.

Ale – lots, see details   P – own huge car park

We assumed that you would not from choice linger in a hotel near Heathrow Airport, but would be there for one night in order to catch an early flight, or after arriving on a late one. There are alternative places to lay your head nearby: the Monkey Island Hotel at Bray, the Castle Hotel at Windsor and the Oakley Court Hotel at Water Oakley near Windsor. London itself is not far away. (See also Airports-Heathrow, page 253).

However, if you must be close to the Airport, we picked out the following hotels, because they have a little more to offer than simply bed and board.

H   **HOLIDAY INN,** Stockley Road, West Drayton, Middlesex — phone 45555

Just north of junction 4 of the M4.

The best of the bunch. It is a modern block, but with its dark red brickwork does not offend the eye too much. The facilities are excellent: a good-sized indoor heated swimming pool with a railed-off area specifically for very young children; alongside is some fitness equipment — static bikes, sit-up benches, etc. Outside are two hard tennis courts and, if your flight is delayed long enough, a nine-hole golf course.

The Farmhouse Kitchen is open daily from 6.30am to 11.45pm and offers a variety of grills, fish dishes, sandwiches, and other snacks and a special children's menu too.

Holiday Inns offer a good deal on rooms: They give free accommodation to children sharing up to the age of 19 and there are 244 double rooms here and each one has two double beds and room for a cot at the normal double room rate. Each of the 156 single rooms has a double bed, so one parent with one child also gets an economic rate.

400 rooms, 244 family   Expensive   Open all year
Farmhouse Kitchen 6.30am-11.45pm
Access/AmEx/Barclaycard/Diners   P — own car park

H   **SHERATON-HEATHROW HOTEL,** London Airport, West Drayton, Middlesex — phone 01-759 2424

On the A4 just west of the Airport.

This is a formidably ugly building, made of a type of breeze block and with small windows — Alcatraz for travellers. But it is pleasant enough inside in the universal style of large 'international' hotels.

Its advantage is the presence of a large indoor swimming pool, with a separate paddling pool.

The Coffee Shop is open from 6am to 11.30pm and provides the usual fast fare of burgers, grills, sandwiches, etc.

Children's accommodation is free up to the age of 16 and most of the rooms will take an extra bed. Parents with two children in tow will usually be offered two double rooms and will only be charged at the single rate for each, ie the children still stay free.

440 rooms 4 sets of adjoining rooms   Expensive
Open all year   Coffee Shop 6am-11.30pm
Access/AmEx/Barclaycard/Diners   P – own car park

H   ***EXCELSIOR*** (THF), *Bath Road, West Drayton, Middlesex –* phone 01-759 6611

On the A4 opposite the Airport.

This is also a rather ugly, very large and sprawling hotel but has the standard THF facilities for families: accommodation is free up to 5 years of age, and from then to 14 costs a nominal £1 per night. There is the usual Coffee Shop which is open all day until 1am and serves the normal array of steaks, grilled chicken, plaice, gammon, burgers and salads. Children have their own menu or can choose half portions from the other menus.

You can have a swim here – but only in the summer. The pool is an outdoor one, with a paddling pool and a patio. There is a well-equipped and well-supervised Fitness Room – lots of static bikes, weights to push, pull and lift, and a running machine. It was very busy when we visited one wet and wintry afternoon.

660 rooms, 12 triples, 3 sets of adjoining rooms   Expensive
Open all year   Coffee Shop 9.45am-1am
Access/AmEx/Barclaycard/Diners   P – own car park

H   ***HEATHROW PENTA HOTEL,*** *Bath Road, Hounslow, Middlesex – phone* 01-897 6363

On the A4.

This is a huge concrete blockhouse situated virtually on one of the runways. We include it as an alternative to the hotels listed above even though the staff in the Reception Area were all far too busy to answer a few simple questions. We got the impression that they might be too busy for their guests.

There is however a very inviting and large indoor heated pool. The usual Coffee Shop, open twenty-four hours a day, offers the usual grills and snacks, and half portions for children.

There is no accommodation charge for children under 12.

670 rooms, 71 sets of adjoining rooms   Expensive
Open all year   Coffee Shop open 24 hours
Access/AmEx/Barclaycard/Diners   P – own car park

Hedge End, Nr Southampton, Hants   map 1

H R   *THE BOTLEIGH GRANGE HOTEL* – phone Botley 5611

On the A334, five miles east of Southampton.

A 16th century mansion, built of stone and covered in ivy, which is rather splendid in an untidy sort of way. It looks like a castle and is surrounded by twenty-five acres of land with marvellous gardens with wide lawns, mature trees and a huge stretch of lily pond, where one might do a spot of fishing. There is a terrace looking out over the gardens and barbecues are held here in the summer. A pity about the hideous little extension.

Half portions are available in the two restaurants: the Cromwell Carvery which offers three courses including a roast, and Squires, which offers steaks, roast duck, etc, for around £9 à la carte. The accommodation charge for children under 5 sharing with their parents is £3.50 and over 5 £4.50.

It's a useful place to stop for a night or a meal – near the New Forest and lots of other touristy spots – Beaulieu, Broadlands, the New Forest Butterfly Farm, Marwell Zoo, etc.

45 rooms, 10 family   Moderate
Open all year   Lunch 12.30-1.45pm – £6.50 (Cromwell Carvery)
Dinner 7.30-9.30pm – £6.50 (Cromwell Carvery)
Access/Barclaycard   P – own car park

Helmsley, N. Yorks   map 4

An attractive market town on the edge of the North York Moors National Park and with its own 12th Century Castle. Both these hotels offer a first class touring base. Close by are an outdoor heated swimming pool, golf, riding and fishing and many places of historic and architectural interest and of course the Moors themselves.

H P R   *THE BLACK SWAN* (THF), Market Place – phone 70466

In the main square.

A lovely-looking stone hotel, partly ivy-clad, facing a splendid square. To the rear is a long modern stone extension and this fits in comfortably with the rest of the building.

There are around half a dozen small lounges, all snug, comfortable and well-furnished, scattered about the ground floor, which has kept much of its 400 year old panelling and ceiling beams. One of these lounges has windows on to a delightful little garden with lots of flower beds and lawns on different levels.

Children's accommodation is free to 5 and costs only £1 up to 14. They also have a special menu and can order half portions from the main menu. The bar snack menu includes soups, salads, and steak and kidney pie, egg and bacon flan, omelettes from 75p to £3.50. The small and varied evening menu changes each day but some examples are: seafood pancake, roast lamb, duckling braised in apricot and brandy sauce, stewed oxtail with dumplings.

37 rooms, 11 family   Expensive   Open all year
Lunch 12-2pm – £5.95 (Sat and Sun only) and bar snacks
Dinner 7.30-9.15pm – £9.50
Access/AmEx/Barclaycard/Diners   P – own car park

H R   ***FEVERSHAM ARMS HOTEL*** (Best Western) – phone 70766

Just on the northern edge of Helmsley.

Another attractive hotel. There's a lovely large stone-walled, carpeted room with table tennis where children can play and several large lawns. There are some children's bikes and the owners' four-year-old daughter shares her toys with visiting children. There is a new tennis court.

At lunchtime there are soup and sandwiches and hot dishes at £2-£4. Children mostly have their evening meal in the bar – chips and things – but are welcome to eat with their parents in the restaurant and will be 'charged according to appetite'. The restaurant menu offers a wide choice of plainish dishes with plenty of fish, steak, chicken, gammon, etc. Lunch on Sunday is in the restaurant.

A cot or extra bed in a room for children under 12 is free.

15 rooms, 5 family   Moderate   Closed 2 weeks at Christmas
Lunch 12-2pm – £2-£4   Dinner 7-9pm – £10
Access/AmEx/Barclaycard   P – own car park

Henley-on-Thames, Oxon   map 1

H R   ***RED LION HOTEL*** – phone 2161

By the bridge into Henley on the A423.

A handsome brick coaching inn, supposedly built in the 16th century, by the Thames. Many famous men have been guests here: Charles I, the 1st Duke of Marlborough, Dr Johnson and Boswell, George III and the Duke of Wellington.

Many of the rooms look out over the river and you can just about see the river from the restaurant if you stand on a table. A nice simple lunch is served, with soup, fruit juice, melon and the like followed by a roast dish, grilled meat, fried fish, omelette, or salad, and standard puddings. The à la carte dinner menu offers more varied fare – smoked salmon, whitebait, mushrooms stuffed with Camembert, etc, followed by grilled meats, escalope of veal, roast duckling, chicken, beef stroganoff, grilled and fried fish and some flambé dishes and the normal dessert trolley. Half-portions can be served in the restaurant.

A place to stop if you have a yen to browse in pretty Henley.

A cot will cost £5 per night and an extra bed £10.

28 rooms, 5 family   Moderate   Open all year
Lunch 12.30-2pm – £4.25   Dinner 7.30-9.45pm – £8 alc
Licensed   AmEx/Barclaycard   P – own car park

Hereford, Hereford & Worcs   map 2

H R   *GREEN DRAGON HOTEL* (THF), Broad Street – phone 272 506

In the main street.

A very smart and quite grand hotel in this famous Cathedral city. The long white Georgian façade disguises a much older building, and within there are some lovely rooms; a stately oak-panelled dining room, a plush bar and a very elegant and comfortable entrance hall and lounge.

There are bar snacks at reasonable prices at lunchtimes – ploughman's, cold meats and salads, pizzas, quiches, lasagne, etc, at between £1 and £3. The restaurant lunch might offer king prawns provençale, roast pork, chicken stroganoff or leg of lamb. Dinner dishes are interesting too, for example, stuffed saddle of lamb, jugged venison, honey spiced chicken, etc. Children can have half portions from this menu and have their own menu too. Their accommodation is free up to the age of 5 and is £1 from 5 to 14.

88 rooms, 9 triple, 2 family, 1 suite   Moderate
Open all year   Lunch 12.30-2.15pm – £5.50
Dinner 7.30-9.30pm – £9   Ale – Bass
Access/AmEx/Barclaycard/Diners   P – car park at rear

Hindon, Wilts

map 2

H R   *LAMB AT HINDON* – phone 225

On the B3089 west of Salisbury.

A solidly built long low stone coaching inn at the village crossroads. An attractive building, parts of which date back to the 17th century. Over the road is a small garden with a few tables and benches and some shady trees.

The lunch at £4.50 for three courses and dinner for £7 offer good value and there is a wide choice of dishes including beef topside cooked in beer, beef curry with no less than six side dishes, Avon trout, poached salmon, rump steak, fillets of sole, etc. Children can be provided with smaller portions at lower prices.

Accommodation for children costs £3 for a cot or £7 for an extra bed, and the latter price includes breakfast.

16 rooms, 2 family   Cheap   Open all year
Lunch 12.30-1.30pm – £4.50   Dinner 7.30-8.45pm – £7
Ale – Wadworth's   Access only   P – space for twelve cars

Hinton Charterhouse, Avon

map 2

R   *HOMEWOOD PARK* – phone Limpley Stoke 2643

The turning, off the A36, is easy to miss, but is directly opposite Hinton Priory.

This small hotel in a lovely 18th century stone manor house, which was enlarged during the 19th century, is approached through extensive grounds and a spacious lawned garden.

The pretty pastel-coloured restaurant offers a menu which is part English and part French, and children are catered for with smaller portions – according to the size and appetite of the child.

There are always interesting dishes to be had here. The set lunch menu might have smoked sprats or red mullet soup followed by grilled pigeon or fricassé of mullet and monkfish with prawns. It's just as difficult to make a choice in the evening: hot trout mousse in puff pastry, game terrine or hot tomato tart: calves liver with parsley purée or best end of lamb. Fresh fish is always featured, especially on Thursdays.

The ladies' lavatory is not really big enough to change a baby, but the owner will find room upstairs.

Closed 25 Dec to 14 Jan   Lunch 12-1.30pm – £8
Dinner 7-9.30pm – £15 alc   Licensed
Access/AmEx/Barclaycard/Diners   P – own car park

Holne, Devon

map 2

P   *CHURCH HOUSE*

Off the B3357.

A handsome white-painted and timbered pub which adjoins the churchyard. Parts of the building date from the 14th century and there is a lovely and comfortable alcoved bar. There is a small garden at the side.

There is a dearth of pubs with children's rooms in this area so that this pub, where children can be taken into the dining room, is included. The owners are not so keen on their presence in the evenings when the dining room functions fully as the pub's restaurant – so lunchtimes only in general.

There are good pub meals here, seven days a week: cold meat salads, steak and kidney pies, plaice and chips, trout and scampi – all under £3 – and steaks at under £5.

Ale – Bass, Blacklawton   P – on street

Hopton Wafers, Shropshire

map 3

P   *CROWN INN,* Nr Cleobury Mortimer

On the A4117 west of Cleobury Mortimer.

A delightful old stone pub, pleasantly ivy-clad, in the depths of the Shropshire countryside. You can approach it from the famous Clee Hill, set high up with a glorious view of rural England, of which A E Housman wrote:

'From Clee to Heaven the beacon burns,
The shires have seen it plain.'

The pub itself has a small patio at the front and a large children's room with a pool table and plenty of other tables and chairs. There is a children's menu (being enjoyed by a hoard of them when we visited one lunchtime) of eggs, burgers, plaice, etc, and chips, and £1 is the maximum you will pay. Adults can go up to £5.50 for a fillet steak, or settle for cottage pie, or steak and kidney pie at under £2.

Ale – Banks, Marston's   P – large car park

Horton, Dorset
map 2

P R   *HORTON INN,* Cranbourne Road – phone Witchampton 840 252

At crossroads at Horton – junction of a minor road with the B3078.

Big white painted inn with black shutters, reminiscent of French country hotels, and in every direction lies the open countryside.

The large and splendid children's room, next to the dining room, has a salad bar every Friday, Saturday and Sunday.

The restaurant – a very pretty room – offers soup, avocado, paté, mousse, some plain grilled fish and meat and some with sauces. Half portions are supplied for children and the 'Ladies' is plenty large enough to cope with a baby's needs.

Bar food is served every day with a huge range of salads, grills, sandwiches, sea-food platter, etc, at 70p to £3 and a Sunday roast, three-course, meal at £5.

Lunch 12-2pm – snack menu   Dinner 7-10pm – £10 alc
Ale – Wadworth's, Hall's
Access/AmEx/Barclaycard/Diners   P – own car park

Horton Heath, Hants
map 1

P   *RISING SUN,* Botley Road

On the A3051.

Plainish but appealing pub with a separate children's room in the large garden which has swings and a climbing frame. The children's room is a large and comfortable wooden garden hut, and is heated during the winter. We think it will appeal to the young fry. Six lanes of Petanque are laid out to one side of the garden and you can chance your arm while you relish your Ricard.

Basic bar snacks are available at all times – sandwiches and rolls – plus a daily 'special', eg cottage pie at around £1.

Ale – Whitbread   P – own car park

Hungerford, Berks
map 2

H P R   *THE BEAR* – phone 82512

On a small roundabout just as you come in to, or go out of, the town. Keep driving – you can't miss it.

An historic inn where tradition has it that both Charles I and William of Orange stayed – the first to lose a throne and the second to gain one. There is a pleasant courtyard where one can sit. Some bedrooms open directly on to it and some overlook the gurgling trout stream at the back of the building.

Accommodation for children costs £7.50.

A range of snacks (eg sausage, beans and chips, chicken and chips) and salads suitable for children is offered and they are welcome in a room off the bar. The bar snacks are excellent – smoked mackerel paté, turkey and salad, steak and vegetable pie, etc – at no more than £3 a time. The cooking is above the ordinary here, and they offer three grades of menu: the tourist at £7.50, the house at £9.50 and the gastronomic at £13.50. The restaurant itself is a particularly attractive room.

Hungerford has many antique shops – a paradise for antique-hunters.

28 rooms, 5 family Moderate Always open
Lunch 12.30-2pm – £7.50-£13.50
Dinner 7.30-9.30pm — £7.50-£13.50 Ale – Arkell's, Morland
Access/AmEx/Barclaycard/Diners P – own ample car park

Huntingdon, Cambs
map 1

You should be warned about the Huntingdon ring road. It is designed so that you can't get into town – each turn-off ends in a cul de sac or car park. We had visions of driving on for ever like a motorised Sisyphus. Head for the Old Bridge instead and have a beer and bar snack.

H R   *OLD BRIDGE HOTEL* – phone 52681

On the ring road around the town.

An attractive Georgian building which is festooned on all sides with ivy. At the back of the hotel there is a patio prettily decorated with hanging flower baskets, and one can also sit on the lawn which is slightly overawed by the surrounding car park.

There is an excellent lunchtime buffet as well as the restaurant menu, from which children can order half portions. The bar snacks have also been created with imagination (Gruyère cheese fritters, lamb sweetbreads, etc) and cost £2-£3 a dish. The restaurant menu is English with plenty of fish dishes – lemon sole with apple, raisin and spiced wine sauce, rainbow trout with nut and yoghurt sauce, etc – and steak, duckling, turkey, veal, lamb, etc – mostly cooked in alcohol-based sauces.

Although there are no family rooms as such, a number of rooms can take extra beds at a cost of £4 and cots are also £4.

You can arrive by boat and moor at the hotel's own jetty on the River Ouse.

26 rooms   Moderate   Open all year
Lunch 12.30-2.30pm – £9 alc   Dinner 7.30-10.30pm – £9 alc
Ale – St Neots (Paine's), Ruddles
Access/AmEx/Barclaycard/Diners   P – own car park

H   ***THE GEORGE HOTEL*** (THF) – phone 53096

Where the A604 joins the High Street.

Typical THF county town hotel – albeit a coaching inn with a long history. No great shakes from the front, but there is a lovely old courtyard, part galleried. Local theatre groups stage plays here occasionally. An alternative for food or accommodation to the Old Bridge Hotel.

Accommodation for children sharing with parents is free up to the age of 5 with a nominal charge of £1 made for children from 5 to 14. The restaurant has a special children's menu and will serve half portions.

21 rooms, 4 family   Moderate   Open all year
Lunch 12.30-2pm – £9 alc
Dinner 7-9.30pm – £9 alc   Ale – Greene King
Access/AmEx/Barclaycard/Diners
P – own car park

Hurdlow, Nr Buxton, Derbys   map 3

P   ***BULL I' THE THORN***

On the A515 about five miles south of Buxton.

The heart of this fine pub, set in the expansive Derbyshire countryside, is a 15th century small manor house. On a massive beam over the entrance are three marvellous wood carvings – the eponymous bull in the thorn bush, an eagle and some hounds. The bar is superb: a long room with a paved floor, wood panelled walls, a wonderfully carved upright chair, wooden settles and a grandfather clock.

The children's room at the back is cheerful enough with bench seats and tables and it opens on to a paved terrace and a big lawn encompassed by a stone wall. There is a swing here too.

Hot and cold meals are served at all times – salads, chicken, scampi, plaice, chips and peas – all below £2.

Ale – Robinsons   P – own car park

Hythe, Kent

map 1

H   *HOTEL IMPERIAL* (Best Western), Princes Parade – phone 67441

On the sea front to the west of the town.

A vast and imposing Victorian pile by the sea with extensive gardens and many facilities including a nine-hole golf course and a large putting green, tennis and squash courts, a good-sized heated indoor pool, a games room and a grassy play area with swings and slides.

Cots cost an extra £3.50 and children under 14 are accommodated for £7. There is a special children's menu available between 5.30 and 6.30pm and half portions are served in the restaurant.

86 rooms, 7 family   Moderate   Open all year
Lunch 1-2pm – £7   Dinner 7.30-9pm – £9.50
Access/AmEx/Barclaycard/Diners   P – own car park

Ibsley, Nr Ringwood, Hants

map 2

P   *OLD BEAMS INN*

On the A338.

Splendid thatched English pub with a lovely beamed and white-painted exterior. The children's room, a small room with tables and chairs, has sliding doors on to the garden and patio.

There is a separate buffet bar serving a good range of hot and cold food, including a roast of the day.

Ale – Wadworth's, Strong's, Whitbread   P – own car park

Instow, Devon

map 2

H   *COMMODORE HOTEL* – phone 860 347

On the A39.

A very pretty modern hotel with a colonial air in lovely spacious gardens overlooking the sand and sea of the Taw-Torridge estuary. Although there are no special facilities for children – other than the basic food, cot, high chair and baby-listening – with it's emphasis on 'quiet good service' it's excellent for an overnight stop.

Accommodation for children up to 12 is half price. Children's meals are charged according to what they want to eat and dinner for children up to 12 is served at 6.30.

21 rooms, 7 family   Moderate   Closed at Christmas
Lunch 12.15-1.45pm – £4.75   Dinner 7-9pm – £7.50
AmEx/Barclaycard   P – own car park

Inveraray, Strathclyde
map 5

P **THE GEORGE**

On the A83 a short walk from Loch Fyne.

A big white-washed inn in this lovely little town, which is full of pretty white-painted buildings, on the shores of Loch Fyne. From a distance, with the sun striking the white façades and glinting on the water there is a reminder of a Mediterranean village. See Inveraray Castle, in all its Gothic splendour, while you're here.

Inside the pub there is a series of stone-walled and stone-flagged rooms including a comfortable lounge just inside the front door where children may sit.

There is a good range of hot and cold meals every day: soups and salads, pies and quiches at an average of £2 a dish. It's a cheerful place for a stop, with a friendly owner and staff, which is more than can be said for the nearby Argyll Arms.

P – on the street

Ipplepen, Devon
map 2

P **PLOUGH INN**

Off the A381.

A white-painted pub in the village high street with a patio at the back where you can eat and drink.

Inside it is spacious and well-furnished with two good sized children's rooms.

Food is served all week – hot meals and snacks – and the landlord offers a traditional Sunday lunch and a children's menu during the summer.

Ale – Ansell's, Tetley's, Hall's   P – on the street

Ipswich, Suffolk
map 1

H **POST HOUSE HOTEL** (THF), London Road – phone 212 313

A modern two-storey building two miles from the centre of the town on the A12.

This is an alternative to doing battle with the Ipswich town planners who make it so difficult to stop in their town (does anyone want to now that Bobby Robson has left?). For example, it is impossible to get near another THF hotel, the Great White Horse, in the town centre, much less to park near it – tough if you have luggage, children, pushchair, etc.

There are plenty of family rooms at reasonable prices. In the garden is a heated swimming pool. Accommodation is free for children up to the age of 5 who share with their parents – from 5 to 14 there's a nominal charge of £1. The Coffee Shop is open from 10am to 10pm and has the normal selection of snacks, grills, burgers and salads.

118 rooms, 59 family   Moderate   Open all year
Lunch 12.30-2pm – £7   Dinner 7-10pm – £10   Ale – Adnam's
Access/AmEx/Barclaycard/Diners   P – own car park

Isfield, East Sussex
P   *LAUGHING FISH*

map 1

Off the A26, north of Lewes.

A pleasant, unpretentious village pub, white-painted, by the old railway station. There is a big, barracky bar where hot and cold food is served every day except Monday – sandwiches, steak and chips, scampi and chips, etc.

The children's room is out at the back of the pub, and is adequate and has lots of tables and chairs. The landlady prefers to call it the family room because she wishes children in the room to be properly supervised by their adults.

There is a pretty little garden by the side of the pub with bench tables, swings and a climbing frame.

Ale – Beard   P – own car park

Jameston, Dyfed
P   *SWAN LAKE*

map 2

On the A4139 west of Tenby.

The interior of this pub is disappointing because the front is pretty – the lounge bar looks all right, the dining room is uglyish and the children's room is a just-about-passable corridor outside the 'Ladies' and the public bar. It has seating and space invaders and a door opening on to a pretty little grass garden.

We were glad enough to find it, though, and have a drink and a hot meal. A good selection of food is on the go from 11.30am to 2.15pm and 7 to 10.15 in the evenings (children out by 9 o'clock please); Quiches, fish dishes, hot dish of the day at around £2; salads at £3-£4; coq au vin at under £3.

It's the best we could find folks.

Ale – Marston's, Ind Coope Burton, Worthington
P – a short walk away

Jedburgh, Borders   map 5

R   ***THE CARTERS' REST,*** *Abbey Place* – phone 3414

Park in the public car park which you can see as you enter from the A68 – and from which you can see the signs to the restaurant which is in a lovely situation immediately opposite the Abbey.

They originally pinched stone from the Abbey (well, it was always being ravaged in the Border fighting) to build this inn. The pub's two bars are rather horrid, but the restaurant is pleasant and well run and offers a children's menu with prices from £1.75 to £3.25. There's also a comfortable coffee lounge next door to the 'Wenches' (oh dear!) which has a large waist-high shelf ideal for nappy-changing. You can breast-feed there too – or 'in the boss's office'.

Closed Sun and Nov-Easter   Lunch 12-2pm
Dinner 6-9pm – main dishes from £3.90   Ale – Younger's
AmEx/Barclaycard   P – two public car parks close by

Keeston, Dyfed   map 2

R   ***KEESTON KITCHEN*** – phone Camrose 710 440

On the main A487 – not in the village.

It doesn't look much more than a shack, but is comfortable and welcoming. Outside is a pretty little sheltered terrace. Coffee is served from 11am, and a good mixture of snacks (things on toast, things with chips, spaghetti) costing up to £3 is served at lunchtime. There's plenty to suit a young palate and, if required, half portions are available. They 'prefer to cater for high chair-size people during the day' (and so say all of us). The evening menu has a mix of plain meat (grilled steak, baked gammon), fish (local salmon with hollandaise sauce, trout with cream cheese and prawns) and 'foreign' (Hungarian goulash, Turkish lamb kebab). It changes all the time. Half portions are also served at dinner time.

The owners would try to help a mother with feeding or changing 'in desperation' although they don't really have the space.

Good inexpensive food at an easily accessible restaurant.

Open all year   Lunch 12-2pm – snacks up to £3
Dinner 7.30-9.45pm – £6.50 alc   Ale – Bass
Access/Barclaycard   P – own small car park

Kelso, Borders

map 5

H   *EDNAM HOUSE HOTEL* – phone 24168

Go to the centre of town and look for the hotel sign.

Grand four-square granite pile – a fishing hotel which was once the home of the Duke of Roxburghe. It and the splendid gardens retain their 'ducal' air: the interior is beautiful with lots of carved wood and ornate plaster. The huge gardens have a croquet lawn and a long balustrade overlooking a lovely stretch of the Tweed. Handy for the town (once described by Sir Walter Scott as the most beautiful in Scotland) and many places of historic interest – and the staff are very helpful in arranging other activities for you and the children: riding, golf, etc.

Sharing with parents, children's accommodation is charged on a rising scale starting at a quarter of the single rate for 2-5 year olds to two-thirds for 12s to 14s.

32 rooms, 2 family   Moderate
Closed Christmas and the New Year   Bar lunches 12.30-2pm
Dinner 7-9pm £8.30
No credit cards accepted   P – lots of parking space

Kentallen, Highland

map 6

R   *THE HOLLY TREE* – phone Duror 292

On the A828 three miles south of Ballachulish Bridge.

A pretty, nicely-furnished restaurant which looks out over Loch Linnhe and the mountains behind. At the front of the building is a coffee shop which is open from 10.30-5.30 and serves snacks and, at the appropriate times, the same food as the restaurant. The coffee shop is closed from mid-November to Easter and the restaurant from mid-November to mid-December. It is then open at weekends only until Easter, after which it is closed on Wednesdays only. Got it?

The owners have three young children of their own and are very sympathetic to parents' needs. Nursing mothers are welcome to use one of the former waiting rooms of Kentallen Station (now B&B rooms). Plan to take a leisurely lunch – the service is unhurried.

There is a special children's menu and half portions even of the very reasonably priced Sunday lunch. There is a very good menu; the food offered is interesting without being too rich; fillet of turkey with mustard seed and apricots (£4.75), local trout baked with hazelnuts and grapefruit (£4.50).

Lunch 12.30-2.30pm Dinner 6.30-9.30pm Licensed
No credit cards accepted P – own car park

Kilchrenan, by Taynuilt, Strathclyde   map 5

H   *TAYCHREGGAN HOTEL* – phone 211

Off the B845, off the A85 from Taynuilt.

Idyllic is the only word to describe this beautiful white hotel which looks south and west from its promontory by Loch Awe. The original house was once a drovers' inn and across a lovely cobbled courtyard is the attractive modern wing. The hotel is surrounded by twenty-five acres of tranquil gardens and behind roll the hills dominated by the heights of Cruachan. The whole atmosphere is relaxed, peaceful and welcoming.

There are boats for hire; trout fishing to be done; and riding and deer-stalking can be arranged as can wind-surfing.

Children under 8 years are accommodated at half price and cots are provided at £5 per day. Half portions are available in the restaurant and there are bar snacks at lunchtime, including hamburgers and salads and a Danish cold table. High teas are also served from 3.45pm.

17 rooms, 10 family Expensive Closed Oct-Easter
Lunch 12-2.15pm – about £2 Dinner 7.30-8.45pm – £10
Ale – Greenmantle Barclaycard/Diners P – own car park

Kildrummy, by Alford, Grampian   map 6

H   *KILDRUMMY CASTLE HOTEL* (Best Western) – *phone 288*

On the A97 south of Kildrummy.

A lovely country mansion built in 1900 in the Scottish baronial style with a delightful lawned and balustraded garden. Next door is the 13th century ruin of Kildrummy Castle in twelve acres of splendidly varied garden. The hotel's interior reflects the overall grand baronial manner with antique furniture, oak panelled *walls and ceilings and large fireplaces in its series of public rooms.*

There is a safely fenced-in play area at the side with a slide, swings, see-saw and a rocking boat. Children are accommodated free to the age of 12; the chef will cook to order for the children's high teas and suppers; and half portions are also served in the restaurant which concentrates on traditional Scottish fare such as salmon, trout and game much of it fresh from the Kildrummy estate.

A lovely place for a tranquil and relaxed stay, especially for fishermen since the hotel has a three mile stretch of salmon and trout fishing on the River Don.

15 rooms, 2 family   Moderate   Closed 4 Jan-beginning Mar
Lunch 12.30-2pm – £6.50   Dinner 7-9pm – £10.50
Access/AmEx/Barclaycard/Diners   P – own car park

R   ***THE MOSSAT SHOP*** *– phone 355*

On the A97 where it meets the A944.

This little craft shop/café complex is well designed. The modern dining room has a simple white-paint and wood interior with pretty table cloths, cushions and curtains also in brown and white. Their speciality is pancakes – savoury and sweet – with some interesting fillings. They sell for between £1.20 and £1.80. Other hot and cold dishes are also available – brunch, lunch, tea and dinner. The craft shop sells some lovely locally made goods – superior to the normal run of 'craft' goods. A good place to stop in an area of great beauty.

Half portions of some of the dishes are served to children.

The owner would help a mother needing to feed or change her baby.

Open 10am-7pm Mon-Fri, 10am-8pm Sat and Sun   Unlicensed
No credit cards accepted   P – plenty of space

Kinclaven, by Stanley, Tayside   map 6

H   ***BALLATHIE HOUSE*** *– phone Meikleour 268*

Off the A93 south of Rattray.

This is a lovely Victorian country house in the baronial style with spacious lawned and wooded grounds which look out over the River Tay. There is one tennis court, croquet lawn and a putting green. Trout fishing can be arranged on a daily basis and there are lots of golf courses including the famous Blairgowrie within an easy car ride. Apart from the garden there

119

is not a lot for children, but it is a peaceful place for a stopover – if your car survives the journey up the badly pot-holed drive.

Cots are charged at £3 per night; children up to 5 are charged at one-third of the adult rate and thereafter at two-thirds of the adult rate. Supper can be served at 6pm or half portions provided in the restaurant.

23 rooms, 5 family   Expensive
Closed end Oct-beginning Mar   Lunch buffet bar and grill
12.30-2.30pm – dishes starting at £1.50   Dinner 7-9.30pm – £9
Access/AmEx/Diners   P – own car park

Kingscote, Glos   map 2

P   ***HUNTER'S HALL***

On the A4135.

A nice old coaching inn of mellow stone, with a huge grassy garden, with lots of tables and chairs. Children may sit in the entrance hall which is a reasonable size with several easy chairs, or they may eat in the very large dining room which offers a range of salads at lunchtimes plus one or two hot dishes – quiche for example. In the evening the menu is more varied, with steak at just over £4, boeuf bourgignon, scampi, etc.

Ale – Bass, Fussell's   P – own car park

Kinloch Rannoch, Tayside   map 6

H   ***RANNOCH HOTEL*** (Barratt) – phone 201

On the B846 at Loch Rannoch.

There is nothing spectacular about the hotel but there is about its setting and facilities. It is part of a leisure centre with apartments to let and self-catering lodges, but manages not to take on a 'holiday camp' atmosphere. It is by the beautiful Loch Rannoch and in glorious countryside. Next to the hotel is a heated indoor swimming pool, games room with pool table, gym area, sauna, solarium, whirl pool, two squash courts and dry ski slope. Add to that the cycling, canoeing and rock-climbing and you could end up very fit here – or in need of a rest. More gentle pursuits are walking, fishing for salmon and trout, golf and pony-trekking.

There is an excellent children's play area which in effect is a mini commando course. A bonus for parents is that each

Wednesday the children are taken off for the day for a nature walk and picnic.

Bed and breakfast for children under 10 is £5 per night, and cots cost £1.50 per night. Half portions are also available in the restaurant.

12 rooms, 6 family   Moderate   Open all year
Grill room 8.30am-10pm   Dinner 7-8.30pm – £8.50
Access/AmEx/Barclaycard/Diners   P – own car park

Kinlochard, Aberfoyle, by Stirling, Central   map 5

H   *FOREST HILLS HOTEL* (Barratt) – phone 277

Follow the B829 from the A821 and you'll see it.

A large leisure complex, to include squash, indoor swimming pool and curling rinks, is in the process of being built. Even before its completion, this is a good place to stop, particularly in view of its splendid location. It stands alone on the shores of Loch Ard. Behind are the hills of Ben Lomond and surrounding the hotel are wide lawns with a heated swimming pool, a super commando course play area, putting green, two tennis courts, croquet lawn, etc. Many other activities can easily be arranged – pony trekking, boating, walks, cycling, etc. One feels that children can run free here in safety. There are plenty of spacious public rooms.

Accommodation is free for children up to 10.

18 rooms, 4 family   Moderate   Open all year
Bar lunches 12.30-2pm   Dinner 7.30-9pm – £8.95
Access/Barclaycard   P – own car park

Kinver, Staffs   map 3

P   *WHITTINGTON INN*

On the A449 near Kinver.

This is a splendid pub, very smart with its black beams and white-painted brickwork, in an area which is pretty barren of such places. The pub itself is on the ground floor and is very spacious and has oak-panelled walls. There is a small alcove room which can be used by children with their adults. At the back is a big patio and very attractive lawned garden enclosed by a wall.

This is not all: upstairs is a wine bar where families are also welcome. It is a lovely room with a big vaulted ceiling and

*white-washed brick walls. Food is served here from 12 to 2.15
and from 7 to 10.15 (slightly shorter hours on Sunday). The
menu comprises a range of salads at prices up to £3, and a good
choice of hot dishes at around £2 – for example lasagne,
moussaka, canneloni, chilli con carne, cottage pie and goulash.
And of course sandwiches. A nice oasis for food and drink.*

Ale – Bass, Courage Directors, Marston's   P – own car park

Knutsford, Cheshire   map 3

R   **DAVID'S PLACE,** 10 Princess Street – phone 3356

In the middle of the town.

*A shop front aspect but a lovely cool and smartly decorated
restaurant which has a pleasantly alcoved appearance with its
three interconnected rooms. Outside there is an enclosed lawn
with a climbing frame. Apart from the full, and catholic,
restaurant menu there is a shorter Brasserie menu with dishes
from £2 at lunchtimes only.*

*The friendly owner will cobble up meals to children's tastes and
charge according to what they eat.*

*Mothers can if necessary attend to their babies in a room
upstairs.*

*A useful place to know in an area that's pretty devoid of
restaurant choice for parents with children.*

Closed – Sun   Lunch 12.30-2pm – £10 alc (Brasserie from £2)
Dinner 7.15-10pm – £8   Access/AmEx/Barclaycard/Diners
P – a car park five minutes away and difficult street parking

---

Lamphey, Dyfed   map 2

H   **THE COURT** (Best Western) – phone 672 273

On the A4139 – you can see the hotel from the road.

*A splendid Georgian mansion with a classically pillared
entrance, it stands dominantly over open fields and next door to
the ruins of Lamphey Palace.*

*There are thirteen acres of lovely gardens, mostly lawns and
trees, in which to roam and detached to one side of the hotel a
well-designed heated indoor pool with a sun terrace.*

*The owner was a little pedantic in her emphasis on bar meals
(not snacks) at lunchtimes, but there are steaks at around £6, a
dish of the day, and ham and chicken dishes and salads at*

around £3. High teas are prepared for children at 6.30 and such things as eggs and soldiers, sausages and fish fingers are available at under £1. The evening menu concentrates on steaks and seafood with some interesting touches such as 'fondue Chinoise'.

Accommodation is free for children up to 16.

20 rooms, 9 family   Cheap   Open all year
Bar lunch 12-1.45pm   Dinner 7.30-9.30pm – £7.95
Access/AmEx/Barclaycard/Diners   P – own car park

Lane, Nr Newquay, Cornwall

map 2

P *KING'S HEAD*

Situated on a road which links the A3075 and the A392.

A large busy roadside pub which we were pleased to find because of the scarcity of choice in this area for families. It has a spacious family room off the main bar with plenty of tables and chairs.

Hot and cold snacks are available all week during the summer, but at lunchtime only during the winter. There are the usual sandwiches and salads and there is a 'daily special' which might be cottage pie, a curry, chicken Maryland, fish and chips or a farmhouse grill. You will pay no more than £2 a time.

Ale – Devenish   P – opposite

Langtree, Devon

map 2

P *GREEN DRAGON INN*

On the B3227.

A good pub at the edge of an ugly little village in the midst of beautiful Devon countryside on a holiday route to North Cornish coast. There is a big homely bar, and the children's room has some electronic games. The large grassy garden has swings, a slide and plenty of tables and chairs.

Food is served all week with a special children's menu.

Ale – Usher's   P – own car park

Lanreath, Cornwall

map 2

P *PUNCH BOWL*

Off the B3359, north west of Looe.

123

Famous 17th century pub — large and rambling with a low-beamed and brass-bedecked interior — whose sign is said to have been painted by Augustus John. Opposite is a Farm Museum.

The family room is operational only during the summer. There are a couple of patios and a stretch of garden.

Food is available all week, including hot and cold buffet lunches — again only during the summer.

Ale — Bass   P — own car park

Lapford, Devon   map 2

P   *OLD MALTSCOOP INN*

In the village near the church which can be seen from the A377.

Pretty 16th century pub with two bars — one for dining.

The children's room is little more than a hallway between the bars and front door. It has a long oak bench table and a fruit machine. The door leads to a tiny patio with benches and tables and through the archway at the side of the pub is another, larger garden also with picnic benches and tables.

There's no food on Sundays and cold food only on Mondays, but from Tuesdays to Saturdays cold snacks are served at midday — baps, ploughman's, salads — and in the evenings steaks, scampi, fish, gammon and the like are served.

Ale — Wadworths, Cotleigh   P — own car park

Lavenham, Suffolk   map 1

H P R   *SWAN HOTEL* (THF), High Street — phone 247 477

One of the most important centres for the wool trade a few centuries ago, this is a wonderful village full of 15th century timber-framed buildings. The Church, also 15th century, is notable especially for its 140 foot tower of flint and stone — worth climbing for the view. Afterwards you can repair the damage at the Swan, one of the finest-looking coaching inns in the land. Its interior is a superb amalgam of heavy beams, oaken doors, uneven floors and huge fireplaces. The restaurant is a fine sight with its high timbered ceiling and minstrels' gallery. Here you can tackle the primarily English dishes such as red lentil soup, East Anglian trout, roast lamb or beef, etc. There is also a buffet lunch available: salads or a hot dish of the day at around £3. Children can choose half portions from the main menu and have their own special menu too.

Their accommodation from 5 to 14 costs a nominal £1 per night, and is free up to 5 years of age.

The hotel has a quiet, secluded and very attractive garden at the back. With a smooth lawn and surrounded by trees and flowers you can sit there and sup some of the amber fluid in peace.

42 rooms, 8 family   Expensive   Open all year
Lunch 12.30-2pm – £8.25
Dinner 7.30-10pm – £9.95   Ale – Bass, Greene King
Access/AmEx/Barclaycard/Diners   P – own car park

Lechlade, Glos

map 2

P   *TROUT,* St John's Bridge

On A417, one mile east of Lechlade.

Lovely old Cotswold stone pub with large garden overlooking a sweep of the Thames. During the summer it has a garden bar, marquee and barbecue which make it even more worth seeking out. Take some Courage and watch the river, quite still here, dream along with you.

The bar as you enter has a flagged floor and low-beamed ceiling and to one side is a well-furnished and airy children's room. It is not available on Saturday night when it becomes a restaurant.

There is a very good range of meals here, and it includes an under-7 menu of fishcakes, or burgers, or sausages and chips at less than £1. You can choose from scallops, paté, prawn cocktail, trout, chicken and mushroom pie, duck and steak and will not pay more than £5. There are also pizzas, burgers, cottage pie, plaice and chips, and ploughman's at under £2.

Ale – Courage   P – own large car park

Leominster, Hereford & Worcs

map 3

H P R   *THE ROYAL OAK* – phone 2610

In the middle of town (on A49/A44).

This is a pleasant, if unremarkable, Georgian building with a welcoming air. The owner has a small room off the main bar (where real ale is quite a feature) where families are welcome and there is a very comprehensive range of bar meals available at lunchtime and in the evenings. The menu includes quiche, scampi, chicken, omelettes, gammon, steaks, salads and sandwiches at prices from £1 to £6.50. Children can order also from their own menu which includes a mini-ploughman's, mini-scampi, mini-omelettes, etc, as well as sausages, fish fingers and things on toast. The thoughtful owner also offers boiled potatoes as well as the ubiquitous chips – hurrah!

Accommodation for children is £2.50 for a cot and about £7 for an extra bed.

17 rooms, 2 suites   Cheap   Open all year
Lunch 12-2pm – £5 alc   Dinner 7-9pm – £5 alc
Ale – Hook Norton, Woods, Theakston's
Access/AmEx/Barclaycard   P – own car park

Lifton, Devon   map 2

H   *ARUNDELL ARMS* (Best Western) – phone 244 or 456

On the A30 east of Launceston and the Cornish border.

The hotel, in an area of stunning beauty, comprises several different stone buildings the main one at the front smothered in ivy. It has a delightful and comfortable interior with slate floors. There is a lawned garden on several levels and a games room and skittle alley which are part of the Old School House standing separate from the other buildings. The games room has bench seats, darts and table tennis. The Arundell is a famous fishing hotel with twenty miles of private fishing on five rivers, including the Tamar.

Accommodation is free for children up to the age of 12 and, indeed, the owners 'like to have children to stay'. A cold buffet is served in the cocktail bar from 12 to 2.30pm and the restaurant serves 'whatever they want' to the children as well as half portions from the adult menus. At lunch the menu is fairly plain – grilled steak, steak and kidney pie, grilled salmon and local trout – and at dinner quite rich and varied – crustade of seafood, banderille of beef, quail, vegetable and cheese pancake, etc, and with some simpler roast and grilled dishes too.

28 rooms, 2 family   Moderate   Closed at Christmas
Lunch 12.15-2pm – £8 alc   Dinner 7.30-9pm – £9.25
Access/AmEx/Barclaycard   P – large car park

Lincoln, Lincs   map 4

H R   *WHITE HART HOTEL* (THF), Bailgate – phone 26222

Bailgate is between the Cathedral and the Castle.

This is a very smart and well-cared for hotel, with a white-painted front, in the Cathedral precinct. The Cathedral itself is a magnificent example of Gothic architecture (completed in about 1280) with an intricately carved stone façade and soaring central tower. The precinct has everything a precinct should have – cobbled closes, rows of Georgian houses and surviving parts of the old city.

The interior of the hotel too is smart and cared for with a handsome and delightful Orangery with a domed glass roof. Here one can order snacks and buffet meals from 10am to 11pm – such things as soups, paté, French bread sandwiches, and a hot or cold buffet at £3.95. The restaurant offers limited table d'hôte dishes – roasts and fish – while the à la carte menu, English in emphasis, offers dishes such as mussel soup, Dover sole, saddle of hare, fillet of pork Wellington, etc.

Children are accommodated free up to the age of 5, and up to 14 with a nominal £1 charge. They have their own special menu and can order half portions from the adult menu.

Should this hotel be full, an alternative is the Eastgate Post House down the road: not too bad a modern building with all the usual THF facilities for families and a licensed coffee shop which is open from 10am to 10pm.

57 rooms, 1 family, 2 sets of adjoining rooms   Moderate
Open all year   Lunch 12.30-2pm – £5.95 (three courses)
Dinner 7-9.45pm (Sun to 8.45pm) – £7.95
Ale – Sam Smith's, Bateman's
Access/AmEx/Barclaycard/Diners   P – own car park

Linwood, Hants   map 2

P   *HIGH CORNER*

Off the A338, but the car must survive a badly pot-holed track to reach the pub. It's worth all the swerving and manic heaving on the steering wheel because the pub is in a lovely woodland setting, and is a very appealing rambling old building with a large garden.

There's a good-sized children's room with space invaders, and they (the children) can also invade the sun lounge which overlooks the garden.

There's plenty of food available at all times. Apart from ploughman's, paté, scampi, chicken and plaice (at up to £2.60), there are usually two dishes of the day at about £2 (a curry and sweet and sour pork when we visited). There are usually half a dozen grilled meals on the go as well – lamb cutlets, trout, chicken Maryland, etc. at prices up to £4.50.

Ale – Bass   P – own ample car park

P   *RED SHOOT INN*

Off the A31 or A338 north of Ringwood.

A large and rambling country pub in open countryside where New Forest ponies safely graze.

There is a large patio and off to the side a separate, slightly scruffy, children's room mainly intended for summer use.

There is plenty of food to choose from every day and this includes a children's menu — fish fingers, burgers, sausages and chips — at under £1. On offer, as well as sandwiches, are omelettes, plaice and chips, quiches and lasagne, at just over £2. More expensive items can be had in the evenings — for example steaks at around £4.

Ale — Whitbread   P — own car park

Litton, Somerset   map 2

P   *YE OLDE KING'S ARMS*

On the B3114 west of Midsomer Norton.

A superb 15th century pub not far from the famous Chew Valley Lake with all its bird life. The pub has some water too — a small stream in its delightful garden with beautifully kept lawns, masses of split-log benches and tables, a slide and no less than six swings.

The pub has several inter-connecting rooms, with stone walls, some wood panelling and black oak beams, and all well-furnished with wooden tables, one or two pew seats, etc. The children's room is in character — oak-panelled with tables and chairs and a big open fire.

There is a good range of food: sandwiches at around £1, paté, smoked salmon, cottage pie, chilli con carne and lasagne at just under £3, salads at £3 to £4, etc.

Ale — Butcombe, Wadworth's, Bass   P — own car park

Llanarmon Dyffryn-Ceiriog, Clwyd   map 3

This village is a paradise of prettiness set in beautiful and peaceful countryside of gentle hills. Its two splendid inns sit opposite each other and we recommend an extended trip — perhaps a morning drink, a walk and lunch. You must in any event visit both establishments. Follow the A4500 from Chirk (birthplace of Billy Meredith, Wales' greatest footballer, and so

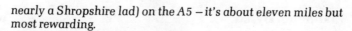

nearly a Shropshire lad) on the A5 – it's about eleven miles but most rewarding.

P R **THE HAND HOTEL** – phone 666

The hotel retains much of the atmosphere of the 16th century farmhouse it once was. The bar is homely with low beamed ceilings, comfortable furniture and log fire and the lovely dining room has stone walls and more beams.

There are two places for children – a large pool room which is much more comfortable than is usual and a little area with bench seats between the dining room and bar. The children can eat from the bar menu at lunchtime, and you will be charged according to their appetites, and can choose a half portion from the menu in the evenings.

The lunch bar menu offers soup, cold meat salads at £2.25 and various meat and fish with chips at up to £3. There's a simple dinner menu with five starters (soup, paté) and five main courses (sole veronique, steak, chicken Maryland).

The owners will usually be able to offer a room for a mother to change or feed a baby.

The garden has an all-weather tennis court, and the hotel has fishing rights on the River Ceiriog.

Open all year   Lunch 12-2pm   Dinner 7.30-9pm £8.50
Access/Barclaycard   P – own car park

P R **WEST ARMS HOTEL** – phone 665

The West Arms too is an ornament to the village. The main building is 16th century – a long low stone building strewn with roses – and the entrance hall can be used by children if the adults fancy a drink. It is a pleasure to sit in with its heavy beams and huge open fireplace. The bar at the back has similar beams, a stone fireplace, excellent and comfortable furniture and antique oak corner cupboards. There is also a 13th century confessional which is said to have been looted (long ago) from Llangollen Abbey. All this plus a lovely big grassy garden alongside the River Ceiriog.

There is a good range of bar snacks throughout the week – sandwiches, lots of fish dishes, gammon, chicken – at up to £2.75, and the dinner menu also concentrates on fish dishes and roasts. Reduced portions for children can be arranged, and the owners would find a spot where a mother could feed or change her baby.

Lunch 12-2pm   Dinner 7.30-9.30pm – £8
No credit cards accepted   P – own car park

Llandeilo, Dyfed

map 2

R   *CAWDOR ARMS HOTEL* – phone 823 500

In the centre of the town.

Don't be put off by the scruffy exterior of this Georgian building. The interior instantly reassures you with its beautiful furniture, elegant dining room and array of fine oil paintings.

There is a light lunch menu which offers excellent value – for example omelettes at under £2, curried chicken at under £3, and fish dishes and grills from £3.50. The evening menu concentrates on local ingredients such as Welsh lamb and, for example, grilled darne of Towy Sewin with chicory salad.

Children's portions can always be made available and there is plenty of space available for mothers to tend their babies. Teas are available to non-residents from 3.30 to 5.30.

Open all year   Lunch 12.30-2pm   Dinner 7.30-9.30pm – £11.50
Access/AmEx/Barclaycard/Diners
P – small car park and street parking

Llandrindod Wells, Powys

map 3

H   *HOTEL COMMODORE* – phone 4401

In the centre of town.

A big red-brick Edwardian building with a partly-tiled façade, the hotel is a little bit tatty in places, but offers reasonable facilities in a town in the heart of Welsh tourist territory. For example the indoor pool is supervised, and there is a paddling pool alongside. There are two squash courts, a snooker room and a games room with pool and space invaders. The hotel staff can also arrange free fishing and free golf from Monday to Friday.

There are plenty of family rooms here and children are accommodated free up to the age of 14. Children's food is available – whatever and whenever required within reason.

An unpretentious hotel, useful to know about for a short stay if touring mid-Wales.

55 rooms, 12 family   Moderate   Open all year
Bar lunch 12-2pm – up to £2   Dinner 7-8.30pm – £7
Ale – Bass
Access/AmEx/Barclaycard   P – own car park

H P R **THE METROPOLE** (Best Western) – phone 2881/2

On the A483.

A spacious spa hotel which was built by the present owners' great grandmother. I wonder what she would have thought of the bilious green of the exterior. It has a large pretty pink bar with a log fire – and a white wrought-iron conservatory, with a lovely old wysteria, which runs along the whole front of the hotel. Here you can sit with the children and have a drink. The garden with tables and chairs is on the opposite side of the road. There is an outdoor unheated swimming pool and free fishing for residents as well as free golf during the week.

The bar serves a good range of meals – lasagne, lamb stew, turkey curry, chicken provençale, salads (cheese, quiche, paté) all at £1.60 and the restaurant has a table d'hôte menu of mostly plain food for lunch and dinner. They allow children to choose half portions or will prepare whatever is required for them.

Accommodation for children sharing with their parents is free up to 12 years.

141 rooms, 9 family   Moderate   Open all year
Lunch 12.30-2.15pm – £5.15 (Bar 12-3pm)
Dinner 7-8.30pm £7.35 (Bar 6-11pm)   Ale – Whitbread
Access/AmEx/Barclaycard/Diners   P – own car park

P   **THE LLANERCH**

A turning off a road which runs parallel to the main A483, but on the other side of the railway line and close to the railway station.

An attractive stone building most of which dates from the 16th century. It comes as a bit of a surprise standing in a side street very close to the railway station and with factory buildings on three sides. The main bar is big, but by no means beautiful, with a large open fire and off to the side is a darkish children's room with plenty of seating and tables. There is a big ugly pool room for over 16s. At the front is a lovely grassy garden where children can play (swings, slide, etc, promised) and at the back a quiet terrace for adults only which looks out on apple trees and green fields.

There is a good range of pub food available every day from 12-2pm and up to 10pm in the evening. For example steak and kidney pie, salads, steak baps, Llanerch pie, bikers butty are all under £2, baked trout is under £3, and a sirloin steak is £4, as well as sandwiches, burgers, etc. Children's portions can be provided.

Ale – Brain's, Bass, Robinson's   P – own car park

131

Llandudno, Gwynedd

map 3

H   *GOGARTH ABBEY HOTEL* – phone 76212

On the West Shore of the town – just keep driving south and you will see the hotel on your right.

A sprawling white hotel which is a little bit drab but has a lot to offer in its situation and amenities. It is at the quiet end of Llandudno and looks out over the sea to the Snowdonia mountains beyond. In its lawned gardens are a putting green, croquet and badminton. Because it encompasses what was once the home of Alice Liddell, there is an Alice in Wonderland theme with figures on the lawn based on the Disney film characters and paintings of them on the walls of the indoor heated swimming pool. Next to the swimming pool is a games room with table tennis, darts, pool, fruit machines and table football.

Lunch is in the bar where you can eat for under £2 – we were unimpressed that a resident was refused even a sandwich at just after 2 o'clock – and there's a different table d'hôte menu each evening – fish, grills, roast meat.

The rates for children sharing their parents' room is free up to two years, 3-10 years £8, 10 and over £10. High tea is served for them in the dining room at 6 pm or they can eat half portions from the adult menu.

42 rooms, 8 family   Moderate   Closed first week Jan
Bar lunch 12-1.45pm   Dinner 7-8.15pm – £8
Access/AmEx/Barclaycard   P – own car park

Llangammarch Wells, Powys

map 2

H   *LAKE HOTEL* – phone 202

Go to the village and follow the sign to Upper Chapel and Brecon.

This is very much a sporting hotel set in wonderful countryside. It's a big rambling place and the Victorian part with its tiled façade is typical of the spa hotels which were built in the 19th century. There is a splendidly grand lounge for instance with a wonderfully ornate china cabinet against one wall. The hotel's barium spring used to be bottled and sent all over the world. The other part of the hotel can best be described as mock Tudor.

The fifty acres of grounds sweep down to the river and the hotel has access to five and a half miles of salmon and trout fishing on the Irfon and the Chwefru. The hotel's lake is stocked with trout and fishing can also be arranged on the Wye. Rough shooting can be arranged, and if your interest in wild life is more passive the surrounding country is full of unusual wild life – polecats, badgers and red kites are regularly spotted.

Other facilities include a nine-hole par-three golf course; a hard tennis court; a putting green; a games room with snooker and table tennis (for over-14s) and an outdoor play area with swings and a climbing frame.

There is a big range of bar snacks available from 12 to 2pm – soup, salads, ploughman's, and lots of things with chips – at prices from under £1 to around £4. Fish of course features strongly on the dinner menu along with game soup and venison. Children are catered for with a high tea at 6pm and can also choose half portions from the main menu. Their accommodation is free up to 2, and up to 14 costs £5.50 a day for bed and breakfast.

An interesting spot for any enthusiasts of the outdoor life.

29 rooms, 10 family   Moderate   Closed Jan
Lunch 1-2pm (bar 12-2pm)   Dinner 7.30-8.45pm – £9.50
Access only   P – own car park

Llangollen, Clwydd   map 3

A picturesque town in the Dee Valley and in the heart of lovely, hilly country. On one side the famous Horseshoe Pass guards the town, which hosts the renowned International Eisteddfod each year.

H R   *THE ROYAL* (THF), Bridge Street – phone 860 202

Right by the bridge.

A comfortable hotel which offers the basic needs for a travelling family, but no additional facilities, except fishing. This can be done from the hotel's terrace overlooking the fast-flowing Dee. The terrace is scruffy, though, and unsafe for children.

Accommodation for children under 5 years is free, and from 5 to 14 the charge is £1. There is bar food at lunchtime and teas for children from 3 to 5pm. They may choose from their own menu or have half portions. Lunch is soup, French bread sandwiches for around £1.50 and a hot dish of the day for under £3. The dining room menu always includes some special Welsh dishes – Caerphilly cheese flan, brithyll a chig moch – as well as roasts, chicken, etc.

There's a large comfy 'Ladies' where you could change a baby.

33 rooms, 3 family, 3 triples   Moderate   Open all year   Lunch
12-2pm   Dinner 7-9pm – £8.50 (four courses)
Access/AmEx/Barclaycard/Diners   P – own car park

P R   *HAND HOTEL* (Mount Charlotte), Bridge Street – phone 860
303

In the centre of town.

*The illustration in the brochure shows the hotel pristine white
with windows framed in black, Why, oh why, did someone
redecorate it in light brown and mud brown? Never mind, the
great advantage of this hotel is that the bar snacks are available
all day from 12 to 8pm. There is a good choice – soup,
ploughman's, plaice, hot dish of the day, sirloin steak, toasted
sandwiches, etc – and the cold table, laid out in the large and
comfortable bar as you enter the hotel, looks most appetising.
Most of the dishes are under £2. There is a special menu for
children with dishes at under £1 and they can also order half
portions from the main menu, and even a 'Baby's Choice' – baby
food or boiled egg and soldiers.*

*The dinner menu is quite extensive and has a touch of
imagination – for example hot 'Hand Hotel' smokie, lamb
cutlets with honey and mint butter, etc.*

*There is a comfortable lounge where you might pause for a drink
with the family, and their short menu of tea and coffee, toast
and sandwiches goes strong from 7.30am to 11pm. So it's a real
haven for the weary, the hungry and the thirsty in this Welsh
town of poetry, song and fable.*

*Accommodation is also available, and is free for children
sharing with a parent or parents.*

*The garden across the road is full of rose bushes and leads
steeply down to the river and a terrace.*

Open all year
Bar snacks 12-8pm   Dinner 6.45-8.45pm – £7.50   Ale – Border
Access/AmEx/Barclaycard/Diners   P – own car park

Llanrhaeadr, Nr Denbigh, Clwyd   map 3

H R   *BRYNN MORFYDD HOTEL* – phone Llanynys 280

Off the A525 south of Denbigh.

*There is nothing outstanding about this building; it's something
of a hotch-potch, but inoffensive enough in its coat of cream
pebbledash. But there are wonderful wide-open views of the
beautiful Vale of Clwyd, and some useful facilities: a nine-hole*

par-three golf course; one hard tennis court; and an outdoor heated swimming pool with a patio and its own bar.

There are various reductions for children's accommodation – a 75% discount under 2, 50% under 6 and 25% under 12. Children can order half portions or whatever they require in the way of burgers, fish fingers and the like. A great advantage is the 'Golfers' Fayre', snack meals which are available from 11am to 11pm. The restaurant concentrates on roast meats, salmon, trout and dishes such as steak Rossini, chicken chasseur, etc.

The forthright and helpful receptionist/manageress warns parents to beware of Saturday nights – there is always a disco.

17 rooms + 4 in annexe, 4 family, 2 suites   Moderate
Open all year   Lunch 12-2pm – £5   Dinner 7.30-10pm – £8.50
Access only   P – own car park

Llanyblodwel, Shropshire   map 3

P   *HORSE SHOE INN*

Signposted off the B4396 over a narrow bridge.

This is a delightful black and white timbered pub by the River Tanat, where one can fish for trout and grayling (the pub owns fishing rights). Inside are a number of low-beamed rooms, and children are welcome in the match-box bedecked pool room or a pretty lounge on the other side of the main bar 'as long as they behave themselves' as the charming landlady rightly and firmly says.

Outside there are tables and chairs by the river and hot and cold pub snacks are always available (except Tuesday evenings in winter).

Despite the village name, which means 'hamlet of flowers', this pub is in Shropshire. The English took the village from the Welsh in the early 18th century which goes to show that even then the Shropshire lads had good taste in pubs.

Ale – Border   P – own car park

London

For Heathrow see 'H'.

Big cities do not like children, and London loathes them. The majority of hoteliers, restaurateurs and publicans undoubtedly wish they did not exist. They want to get businessmen and foreign tourists through the doors and charge them the earth. In our researches we soon began to recognise the look of incomprehension when we asked about facilities for children and also to recognise the often smug and often curt denial of any such facilities.

Hotels

Does London have the most expensive hotels in the world? Their prices are crippling unless you are staying on a package deal or weekend break basis. Very few of them meet the Guide's basic criteria of providing cots, high chairs and a baby-listening facility. The latter service is the one which is usually missing since most of the hotels are only willing to arrange baby-sitters – at extra cost of course.

We have listed the few hotels we could find, and fortunately these are quite well-spread around Central London.

Restaurants

The London eating experience for families would comprise burgers and chips. A Saturday lunchtime in Beauchamp Place, Knightsbridge, one of the most popular streets for restaurants, sums up our research. We visited the dozen or so which were open and not one had a high chair. In the same way a couple of miles of the Kings Road, Chelsea, brought not a single high chair.

It's the same story as for hotels: restaurants in London have no interest in providing facilities for adults with children. They prefer to charge fat cats and tourists exorbitant prices instead. Thank goodness for the department store restaurants.

Pubs

We found only two pubs in London with children's rooms. So parents can only pop out for a drink with their children to pubs with gardens or patios on those rare summer days.

Department Stores

Head for the ones we have listed if you are seeking food or if you need to deal with a baby. Their facilities are object lessons to the rest of London.

H R   **BARKSTON HOTEL** (THF), Barkston Gardens, S W 5 – phone 01-373 7851

An hotel which is housed in a big Victorian mansion block. It faces a small garden square, and is just off the north end of Earls Court Road.

Accommodation for children is free up to 5 years and then costs £1 up to the age of 14. Children can choose from their own menu or have half portions from the main menu. The lunches are

*excellent value: a good choice of salads at under £2: and a steak
and kidney pie or hot dish of the day is also under £2. Dinner is
good value too with plenty of fish dishes, steaks and other grills.*

74 rooms, 8 triple   Moderate   Open all year
Buffet lunch 12-2pm – £2   Dinner 6.30-9.30pm – £8 alc
Access/AmEx/Barclaycard/Diners   P – NCP nearby

H   ***CHARING CROSS HOTEL,*** Strand, W C 2 – phone 01-839 7282

---

*One of the great railway hotels, which has now been unloaded
by British Rail to a private owner. It is a remarkable essay in
Victorian style, built in 1864, and beloved of John Betjeman
who wrote of it: 'the real splendour of Charing Cross was in the
interior of the hotel and much of this happily remains'.*

*The hotel is in a very central position – not many of London's
attractions are too far away. Children's accommodation costs
£6 for a cot and £10 for an extra bed, and in the Carvery
Restaurant they eat free up to the age of 5 and at half price
between 5 and 10 years. The three-course menu here concentrates on traditional roasts plus a dish of the day.*

211 rooms, 15 family   Expensive   Open all year
Carvery open from noon to 11pm   Ale – Bass
Access/AmEx/Barclaycard/Diners   P – very limited, NCP nearby

---

R   ***CHUEN CHENG KU,*** 17-23 Wardour Street, W1 – phone 01-734
3509

---

*A very big Chinese restaurant in the heart of London's Chinese
quarter just off Leicester Square. It's a long room with a
cafeteria-like air and a similarly long menu. There are lots of
varieties of Dim Sum at under £1 and the rest of the main dishes
vary between £3 and £5. There are also the set menus – for 2
persons at under £10, 3 persons at under £15, and so on.*

*Half portions are not on the menu, but it is easy to order up a
meal suitable for a child from such a list.*

*There is a table in the 'Ladies' where mothers might change a
baby.*

Open 11am-11.45pm (Sun to 11pm)   Licensed
Access/AmEx/Barclaycard/Diners   P – street or public

H   ***COBURG HOTEL*** (Best Western), *Bayswater Road, W2 – phone*
01-229 3654

A large 'mansion block' with a distinctive domed roof, the hotel is in an excellent position overlooking Kensington Gardens — quite a sizeable garden for guests to enjoy. It's a couple of miles from Marble Arch and a brisk stroll across Hyde Park will bring you to Knightsbridge and its shops. For children of all ages the London Toy and Model Museum is nearby.

Cots are free and the charge for older children who require a bed is £5, and this includes breakfast. The restaurant will organise half portions for children.

125 rooms, 4 family   Moderate   Open all year
Lunch 12.30-2.30pm – £7   Dinner 6.30-9.30pm – £8
Access/AmEx/Barclaycard/Diners   P – public car park nearby

R   ***CRANKS,*** 8 Marshall Street, W1 – phone 01-437 9431

The well-known vegetarian restaurant is in a pleasant modern building quite close to tawdry Carnaby Street. They have high chairs but nothing else as we were snappily and impatiently told by, we imagined, the manageress.

The best plan is to order your salad or hot savoury dish and ask for a separate empty bowl for your small child. A small salad is just over £1 and a large one just over £2; hot savoury dishes are about £2.

Closed Sunday and Bank Holidays Open 10am-10.30pm,
Lunch from 11.30am   Licensed
Access/AmEx/Barclaycard/Diners   P – street or public

R   ***CUMBERLAND HOTEL,*** Marble Arch, W 1 – phone 01-262 1234

The Coffee Shop, busy as it is, is a haven from the terrors of Oxford Street. It is open from 10.30am to 1.30am and offers a whole range of snacks, omelettes, grills, burgers, pastries or just tea and toast if you wish. Prices range from just under £1 to just over £5. The children have their own menu or can choose half portions from the adult menu.

Open 10.30am-1.30am   Licensed
Access/AmEx/Barclaycard/Diners
P – difficult, public car parks nearby

H   ***CUNARD INTERNATIONAL HOTEL*** (Trafalgar House), Short-lands, W 6 – phone 01-741 1555

You can see this huge hotel from the Hammersmith flyover and it gets no marks for aesthetic appeal. It reminds us of airports and is geared to conferences, businessmen and package holiday-makers, especially from the USA.

But it is not quite so horrendously expensive as some central London hotels and it is a few minutes by bus, tube or taxi to the centre. It is also close to one of London's finest pubs (though it has no children's room), The Thatched House, in Dalling Road. (NB from Jill – Malcolm spends every Friday night there, he should know.)

Children under 12 are accommodated free and there are lots of triple rooms. If any of these are free they are used for two adults plus one child at the normal twin-bedded room rate. Children's portions are served.

640 rooms, 42 triples, 10 suites, 10 sets intercommunicating
Expensive   Open all year
Lunch 12.30-2.30pm – £8.75 (Master Carver)
Dinner 5.30-10.30pm – £8.75 (Master Carver)
Access/AmEx/Barclaycard/Diners   P – own car park

R   ***DEBENHAMS, SPRINGLES RESTAURANT*** (basement), Oxford Street, W1 – phone 01-580 3000

An Oxford Street store that makes an attempt to cater for families out shopping. There is a good mix of food – steak and kidney pie, fish and chicken every day, with specials like cottage pie, lasagne and chicken and vegetable pie all at about £2. The 85p children's meal is, as usual, something with chips and mostly there's only one dish on offer. There's soup and salad, though, and some good open and toasted sandwiches at up to £1.50. It's a pretty room with lots of pine and space (and it's air-conditioned).

There's a ladies' cloakroom on the 3rd floor which is adequate for dealing with a baby – but no special room which one would expect in a store this size.

Mon-Sat 9.30-5.30pm (7pm Thur)   Unlicensed
Access/AmEx/Barclaycard/Diners
P – several public car parks at the back of the store

R   ***DICKINS AND JONES***, Regent Street, W 1 – phone 01-734 7070

Here is a store which looks after families really well. You can eat in the Rose Restaurant (4th floor) or in one of the three coffee shops – The Coffee Shop (3rd), the Piazza (2nd) or the Patio *(lower ground) and between them they can provide anything from vegetables mashed in gravy for a tiny baby to carrot cake for a vegetarian. Thanks to Miss Saunders and Mr O'Neill for their help and enthusiasm.*

The Rose Restaurant is the place for babies – as well as providing food, they will re-heat food you may take with you. You can eat from the Carvers Table or the Cold Buffet at £5.50 or have salad at £2.50 to £5.50 and other hot dishes like quiche at £2 and fish and chips at £3.25. English breakfast costs £2.25 and a cream tea £1.95. Half portions are available for children up to 10. There's a large and comfortable 'Ladies' on the 4th floor with lots of tables and seating although the real mothers' room is on the 3rd floor. The Coffee Shop here is which serves snacks like toasted and open sandwiches at about £1.50.

Going down a floor in a delightful new and colourful children's department is the Piazza where the food is mostly vegetarian including carrot cake, vegetarian pie and other wholemeal cooking. Here you can choose from a fine array of herbal teas and can drink fresh-squeezed orange juice.

The Patio on the lower ground floor is more of a wine bar – at lunchtime anyway – and is probably more for the 'young and beautiful' – it's the only one of the four which plays music all day. It offers good cheap snacks and meals – salad bowls and plenty of meats and salads as well as some hot dishes all at around £2. It also serves marine ices in many flavours.

Rose Restaurant Mon-Fri 9.30-5pm
Coffee Shop & Piazza Mon-Fri 9.30-5.15pm (6.45 Thur)
Patio Mon-Sat 9.45-5.30pm   Licensed
Access/AmEx/Barclaycard/Diners
P – meters and public car parks

Next door is LIBERTY'S whose restaurant has a most beautiful antique high chair. A new restaurant, however, was being planned so we can give you no details.

R   **L'ESCARGOT,** 48 Greek Street, W1 – phone 01-437 2679

A busy and famous restaurant in the heart of seedy Soho. However, for a place of its reputation it is not so blindingly expensive as many of its competitors. There is always lots of fish – sole, turbot, scallops, etc, at about £7 a dish – as well as poultry, beef and lamb. The Brasserie menu runs concurrently on the ground floor and for longer – 10am to 3pm and 5.30 to 11.30pm Monday to Friday (evenings only Saturday). Lighter meals are served here: smoked lamb at £3, chicken curry at £4, steak and mushroom pie and calves liver at around £4.50.

Half portions are served for children. There is a table in the 'Ladies' which is spacious, and a mother could breast-feed a baby in the office.

Closed Sat lunchtimes & Sun   Lunch 12.15-2.30pm – £10 alc
Dinner 6.30-11.15pm – £10 alc   Licensed
Access/AmEx/Barclaycard/Diners   P – street or public

R   **D H EVANS, RIVER RESTAURANT** (5th floor), Oxford Street, W1 – phone 01-629 8800

The theme of the restaurant is the Thames and it is divided into four sections – Embankment, River Park, Tower and Armoury – with each suitably decorated. Children will probably prefer the River Park where you eat in a bandstand surrounded by a mural of Guards in red uniforms and bearskins, and adults the Embankment with a mural which faithfully depicts famous landmarks along the Thames. ASH will like the fact that no smoking is allowed in the Tower or the Embankment.

There's a huge self-service counter offering a good selection of food with hot meals available throughout the day, starting with breakfast for £2.45 which is served until 11.15, lunch at which there is always a roast at about £3.50, salads up to £2.50, fish dishes at £1.75 to £2.50 and open sandwiches at £1.50. For vegetarians there's a help-yourself salad which includes nuts and fruit at £3.25 and, although the special children's menu is the inevitable things-and-chips (£1), there's no minimum and they can have soup or various salad portions at 50p each.

Although the restaurant is very jolly, the 'Ladies' on the floor below is rather grim but you could just about manage to look after a baby's needs. Better, if you're out with a nappy-filling, breast-feeding baby, to go to one of the other Oxford Street stores where your needs are better served.

Open Mon-Sat 9.30-5.45pm (7pm Thur)   Licensed
Access/AmEx/Barclaycard/Diners
P – large and expensive car park in Cavendish Square

R   **THE GARDEN CAFE**, White House Hotel, Albany Street, W1 – phone 01-387 1200

A big and busy coffee shop not far from Madame Tussaud's. It's open all day and serves snacks, soups, omelettes, several types of salad up to £5.25, fish, grills (a rump steak costs £6) and burgers. There are also dishes of the day – for example braised lambs liver at just over £3 and goujons of plaice at under £4.

Children's portions can be ordered and mothers will find space to feed or change a baby in the 'Powder Room'.

Open 7am-11.30pm all week   Licensed
Access/AmEx/Barclaycard/Diners   P – public

R   ***GEALE'S FISH RESTAURANT,** 2 Farmer Street, W 8 – phone 01-727 7969*

A real good fish and chipper – always bustling with life and noise.

The fishy starters include fish soup, crab soup, mackerel fillet, prawn cocktail at between 50p and £1.50, followed by a choice of marvellously fresh fish at prices ranging from under £2 to about £2.50 according to size and availability. Chips, peas and side salads are an extra 30p-50p and there are a few puddings – apple crumble at 70p and chocolate éclairs at 85p.

It is not reasonable of course to expect half portions of fish, but two children can share one dish or a really small child can have a plate and eat some of its parents' food.

The upstairs restaurant is not open at lunchtime and can then be used by a mother to attend to her baby in comfort and privacy.

Closed 2 weeks at Christmas, 5 days at Easter, and mid-August for 3 weeks
Lunch Tue-Sat 12-3pm   Dinner Tue-Fri 6-11.30pm (Sat to 11pm)
Licensed   Access only   P – quite difficult street parking

R   ***GROSVENOR HOUSE HOTEL,** Park Lane, W 1 – phone 01-499 6363*

We include this grand and stately hotel as a refuge for lunch and afternoon tea. The Pavilion restaurant, bright, pretty and airy, looks out on Park Lane and you will find an excellent choice of cold food and hot dishes of the day, including a daily roast. The price of £12 includes two other courses and half a bottle of wine per person. Children can order half portions and also have their own special menu.

Teas are served in the elegant lounge from 3.30 to 5.30pm – sandwiches, scones, pastries and gateaux and a good selection of teas. The cost is from £2.50 to £5.25 and worth it to relax in such pleasant surroundings.

Lunch (The Pavilion) 12-3pm – £12

Dinner (The Pavilion) 6-11pm – £12
Access/AmEx/Barclaycard/Diners
P – underground car park opposite

R   *L S GRUNTS*, 12 Maiden Lane, W C 2 – phone 01-379 7722

Quite close to the Covent Garden Piazza, this big and busy
Chicago pizza pie restaurant lies back from the street. The range
of pizzas is large and each one is for two people (so don't go
alone). They cost £4 to £5. They only do these large pizzas – half
portions are not on the menu, so judge whether you need a
regular or large version according to the sizes and numbers of
your children.

Although the children are given balloons and cartoons on the
large screen video, there is nowhere to change or feed a baby in
comfort.

Closed Sundays   Open 12-11.30pm Mon-Sat   Licensed
Access/Barclaycard   P – street or public

R   *HAMLEYS*, Regent Street, W 1 – phone 01-734 3161

A bright, bustling self-service restaurant on the 4th floor of this
children's paradise, parents' purgatory. It's a room which will
delight children, with 'park' chairs and cut-out buses. It has a
large no-smoking area which will delight ASH.

The menu does tend to concentrate on the burger-and-chips,
sausage-and-chips sort of food, but there are other hot dishes
each day as well as sandwiches, salads and baked jacket
potatoes with various fillings. Pastries and cream teas are also
served. Prices range from about £1 to £3.50.

There is a spacious mothers' room right next to the restaurant,
with a long bench for changing and some seating.

We don't recommend you try to eat here at lunchtime during the
school holidays unless you have unlimited strength and
patience.

Open 9.30-5.30 Mon to Sat (9.30-8pm Thur)
Lunch 11.30-2.30pm   Unlicensed
No credit cards accepted   P – meters or public car park

P   *HAND IN HAND*, 6 Crooked Billet, S W 19

There is a very busy and popular pub, especially at weekends,
by the west side of Wimbledon Common and not far from that

marvellous golf course, Royal Wimbledon. It's a rather charming pub with a small courtyard at the front with a few benches. Inside there is a big open bar and at one side a spacious children's room with rows of tables and chairs. It is utilitarian but what a haven for parents tired and thirsty after football, cricket or just coping on the Common.

There is pub food available every day – salad baps, burgers, chilli con carne, chicken and chips, pies, etc, and the most expensive item is £2.50. Most are below £2.

Ale – Young's   P – roadside parking

R   **HARRODS GEORGIAN RESTAURANT,** Brompton Road, S W 1 – phone 01-730 1234 ext. 3467 or 2888

Two bright and beautiful rooms – one with an ornate plaster ceiling and the other with a large skylight. There is also the Terrace Bar with pretty conservatory cane furniture and hanging baskets. The full English breakfast is £4.50 – and it is full – and Continental £2.95. The three-course lunch is £9.25 and is good value for those with a hearty appetite: There are starters such as pasta tricolore, tuna salad and ham mousse, and the main course can be chosen either from the Cold table (presided over for some fifteen years by the helpful and efficient Anne) with its splendid array of meats, fish and salads or from the Carvery which in addition to rib of beef and roast pork, offers goulash, plaice bonne femme, etc. There's then a good choice of rich and sticky puddings. There's a choice of rich and sticky cakes at tea time, plus cream teas, sandwiches, fruit dishes, etc. The tea costs £3.95.

Half price is charged for children up to 12 and discretion is used for infants who clearly aren't going to eat as much as a half portion. (Polly has always eaten from Jill's plate at no charge.)

This restaurant is the only one in Harrods with high chairs. It is on the 4th floor as is a ladies' cloakroom with a separate little room for breast-feeding and nappy-changing – by the old maps and prints department. There is another mother and baby room on the 1st floor in the children's clothes department.

Open Mon to Sat   Breakfast 9-11am   Lunch 12-2.30pm
Tea 3.30-5.30pm (4.30pm Wed & Sat)   Licensed
Access/AmEx/Barclaycard/Diners
P – own car park, but it's often full

H   **HOLIDAY INN,** King Henry's Road, N W 3 – phone 01-722 7711

A reasonable-looking modern hotel which is only a short ride by bus, tube or taxi to the 'West End' and has the delights of Hampstead and its Heath just up the road.

There is an excellent indoor swimming pool of a good size with an area roped off for small children, and an exercise area alongside with a static bike, jogging machines and other equipment (properly supervised). There's a pool table here and at weekends a table tennis table.

The coffee shop, open from 11am to 9pm, has a range of snacks, omelettes, ravioli, burgers, salads, etc, plus a special children's menu.

At weekends a baby-patrol is in operation – a free service. But you have to pay for this during the week. Nevertheless we include this hotel because of its useful position and its positive economic advantages for a family of four who can occupy a twin-bedded room with two double beds at the standard price.

276 rooms, 176 family   Expensive   Open all year   Lunch 12.30-2.30pm – £6.75   Dinner 6.30-10.30pm – £11
Access/AmEx/Barclaycard/Diners   P – 120 spaces

H R   **HOLIDAY INN,** 17 Sloane Street, S W 1 – phone 01-235 4377

A smart modern hotel in one of the more elegant parts of London and close to the Victoria and Albert, Science and Natural History Museums as well as many good shops, including Harrods and Harvey Nichols. It is five minutes' walk from Hyde Park too.

The hotel has many rooms with two double beds, and children (up to the age of 19) can share a room with two adults. The pretty, bright glass-covered restaurant is set around the swimming pool giving the feeling of eating out of doors. There is a lunchtime buffet – a good choice of salads and some hot dishes of the day – and a coffee shop menu is in operation (in the restaurant) from 11am-6pm. You can eat soup, omelettes, kebabs, etc. The children's menu is the usual things and chips at around £1.50 and there is a full à la carte menu in the evening.

A 'hostess' is on duty to look after children in the evenings at weekends – the baby-patrol is available from Friday to Sunday inclusive – so that parents can have their freedom. Otherwise you must arrange and pay for baby-sitters.

206 rooms, 24 family, 4 suites   Expensive   Open all year
Buffet lunch 12.30-2pm – £8.50   Dinner 7-11pm – £14 alc
Access/AmEx/Barclaycard/Diners   P – very limited but there is a public car park at the rear of the hotel

H R *HOLIDAY INN,* George Street, W 1 – phone 01-723 1277

Off the Edgware Road, near Marble Arch.

The usual Holiday Inn set-up – and handily placed in the West End. Its great advantage is the provision of two double beds in every twin room. If you happen to be in London with two children, a stay here makes some kind of economic sense since four cost the same as two.

There is an indoor pool of a reasonable size and alongside a small exercise area with a static bike and a jogging machine. The Brasserie is open all day and has a good selection of snacks and meals – lots of salads, goulash soup, quiches, casseroles, cutlets, chicken and fish dishes. For example boeuf bourguig-nonne costs £5.80 or spaghetti bolognese £3.50. Children have their own menu – burgers, fish fingers, chicken drumsticks, etc or can order half portions from the main menu.

243 rooms, 136 family   Expensive
Open all year   Brasserie 7am-10.30pm
Access/AmEx/Barclaycard/Diners   P — own car park

H *HYDE PARK HOTEL* (THF), Knightsbridge – phone 01-235 2000

You need to be very rich to stay here. It is a very elegant and stately pile whose rear rooms overlook Hyde Park and a premium is charged to stay in them. There's a lot of marble about as you climb the wide stairs to the entrance hall (shouldn't they carry you at these prices?) The Park Room restaurant is particularly attractive and its tall windows look out on the Park. There is also the Cavalry Grill (closed on Saturdays) which offers a businessman's lunch at £11. Both serve half portions.

The lunchtime buffet menu (you help yourself) costs over £9: fish dishes to start and a cold buffet or a hot dish of the day to follow. Afternoon teas are served from 3.30 to 6pm – handy for the footsore Knightsbridge shoppers.

Cots are free and older children up to 14 are charged at a nominal £1 per night.

By the way, someone will park your car for you if you are staying at the hotel.

180 rooms, 20 suites   Expensive
Open all year   Lunch (The Park Room) 12.30-2.30pm – £14 alc
Dinner (The Park Room) 6.30-11pm – £14 alc
Access/AmEx/Barclaycard/Diners   P – public or street parking

R   *PETER JONES, Sloane Square, S W 1 – phone 01-730 3434*

There are two restaurants – The Restaurant and The Crock Pot – next door to each other on the 4th floor and a Coffee Shop on the 5th floor, in all of which you can get something to drink or eat during store opening. The Restaurant serves a special children's menu at £1.75 all day: homemade fish cakes or sausages with beans and potatoes or spaghetti bolognese followed by ice cream and chocolate sauce or jelly and ice cream. At lunchtime (11.45am-2.30pm) a wide choice of cakes, pastries, salads, sandwiches and omelettes in a price range of about 50p to £3 is available and 'High' and 'Afternoon' teas are also served – such as fried plaice or grilled ham with tea and a pastry at £3.80 or toast, sandwiches, cakes, etc. The Crock Pot offers open and toasted sandwiches at £1.30 and pastries in the mornings (9.30-11.45am), two hot dishes, patés and omelettes at lunchtime (11.45am-2.45pm) of which half portions are available for children, and club or toasted sandwiches or buttered tea cakes and pastries in the afternoon. All day the Crock Pot serves some tooth-rotting ice-cream 'cups' – mixtures of fruit, nuts, sauces. The Coffee Shop serves a good selection of salad snacks (pitta and taramasalata £1.60, slimmers salad £2.35), wholemeal bread, fresh fruit salad, cakes and pastries all day.

Seats and tables are available in the ladies' cloakrooms on the 2nd, 3rd and 4th floors.

Open Mon-Sat 9.30am-5pm (6.30pm Wed)   Licensed
No credit cards accepted   P – street parking, often difficult

---

R   *JOHN LEWIS, THE PLACE TO EAT* (3rd floor), Oxford Street, W 1 – phone 01-629 7711

This is an exceptionally bright pretty self-service restaurant with a scheme of white, pink and green. It has seven different sections offering different kinds of food – Breakfast All Day, Crockpot, Patisserie, Cold Table, Créperie, Seafood and the Soda Fountain. Something as you see to suit most palates and at reasonable prices – ranging roughly from £1 to £4. There's a better choice than usual for those anxious that they and their children don't suffer from fatty heart – cereals and muesli at the breakfast bar, salad portions at 70p each (or £2.95 for all six salads) at the Cold Table and children's crockpot (£1.30). The staff are extremely helpful and take a great pride in the place. It gets very busy though – 'best advice going is to lunch before 12', said the assistant who showed me round.

The mother's room is far and away the best we've seen — it's smashing with a large changing area with mats provided and nappies available (Peaudouce, of course); and a feeding area with plenty of chairs and bottle warmers. A mother with a young baby I met there plans her shopping trips around John Lewis because of their splendid facilities.

The great care and pride the store takes is reflected everywhere, but even they haven't got it quite right — the mothers' room is the only part of the store which can't be reached by lift and the flight of stairs to it is pretty daunting to a mother with shopping, baby and pushchair. (Please JL — at least a ramp?)

Sat 9.30am-12.30pm Thur 9.45am-7.30pm, Mon, Tue, Wed & Fri 9.30am-5pm
No credit cards accepted
P — Cavendish Square is easiest if you're rash enough to take the car

---

R   **MACARTHURS** — three branches at:
147 Church Road, Barnes, S W 13 — phone 01-748 3630
248 Upper Richmond Road West, S W 14 — phone 01-876 4445
50/54 Turnham Green Terrace, Chiswick, W 4 — phone 01-994 3000

These are appealing, brightly decorated restaurants and they serve some of the best burgers in the West. There is a whole range of them (4, 8 or 12oz) from around £2 to just over £3. Rump steak is an alternative and there are various salads, baked potatoes, etc.

The Barnes branch stays open to midnight on Fridays and Saturdays.

The 'Junior Mac' is a half-size burger at just over half price. There are no special facilities available to change or feed a baby.

Closed public holidays   Mon-Fri 12.30-2.30pm & 6-11.30pm
Sat/Sun 12.30-11.30pm   Licensed
Access/Barclaycard   P — street parking

R   **MILBURNS at the VICTORIA & ALBERT MUSEUM,** Cromwell Road, S W 7 — phone 01-589 6371

Some time during the summer of 1984 Milburns will be opening a new restaurant in the Henry Cole Wing of the Museum. The old one, meantime, is a very useful place for a good self-service snack or meal if you're in this part of London. It is not just used by visitors to the Museum, though it's hard to resist a bit of culture even if you've dropped in for a quick bite.

There's a good range of food at lunchtime – soup, quiche, salads – and interesting hot dishes are offered each day such as devilled sausages, cauliflower cheese, pigeon casserole, kedgeree, steak and kidney pie. In the morning and afternoon pastries, sandwiches, and so on are available, but in the old restaurant there is a gap in service from 11.45 to noon and 2.30 to 3pm – in the new restaurant there will be no interruption of service. Half portions are available for children with a minimum at lunchtime of 50p.

There is shelving in the cheerless museum ladies' room close to Milburns where it would be easy to change a baby, but nowhere to sit to breast-feed. It is hoped that the new restaurant will have its own lavatories so comfort for feeding mothers may improve.

Open Mon to Sat (closed Fridays) 10am-5pm, Sun 2.30-5.30pm
Licensed   No credit cards accepted
P – meters or public car parks

R   ***PORTERS,*** 17 Henrietta Street, W C 2 – phone 01-836 6466

A couple of streets away from Covent Garden Piazza is this smart, cheerful and bustling restaurant. It specialises in pies at around £3 – cottage, lamb and apricot, Billingsgate, steak, oyster and clam, and several others. There are salads and baked potatoes and puddings redolent of childhood (the kids won't like them) – bread and butter pudding, steamed syrup sponge and jam roly poly.

Children's portions are available at Sunday lunchtimes but not otherwise. There are no facilities to change or feed a baby.

Closed Christmas & Boxing Days   Lunch 12 noon-3pm
Dinner 5.30-11.30pm (10.30pm on Sun)   Licensed
Access/Barclaycard   P – public parking

P   ***PUNCH AND JUDY,*** The Piazza, Covent Garden, W C 2

An interesting pub in the centre of the Covent Garden development. Its main bar is amongst vaulted brick cellars and pleasant it is too, even if the music is intrusive. You can sit with your children in a separate area at one end of the pub or outside under the roof of the Piazza.

Food is served from 11.30-2.30 and from 5.30 to 7.30 Monday to Saturday and at lunchtimes on Sunday. It is mostly under £2 – salads, beef in Guinness, savoury mince, navarin of lamb, etc.

Ale – Courage   P – public parking

149

R   **RICHOUX** – *two branches at:*
         172 Piccadilly, W 1 – phone 01-493 2204
         41a South Audley Street, W 1 – phone 01-629 5228

There is a pleasant tea shop atmosphere to these two restaurants. You can order whatever you wish at any time, the only exception being the breakfast menu which stops at 11.30am. There is a huge choice – egg dishes, salads, grills, pies, beef stroganoff, chicken kiev, sandwiches, pastries and ice creams at prices from £1 to £6.50.

The children's menu is served all day – fish fingers, burgers, spaghetti, fish and chips at under £2. The 'Ladies' are spacious though without tables on which to change a baby.

Picadilly 8.30am-11.30pm (except Sun – 10am-11.30pm)
South Audley Street 8.30am-11pm (except Sun – 10am-11pm)
Licensed   Access/AmEx/Barclaycard/Diners
P – street or public

R   **SELFRIDGES,** Oxford Street, W1

At the time of going to press the old Selfridges Top of the Shop on the 4th floor, which is the one with high chairs, was about to close to make way for a new restaurant due to open shortly after our publication day.

I can only tell you that the Manager intends to provide a good eating place for parents out with their children at prices which they expect to start at about 30p.

As the opening of the new restaurant coincides with their 75th anniversary perhaps it will be worth celebrating with them by giving the new place a try.

They do have a mothers' room on the floor below.

R   **SIMPSON PICCADILLY RESTAURANT,** 203 Piccadilly, W 1 –
         phone 01-734 2002

Somewhere with high chairs right in the centre of London. From breakfast through to tea there's always something hot available at Simpsons, although during the week it's best to avoid the lunchtime businessmen's crush; Saturday is family day. For breakfast there are plenty of meals at around £2 – eggs, bacon, mushrooms, sausages, omelettes, kippers, as well as sandwiches and pastries. At lunchtime there's a choice of cold buffet and plainish hot dishes – plaice, steak and kidney pie, omelette, *roast beef, poached salmon – at prices ranging from £3 to £8. For afternoon tea, too, there's a good choice of sandwiches, omelettes, snacks on toast, and pastries for £1 to £2.25. Try the tea, made with water from their own artesian well.*

Half portions are served to children.

You could cope with a baby in the nearby 'Ladies' – though there's no special mothers' room.

Mon to Sat 9am-5.30pm (Thur 6.30pm, Sat 6pm)   Breakfast 9-11.30   Lunch 12-2.30   Tea 3.30-5.15   Licensed
Access/AmEx/Barclaycard/Diners   P – public parking only

H   ***STAKIS ST ERMIN'S HOTEL,*** Caxton Street, S W 1 – phone 01-222 7888

In a strategic position between the Houses of Parliament, the Embankment, Buckingham Palace and Victoria Station, this is a great big red-brick edifice.

There is no charge for cots in parents' rooms, and an extra bed costs £13. Of the two restaurants, the 'Carver's Table' is the more reasonably priced. It has a children's menu at about £1.50, and half portions can be ordered from the main menu, which is of the prawn cocktail and roast variety.

244 rooms, 12 triple, 4 quadruple   Expensive
Open all year   Lunch 1-2pm – £8.75   Dinner 6-9.15pm – £8.75
Access/AmEx/Barclaycard/Diners   P – restricted

H   ***STANHOPE COURT HOTEL,*** 46-52 Stanhope Gardens, S W 7 – phone 01-370 2161

By London standards this is a reasonably-priced hotel, which is tucked away near Cromwell Road. It's a big Victorian mansion block, with a small lawned garden at the side, and it overlooks a lovely garden square packed with trees.

The charge for cots is £2.50 a night, and for children from 2 to 14 years £5 which includes breakfast.

The hotel is quite close to Knightsbridge, the Natural History Museum, Hyde Park, etc.

125 rooms, 15 family   Cheap   Closed Christmas week
Lunch 1-2pm – £4.25   Dinner 7-8.30pm – £5.50
Access/AmEx/Barclaycard/Diners   P – NCP nearby

H R **TOWER HOTEL** (Thistle), St Katharine's Way, E1 – phone 01-481 2575

A huge modern hotel, built in a slightly brutal style, but in a magnificent position with Tower Bridge and the Tower of London on one side, the Thames on another, and St Katharine's Dock with its many attractions (including the Historic Ships Museum) on another.

Children are accommodated free up to the age of 14, and there is a special children's menu of the 'things and chips' variety in the Picnic Basket restaurant. There is a reasonable choice here of salads, toasted sandwiches and grills from £1 to £6. The other two restaurants, the Princes Room and the Carvery, are quite expensive and offer no concessions, such as half portions, for children.

An interesting place to stay or a place for a quick snack if you have been traipsing around the Tower.

834 rooms, 20 family   Expensive   Open all year
Picnic Basket open from noon to 1am
Access/AmEx/Barclaycard/Diners   P – 124 spaces

Long Melford, Nr Sudbury, Suffolk   map 1

One of the finest small towns in Suffolk, it was once a centre for the wool trade, and has a wonderful wide main street. The 15th century Church of the Holy Trinity is truly magnificent with its plethora of fine windows, and Melford Hall a notable red-brick Elizabethan manor house.

H **BULL HOTEL** (THF) – phone Sudbury 78494

Right in the centre of the village.

This is a striking example of a 15th century half-timbered coaching inn with a wonderful interior of black oaken beams, carved wood and open fireplaces. It has a paved central courtyard with a few tables and chairs.

Accommodation is free for children up to 5 and a nominal charge of £1 is made for children aged from 5 to 14. Half portions and a special children's menu are available in the restaurant.

25 rooms, 15 family   Expensive   Open all year
Lunch 12.30-2pm – £7.75   Dinner 7.30-10pm – £9.95
Ale – Greene King, Bass, Mauldon's
Access/AmEx/Barclaycard/Diners   P – own car park

152

P   ***CROWN INN HOTEL,*** Hall Street

On the A134, half way down the main street.

A lovely old inn dating back to the 17th century, some of it re-built when it was burned by rioters in 1885. Most of it was saved but only after the Riot Act was read from its steps. There is a comfortable and beautifully maintained reception area, with easy chairs, which can be used by children. There is also a pretty walled garden bedecked with flowers and with plenty of bench tables.

A range of bar snacks, hot and cold, is available at all times.

Ale – Adnams, Greene King, Mauldon's   P – own car park

Longframlington, Northumberland   map 5

R   *BESOM BARN – phone 627*

On the A697.

This is a very handsome stone ex-barn in rolling Northumbrian countryside. When we arrived one afternoon the owner was baking the bread rolls and this is symptomatic of his approach: good natural ingredients, good value and a friendly and efficient outlook. The Besom Byre, a separate building to the Barn has such things as steak and kidney pie at under £3, besom broth at under £1 and smoked quail legs in garlic mayonnaise at just over £1. There is a fuller menu in the evening in the Barn at £9 for three courses.

The restaurants are handsome inside too with scrubbed pine tables and wood-burning stoves. Children can be served half portions and baby food can be produced if necessary.

Mothers can tend their babies in the adjoining house if the need arises and it has been known for a baby-sitter to be pressed into service for the benefit of diners-out.

We were impressed in every way by this restaurant. The buildings are handsome inside and out; the menus are interesting and offer excellent value; but above all the owner was obviously used to dealing with families and clearly very happy to welcome them. A clear winner in the restaurant category.

Closed Sun, Mon   Besom Byre Lunch 10-2.30pm
Dinner Besom Byre 7-10pm   Dinner Besom Barn 7-9.30pm – £9
No credit cards accepted   P – own car park

Longhorsley, Nr Morpeth, Northumberland   map 5

H P R   *LINDEN HALL HOTEL* (Prestige) – phone Morpeth 56611

On the A697 north of Morpeth.

At the end of a long driveway you will find this glorious Georgian mansion built in 1812 for a local bigwig and set in 300 acres of splendid grounds and parkland. The interior is beautifully maintained and elegantly furnished and there are excellent facilities: a hard tennis court, putting green, croquet lawn, and large playroom in a vaulted cellar with table tennis and snooker (for adults) and a Wendy house and lots of toys and mini-furniture for mini-children.

Accommodation is free for children up to 12. They have a special children's menu from 6-7pm and can choose half portions from the restaurant menu.

Behind the hotel is the Linden Pub, built of attractive stone like the hotel. There is a large children's room under the rafters with high chair and a terrace outside with plenty of tables and chairs and a giant draughts board to the side. They serve hot and cold meals – salads, sandwiches, boeuf bourgignonne – and a special children's menu (burgers, fish fingers, etc) as well as half portions. Their hours for meals are 12.30-2.30pm (Sunday 12-2pm) and 6.30-9.30pm (Sunday 7.30-9.30pm) so there is a choice here between the hotel restaurant and the pub meals.

45 rooms, 10 family, 3 suites   Moderate   Open all year
Lunch in hotel 12-2pm – £12 alc
Dinner 7-9.30pm – £12 alc   Ale – Theakston's (in the pub)
Access/AmEx/Barclaycard/Diners   P – own car park

Loweswater, Cumbria   map 5

P   *KIRKSTILE INN*

Off the B5289 south of Cockermouth.

A splendid and unspoiled 16th century pub in a superb lakeland setting, close to Crummoch Water and with the dramatic Melbreak Fell lowering in the background. It has a lovely interior too, with beamed ceilings, rough stone walls and wooden settles. There is a separate, cosy dining-room and a veranda at the back of the pub leading to a small lawn.

The children's room, the 'Little Barn', has plenty of tables and chairs, bar billiards and a juke box.

154

Food is served every day and all day and there is plenty of variety: Haddock, scampi and plaice cost just over £3, or you might fancy a sirloin steak at £5.50. There are also sandwiches, burgers and pizzas.

Ale – Jennings   P – own car park

Ludlow, Shropshire map 3

This is a wonderful old town of narrow cobbled streets, packed with Tudor and Georgian houses; John Betjeman thought it one of the loveliest towns in England. There is a fine Norman castle, partly ruined, from which medieval Welsh princes attempted to govern the turbulent Celts and where the 'Little Princes' were lodged before they made their last journey to the Tower of London in 1483; and the Church of St Laurence is one of the biggest parish churches in the land.

H   *FEATHERS HOTEL*, Bull Ring – phone 5261

In the town centre.

Built in 1603 this is one of the ornaments of the town. It's a superb half-timbered building with gables and leaded windows, and with an extraordinarily elaborate carved façade. The interior is just as fascinating with its fine panelling and ceilings and a splendid banqueting room.

On the banqueting side there is a cold buffet during the summer, but sandwiches and ploughman's only in the winter at lunchtimes. The restaurant's set lunches and dinners contain some sound English dishes such as Ludlow broth, curried eggs, leek and potato soup and stuffed tomatoes; and main dishes include lemon sole, braised oxtail, chicken and cider casserole, roast lamb and duck, etc.

There is no charge for cots, but no extra beds available; family rooms only which add £10 to the bill.

35 rooms, 3 family   Expensive
Open all year   Lunch 12.30-2pm – £5.95   Dinner 7-9pm – £8.95
Ale – Flowers, Whitbread
Access/AmEx/Barclaycard/Diners   P – own car park

R   *EAGLE HOUSE RESTAURANT*, 17 Corve Street – phone 2325

In the main street of the town.

An old half-timbered coaching inn with a pretty courtyard where there are tables in the summer. There are two dining rooms: a high-ceilinged refectory type of room upstairs where one can eat from a large collection of snacks and grills from £1 to £4.50; and downstairs a restaurant proper which serves roasts, fish and grills. Hot meals are available all day, starting with breakfast at 9am. The set lunches and dinners are very good value: for example home-made soup, roast beef and Yorkshire pudding and a sweet for lunch; herb egg mayonnaise, lemon sole and a pudding for dinner.

Half portions are served to children and there is a large 'Powder Room' upstairs which mothers and babies may use.

Open all year from 9am-9.30pm Lunch 12-2.30pm – £4
Dinner 7-9.30pm – £5.60 Licensed
No credit cards accepted P – own car park

Machynlleth, Powys   map 3
H P R *WYNNSTAY HOTEL* (THF) – phone 2003

On the A 487 in the town centre.

Typical THF town hotel – it would be wrong to describe it as ordinary in that it compares so well with what else is around in this popular touring area which should be overflowing with superb hotels – but isn't.

There are two comfortable lounges where you can sit with the children while having a drink. Lunch can be taken in the bar or one of the lounges (they'll move a high chair wherever you want it). The lunch menu offers four starters (paté, soup, etc), four main courses all under £2 (cold meat and salad, daily special, steak and kidney pie, fish) and the usual sort of puddings. The dinner menu has special Welsh dishes each day – when we called a starter of Cenn Popty a Thost* and main course of Cyw Iar Mewn Saws Llandrillo* as well as salads, roasts and fish. The dining room is comfortable enough.

For children under 5 there is no accommodation charge and for 5s to 14s it's only £1. Children are offered a special menu or half portions.

At the top of the stairs there is a ladies' powder room and bathroom where a baby can be fed and changed in comfort.

27 rooms, 2 family Moderate
Closed at Christmas Lunch 12.15-2pm Dinner 7-8pm – £8.50
Access/AmEx/Barclaycard/Diners P – own car park

*Leeks on toast glazed with cheese, chicken breasts with mushrooms and Welsh liqueur sauce.

Magham Down, Nr Hailsham, East Sussex map 1

R *WALDERNHEATH COUNTRY RESTAURANT –*
phone 840 143

Just outside Hailsham at Magham Down on the A271 to
Herstmonceaux.

An attractive restaurant in a 15th century brick and tile country
house in a large lawned garden with a swing and a patio.

The set menus offer a good choice of food – home-made soup,
patés, smoked fish, melon, avocado to start; plenty of roast and
grilled meat and fish – beef, pork, lamb, capon, duck, steak,
plaice, sole, and some rich puddings – chocolate walnut fudge,
meringue glacé chantilly, fresh fruit pies and crumbles, and the
like. As well as the main menus there are snacks, eg club
sandwiches, patés, pancakes, etc. 'Any child may choose any
sized portion, and we'll charge accordingly' say the owners who
have two children of their own.

The ladies' lavatory is spacious and mothers can change their
babies there.

Closed – Monday/Sunday dinner/Christmas and New Year/2
weeks end Oct Lunch 12-2pm – £4.50 2-course, £5.25 3-course
Dinner 7-9pm – £6.75 2-course, £8.25 3-course Licensed
Access/AmEx/Barclaycard/Diners P – own car park

Maldon, Essex map 1

H *BLUE BOAR HOTEL* (THF), Silver Street – phone 52681

In the centre of the town.

Is there a reason for visiting Maldon? We are told it is a 'yachting
centre'. Well, if you are a sailor, you might stay at this ancient
inn part of which dates from the 14th century, although it has a
rather unremarkable brick façade. But there are lovely
half-timbered rooms and an oak-panelled restaurant.

Accommodation is free for children up to 5 sharing with their
parents, and £1 from 5 to 14. A special children's menu and half
portions are available in the restaurant.

26 rooms, 4 family Moderate Open all year
Lunch 12.30-2.15pm – £7.50
Dinner 7-9.30pm – £7.50 Ale – Adnams
Access/AmEx/Barclaycard/Diners P – own car park

Malmesbury, Wilts
map 2

H   *OLD BELL HOTEL,* Abbey Row – phone 2344

By the Abbey.

This is one of the oldest towns in England (its charter dates back to 930), and a very attractive one. The hotel is a lovely wisteria-clad Cotswold stone building in the lee of the famous Norman Abbey. It is built on the site of a 12th century castle which may have bequeathed one of its walls to the inn. The very pretty garden at the back is quiet and sheltered.

No charge is made for cots and up to 12 years of age the charge for children sharing with parents is £5 including breakfast. The restaurant will serve half portions for children and the cooking is mostly British traditional. You might lunch on smoked trout fillets or whitebait followed by a roast or chicken and cider casserole; or dine on cucumber and cream cheese mousse, roast duck, best end of lamb or local trout.

19 rooms, 1 suite   Moderate   Closed Christmas Day to 1st Mon in Jan   Lunch 12.30-2pm – £6.50 Dinner 7.30-9.30pm – £9   Ale – Wadworth's Access/AmEx/Barclaycard/Diners   P – own car park

Marlborough, Wilts
map 2

An attractive town with a broad main street (you can park in the middle) with many Georgian houses and a couple of fine churches. There was a great fire here in the mid-17th century and not much survived. It's a good centre for tourists; Savernake Forest is close and there are many Roman sites nearby.

H   *CASTLE AND BALL* (THF), High Street – phone 52002

In the main street.

A very distinctive 17th century coaching inn with a colonnade with pillars supporting the two tile-fronted upper storeys. Pepys described the building as 'penthouses supported by pillars' when he visited in the 1660s.

There are plenty of bar snacks including salads and hot dishes such as lamb chops, plaice and chips, veal and rice, etc, at around £2. There are set lunches and dinners with a reasonable choice of British food. Children can choose from their own special menu or half portions from the main menu. Their accommodation is free up to 5 years, and from 5 to 14 costs £1.

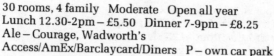

30 rooms, 4 family   Moderate   Open all year
Lunch 12.30-2pm – £5.50   Dinner 7-9pm – £8.25
Ale – Courage, Wadworth's
Access/AmEx/Barclaycard/Diners   P – own car park

R   **POLLY,** High Street – phone 52146

In the main street opposite the Castle and Ball.

A traditional English tea shop with food available all day. Large breakfasts are available until 11.30 and then lunch takes over and in between times there is a great variety of home-made cakes, scones, gateaux and other snacks. During the lunchtime period, which is fairly flexible, you can choose from amongst the cold buffet with a good array of salads and such dishes as chicken in mustard mayonnaise, stuffed fillets of sole, fricadelles of veal and ham in a tomato and herb sauce, etc – at between £2 and £3. There is always smoked local trout, and gammon, and some hot dishes of the day at about £3.50, for example moussaka, steak and mushroom pie, liver with avocado and so on.

The ladies' lavatory is too small to cope with feeding and changing a baby, but the owner will find somewhere for you if you ask.

Open 8.30am-6pm Mon-Fri (7pm at weekends)   Licensed
Access/AmEx/Barclaycard/Diners   P — in the main street

Marlow, Bucks   map 1

H   **COMPLEAT ANGLER HOTEL** (THF) – phone 4444

By Marlow Bridge.

A fine and very expensive hotel in an unrivalled position on the banks of the Thames in a town famed for its Regatta and immortalised by Izaak Walton. You can sit and drink and dream on a lovely terrace and lawn by the river; or be even more tranquil in the back garden. There is a hard tennis court tucked away here.

It does not quite fit the THF mould: for instance there is no children's menu, but the restaurant will provide children's dishes to order at lunchtime. Children under 6 are not accepted in the dining room in the evening – just as well at around £25 per head. However, children under 5 are accommodated free and there is the usual THF nominal charge of £1 for children up to 14.

A grand place to stop, briefly, if you are feeling flush.

42 rooms, 4 family, 4 sets adjoining   Expensive
Open all year   Lunch 12.30-2.30pm – £25 alc
Dinner 7.30-10pm – £25 alc
Access/AmEx/Barclaycard/ Diners   P – own car park

Matlock Bath, Derbys

map 3

H   *NEW BATH HOTEL* (THF), New Bath Road – phone Matlock
3275

On the A6, south of Matlock.

This is a very odd-looking hotel: There is a pleasant enough
Georgian building; then a rather forbidding Victorian block
(was it built for Bradley Hardacre?); and to complete it a rather
dire modern block.

But it has one of the biggest and best outdoor pools that we have
seen and it is naturally heated from a thermal spring beneath
the hotel. It is set in a spacious and pretty garden. The original
thermal plunge bath is still in use in its rather cavernous
vaulted room. There is a hard tennis court too.

Accommodation is free for children up to 5 and costs £1 for
children from 5 to 14. They have their own menu and can order
half portions as well.

We included the hotel partly because of its superb swimming
pool and also because the area is popular for walkers and
amateur archeologists.

56 rooms, 21 family   Moderate   Open all year
Lunch 12.30-2pm – £6.50   Dinner 7-9.30pm – £8.50
Access/AmEx/Barclaycard/Diners   P – own car park

Mawgan Porth, Cornwall

map 2

H   *BEDRUTHAN STEPS HOTEL* – phone St Mawgan 555

On the B3276 – the main coast road from Newquay to Padstow.

The hotel takes its name from the array of huge rocks by the
beach – said to be the stepping stones of the legendary giant,
Bedruthan.

Very well designed modern hotel overlooking Mawgan Porth
Bay. There are excellent facilities for adults including two
squash courts, indoor and outdoor heated swimming pools,
tennis courts, a cinema, etc. The facilities for children are
outstanding: as well as the swimming pools there are two
adventure playgrounds, children's films, a special dining room

for the under-6s, etc. To take the children off your hands there is a crèche every morning except Sundays and the Cherokee Club for 6 to 13 year olds. The Cherokees are kept well occupied with all day outings, their own disco, a special dinner and their own bar. Although a bit 'holiday camp', highly recommended for parents with very small children.

Children under 2 sharing their parents' room are charged one-third of the single rate; and so on up to 12 years old when they pay 75% of the single rate.

56 rooms, all family   Cheap   Closed Dec-Feb
No credit cards accepted   P – own car park

Meeth, Devon
map 2

P   **NEW INN**

On the A386.

A pretty thatched pub dating back to the 16th century. There's a small garden with tables and chairs and a separate dining room.

A large pool room serves as the children's room and hot and cold food is served every day.

Okay for a quick drink.

Ale – Flowers, Hancocks, Ushers   P – own car park

Melling, Lancs
map 3

H P R   **MELLING HALL HOTEL** – phone Hornby 21298

On the A683 north of Lancaster.

A really delightful 17th century manor house built on classical lines in stone in the pretty Lune Valley. It is handily placed for holidays in the Lake District or the Yorkshire Dales. The hotel has a marvellous entrance hall with a fine staircase and a minstrel's gallery, and plenty of space for children to park themselves. There is a pool room with a juke box and space invader machines off the main bar, but you might prefer the coffee lounge off the hall. There is a big grassy garden with a swing.

Bar meals are available from 11am to 2.30pm, and there is a good choice – sandwiches at up to £1, steak for around £4, and Lancashire hot pot, chilli con carne, pizzas, plaice, etc, at under £2. The evening menu offers paté, smoked salmon and mackerel, trout, Lune salmon and Windermere charr as well as

161

chicken and steaks. Children's portions can be ordered and extra beds cost £4 per night with no charge for cots.

13 rooms (most will take extra beds) Cheap Open all year
Lunch 11-2.30pm Dinner 7-9.30pm – £9 alc
Ale – Hartley, Tetley, Yates & Jackson (summer only)
Access/AmEx/Barclaycard P – own car park

Midhurst, West Sussex   map 1

H R **SPREAD EAGLE HOTEL** (Best Western), South Street – phone 2211

In the middle of the village.

This is a very pretty country town, its streets lined with Tudor and Georgian houses and with many tourist attractions nearby; the ruins of Cowdray Castle are on the edge of the town and Petworth House is not far.

The hotel is comprised of two buildings – a superb 15th century half-timbered part with an overhanging second storey and a 17th century Jacobean hall of brick and stone. The interior is delightful with its oak beams and open fireplaces and outside is a small garden and patio.

The charge for children sharing a room with their parents is £7.

Traditional English food is served in the restaurant where half portions are available for children. You can eat poached trout, leg of lamb with wild garlic sauce, poussin in lemon and artichoke sauce, sirloin of beef, salmon in Champagne sauce, etc. Lunchtime snacks are available too – salads, a dish of the day, sandwiches or ploughman's at prices up to around £2.

27 rooms, 4 family Moderate Open all year
Lunch 12.30-2.15pm – £6.25 Dinner 7.30-9.15pm – £8.75
Ale – Ballard, Hall & Woodhouse
Access/AmEx/Barclaycard/Diners P – own car park

Milton Damerel, Nr Holsworthy, Devon   map 2

H P **WOODFORD BRIDGE HOTEL** – phone 481

On the A388.

A superb thatched and white-washed 15th century building with some additions which fit in perfectly with the original. There are twenty acres of gardens in which is a separate development of very smart suites. The whole effect is stunning and a great find whether to stay or just to stop for a drink.

Also in the grounds is an excellent indoor swimming pool, two squash courts, a skittle alley and an all-weather tennis court. Approximately seven miles of trout fishing on the River Torridge is available to guests.

Babies up to 2 are accommodated free and children from 2 to 10 are charged at 75% of the single rate.

The pub has an extensive menu all week and a children's room. The restaurant has a short, pleasing menu which changes each day and always include a 'Taste of England' dish.

16 rooms, 2 family   Moderate   Open all year
Bar lunch   Dinner 7-8.30pm – £10   Ale – Swimbridge
No credit cards accepted   P – own car park

Milton Street, Nr Alfriston, East Sussex   map 1

P   *SUSSEX OX*

Watch out, it is easy to miss: take the road to Alfriston off the A27. Turn left on the road to Litlington and left again to Milton Street.

A secluded country pub set in lovely Sussex countryside near the picture postcard village of Alfriston.

It has a pleasant family room and a splendid large garden with climbing frames, a toy house, etc.

The landlord serves hot and cold food at lunchtimes from Monday to Friday and every evening. Apart from sandwiches and ploughman's, you can choose from the dishes of the day such as steak and kidney pie, risotto, hot pot at around £2 or a sirloin steak at around £4. Saturday and Sunday lunchtimes bring a cold buffet.

Ale – Harvey's   P – own car park

Mitchell, Nr Truro, Cornwall   map 2

P   *PLUME OF FEATHERS*

On the A30.

A pleasant white, stone-walled pub with a friendly and cosy atmosphere. John Wesley stayed here in 1771. The children's room is at the side. There is a garden with tables, chairs and a see-saw.

Pub meals are always available and include the usual

ploughman's, rolls and salads; chicken and chips; scampi, plaice, cod and chips; and cold meats and salads. Prices do not go beyond £3.

Ale – Devenish   P – own car park

Monksilver, Somerset   map 2

P   *NOTLEY ARMS*

On the B3188.

A large attractive white-painted pub in a small village. It is spacious, comfortable and well-furnished. The children's room, though, with piano and space invaders, was a mite scruffy when we last saw it during the winter. The skittle alley can also be used by children.

There is a large garden where barbecues are held in summer and an excellent range of food is offered all week. There are no chips served in this pub (hurrah!) but lots of salads, jacket potatoes with various toppings, 'munchers' – French bread with hot beef or sausages, chicken and mushroom pies, curries, trout, etc.

Ale – Usher's   P – own car park

Moonfleet, Nr Weymouth, Dorset   map 2

H   *MOONFLEET MANOR* – phone Weymouth 786 948

Off the B3157, north of Weymouth.

Of 16th century origin and restored in 1896 this elegant building has associations with the children's adventure classic Moonfleet. Inside is a heated swimming pool and children's pool, three squash courts and a spacious cellar games room with pool, table football, space invader machines. Outside a BMX bikes track, adventure playground and hard tennis court.

Children sharing with 2 adults are charged at £2.50 under 6, £4 to 12 years and £5 over 12. Baby-sitting can be arranged.

A 'businessmen's lunch' at £1.75 is served Monday to Friday and on Sunday during the summer there is a barbecue from 12.30-1.30. Bar snacks are also available and a special children's menu.

40 rooms, 10 family   Moderate   Open all year
Dinner 7-9pm – £6.50   Ale – Hall & Woodhouse
AmEx/Diners   P – own car park

Moreton-in-Marsh, Glos

map 2

H   **WHITE HART ROYAL HOTEL** (THF), High Street – phone
    50731

In the middle of the town.

The hotel is in a street which is part of the Roman Fosse Way. It
is a very attractive building partly Cotswold stone and partly
timbered and dates from the 16th century. There is a patio or
courtyard where you can sit on summer days and a tea room
here which is open during the summer from 9am to 6pm. Apart
from tea, coffee and snacks, there is a buffet lunch also served in
the hotel.

The restaurant's evening meals are English in tone and are
devised to renew you after a hard day's tourist activity in the
beautiful Cotswolds; shirred eggs, baked duck, leg of lamb, etc.
There is a children's menu and baby food too can be supplied.

Accommodation for children sharing with parents is free to the
age of 5 and £1 from 5-14.

27 rooms, 2 family   Moderate   Open all year
Lunch 12-2pm   Dinner 7-9.30pm – £7.95
Access/AmEx/Barclaycard/Diners   P – own car park

Moretonhampstead, Devon

map 2

H   **MANOR HOUSE HOTEL** – phone 355

On the B3212 west of Moretonhampstead.

A stately baronial mansion in the tradition of hotels once
owned by British Rail. The trout-filled River Bovey flows
through the grounds and criss-crosses the first half of the
excellent eighteen-hole golf course. There are two tennis courts
and one squash court. Fishing is available for guests.

There's a wide selection of bar snacks and brunches –
sandwiches of all sorts, a good array of savoury dishes such as
Devon beef stew with vegetables and dough balls, chicken and
cheese omelette with mornay sauce, Welsh rarebit with chutney
and bacon and fisherman's platter of smoked mackerel,
sardines and mussels. At dinner there are offerings like chicken
liver omelette, grilled half spring chicken, roast beef or a choice
of cold meats and salads.

A bed for a child is £10 and a cot £2.

68 rooms, 17 family   Moderate   Open all year

Lunch 12-2.30pm – bar lunches   Dinner 7.30-9pm – £9.75
Access/AmEx/Barclaycard/Diners   P – own car park

Mudeford, Nr Christchurch, Dorset map 2

H   *AVONMOUTH HOTEL* (THF) – phone Christchurch 483 434

On the B3055, east of Christchurch.

*A white-painted and typical seaside hotel in lawned gardens
with shady trees. In the gardens are croquet lawn, adventure
playground, paddling pool and a good heated swimming pool
with poolside patio and snack bar. The adventure playground
has a slide, climbing frames and swing. From the rear garden is
a good view of the placid Christchurch harbour full of small
craft.*

*Inside is a sizeable games room with table tennis, snooker and
table football. During the summer there is a supervised crèche
open from 9.30 to 12.30, Monday to Friday.*

*Fourteen of the family rooms are in garden bungalows.
Accommodation for children sharing is free up to 5 years and a
nominal charge of £1 is made from 5 to 14.*

*Children's high teas and barbecues are served and a special
children's menu and half portions are available in the
restaurant.*

*Not a restful hotel – definitely for families – but the facilities are
good and of course there's the crèche.*

41 rooms, 25 family   Expensive   Open all year
Buffet lunch 12.30-2pm – £3.50   Dinner 7-8.45pm – £8.25
Access/AmEx/Barclaycard/Diners   P – own car park

Mullion, Cornwall map 2

H   *POLURRIAN HOTEL*, Polurrian Cove – phone 240 421

---

*Follow your nose through Mullion, past the cricket ground – you
may have to ask.*

*The hotel has a stunning view over Polurrian Cove and is set in
twelve acres of gardens. There is a heated outdoor swimming
pool, tennis court, badminton court, two squash courts and
superbly equipped play area (which is fenced in for parents'
peace of mind). The ballroom doubles as an indoor playroom*

pool, table tennis, space invaders, and there are plenty of other indoor games for children. High teas are provided from 5.30-6pm. Below the hotel is a superb private beach. One of those hotels which really has everything parents need for a relaxing break.

Children are accommodated free up to the age of 15.

45 rooms, 18 family   Expensive   Closed November-March 31st
Access/Barclaycard   P – plenty

P   *OLD INN*

A visit to the Old Inn entails a short detour off the A3083 – worthwhile in an area very short of good family pubs.

It has a cosy interior and a bright children's room with caged birds, games, magazines, etc. There is a small patio with picnic benches at the front.

The friendly landlord offers hot and cold food all week – sandwiches, cottage pie, spaghetti, jacket potatoes with various fillings, steak, chicken and scampi with chips, etc. Most of the meals are under £2 and a steak is under £4.

Ale – Devenish   P – own car park

Nailsworth, Glos   map 2

P   *WEIGHBRIDGE INN, Avening Road*

On the Avening/Tetbury road B4014, and not far from Amberley and Minchinhampton Common.

This is a fine pub in every way: a very pretty white building with an interior of rough stone walls and good wooden furniture. There are two rooms where children may go: a small one off the bar with a fireplace; and upstairs a superb high-ceilinged beamed room with an array of polished oak tables and chairs. It leads out to a small grassy garden with a swing and a small patio with a few tables.

There is a wide choice of food available at all times including sandwiches and salads, steak and mushroom pie – delicious with its freshly-baked pastry and under £2, cauliflower cheese, two-in-one-pie, etc – all wonderful value.

There is also a resident and very talkative parrot.

Ale – Wadworth's, Simpkiss   P – own car park

Nairn, Highland   map 6

These two hotels, by the Moray Firth, are related and guests of one may use the facilities of the other. They are both signposted off the A96 on the west side of Nairn.

H   ***GOLF VIEW HOTEL,*** Seabank Road – phone 52301

This big stone hotel has an excellent outdoor heated pool and close by it a play area with a climbing frame and a trampoline. These are in the gardens which sweep down to a large sandy beach by the Moray Firth. There are also two tennis courts and a putting green. Indoors is a large, rather gaunt, white-washed games room with table tennis, pool, table football, space invaders and lots of toys.

Accommodation is free for children up to 5 years; up to 12 it costs £8 per day (dinner, bed and breakfast). High teas are served to residents' children at 5.30 and half portions can be served in the restaurant.

Close to Culloden and Cawdor Castle where perhaps still 'the Thane of Cawdor lives a prosperous gentleman'.

55 rooms, 18 family, 4 suites   Moderate   Open all year
Lunch 12-2pm – £4.95   Dinner 7-9.15pm – £9.50
Access/AmEx/Barclaycard/Diners   P – own car park

H   ***NEWTON HOTEL*** – phone 53144

One of those marvellous Scottish baronial houses that has not had its interior ruined. The pine panelling, period furniture and ornate ceilings are in keeping with its exterior. There are extensive gardens all around (the moat is now empty) with wooded areas, putting green, two tennis courts, croquet, a fountain and lawns. In the separate annexe, beautifully converted from the stables and granary, is a sauna, solarium and a mini-gym. Close by are nine-hole and eighteen-hole golf courses and all the facilities of the Golf View Hotel are also available.

Accommodation is free for children up to 5, from 6 to 12 years it costs £8 and from 13 to 15 years it costs 50% of the adult rate. High teas can be served to residents' children – pretty much what they want when they want it. Half portions are also available in the restaurant.

44 rooms, 3 suites and 1 triple   Moderate   Closed Oct-Apr
Lunch 12.30-2pm – £4.95   Dinner 7-9.30pm – £10.50
Access/AmEx/Barclaycard/Diners   P – own car park

Nantwich, Cheshire

map 3

R   *CHURCHE'S MANSION*, Hospital Street – phone 625 933

On the east side of the town on the A52.

A magnificent oak framed mansion which was built in 1577 for Richard Churche, a wealthy landowner. It is built in the traditional Elizabethan black and white style and the interior, lovingly restored, is all oak panelling, heavy beams and fine fireplaces. The furniture, also oak and mainly 16th and 17th century adds to the whole pleasureable effect, and even the high chair is oaken and venerable. At the back there is a very pretty lawned garden.

It is open most of the day, since coffee is served from about 10am and during the summer season afternoons you can look around the building and have a cup of tea.

The menus are comprehensive. At a typical lunch you can choose from roast lamb, chicken, plaice, blanquette of veal, Lancashire hot pot, braised ox tails, rabbit casserole, etc. Dinner might tempt you with sliced smoked lamb, scallop au gratin, wild duck, Holyhead scallops, calves sweetbreads, etc. Reduced portions are available for children.

Sorry – nowhere to change or feed a baby.

Closed Sun evenings.   Christmas & New Year.
Lunch 12-2pm – £4.95   Dinner 7-8.30pm – £9.95   Licensed
No credit cards accepted   P – own car park

Near Sawrey, Cumbria

map 5

P   *TOWER BANK ARMS*

On the B5285.

An ordinary looking country pub, with a small patio with bench tables, very close to Lake Windermere and in lovely surroundings with a good view of Claife Heights. It is owned by the National Trust and backs on to the farm which was once Beatrix Potter's home and now has a museum. She wrote of Sawrey: 'It is as nearly perfect a little place as I ever lived in.'

Inside is a nice-looking bar with flagged floors, wooden pews and an old oven range. The dining room where children can go is slightly scruffy but adequate enough.

Basic pub food – quiche, meat salads, paté – is available every day with children's portions at £1.

Ale – Hartley, Matthew Brown   P – own car park

Needingworth, Nr St Ives, Cambs   map 1

P   *PIKE AND EEL HOTEL*

Go into the village and look for the sign to the pub on the main street.

A big and attractive stone pub, which is partly Tudor, by the River Ouse. It was once owned by Ramsey Abbey and was the site of an old chain ferry. There is a big terrace with long lawns which sweep down to the river's edge with its presiding willow trees and small boats. It also has a large tract of lawned garden with lovely trees to the side and rear.

Inside there is a spacious bar (and a separate restaurant) and two rooms which children can use. Both are heavily beamed and low ceilinged in the original Tudor part of the inn and very comfortably furnished.

A range of bar food – chicken and chips, salads, etc – is available seven days a week.

Ale – Bass, Greene King   P – lots

Nevern, Dyfed   map 2

P   *TREWERN ARMS*

On the B4582 off the A487 east of Fishguard.

An old stone pub which straggles rather untidily, alongside a brisk stream, in the open countryside. Inside there are several rooms, mostly stone-flagged, and the main bar with beams and big open fireplace is rather attractive.

Children may frequent a pool room with several space invader machines, or a long, large dining area, somewhat cafeteria-like with its formica tables and benches. There you can eat a good range of pub meals at good prices: sausages and chips at £1, burgers, chicken, cod and chips at around £1.50; and crab salad at £2.50. Children's portions are available at under £1.

The restaurant is really attractive, easily the nicest room in the pub, but unfortunately had no high chairs. The cheery owner said she would pop out and get one 'tomorrow' – we'll check next year. There is also a grassy garden and a patio. It's a useful pub to know about in an area with very little choice at present.

Ale – Flowers   P – own car park

170

Newbury, Berkshire map 1

H   *CHEQUERS HOTEL* (THF), Oxford Street – phone 43666

In the centre of the town.

Once a posting house between London and Bath, this is an archetypal THF town hotel – the façade is ordinary but the hotel is extended well behind and the public rooms are smart and attractive.

The snack lunch menu has salads and quiche and dishes of the day at about £2; and the restaurant primarily English dishes.

Accommodation is free for children up to 5 sharing with their parents, and from 5-14 a charge of £1 is made. The restaurant offers a special menu and half portions for children.

69 rooms, 4 family   Moderate   Open all year
Lunch 12.30-2.15pm – £6.50   Dinner 7-9.30pm – £7.50
Ale – Courage, Andover, Bourne Valley
Access/AmEx/Barclaycard/Diners   P – own car park

H   *ELCOT PARK COUNTRY HOUSE HOTEL* (Best Western) – phone Kintbury 58100

About five miles from Newbury on the A4 to Hungerford. Watch carefully for a very small and badly placed sign – you have no advance warning of a turn off a fast and busy road.

A grand mansion built in 1678 standing in sixteen acres of parkland and with sweeping views over the Berkshire countryside. There is a hard tennis court.

There is free accommodation for children aged 12 and under sharing with their parents. The restaurant serves reduced portions for children. Buffet lunches are only available when there are business meetings at the hotel – this seems to be on most weekdays.

This is an alternative to the Chequers and is in a lovely spot. It affords some peace and quiet within its pretty gardens. Perhaps the inside needs some smartening up.

22 rooms, 5 family   Moderate   Open all year
Buffet lunches at times   Dinner 7.30-9.45pm – £9.95
Access/AmEx/Barclaycard/Diners   P – own car park

Newby Bridge, Cumbria map 3

H P R   *SWAN HOTEL* (Inter) – phone 31681

Right by the Bridge itself (built in 1832 for £90).

In a superb situation at the end of Lake Windermere, the hotel has its own marina, a stretch of river for trout and salmon fishing and is close to the Newby Bridge steam railway. Outside is a terrace overlooking the river and a long lawned garden runs along the stretch of the marina at the end of which is a children's play area.

There are three bars one of which, the Cygnet Bar, serves snacks from 10am to 5pm with a soup and hot dish of the day served between 12 and 2pm. The Tithe Barn Restaurant – mock stone and beamed – is open for lunch on Sundays only and serves dinners each evening with a good choice of plainish fish and meat dishes.

A cot in your room will cost £2.50 and the charge for children up to 12 is £6.50. Dinner for a child is £6 or they can have whatever they want served to them in their rooms.

This hotel is just on the right side of naff – but they offer good service in lovely surroundings.

36 rooms, 12 family   Moderate   Open all year
Bar snacks 10am-5pm from 60p
Lunch (Sundays only) 12.30-1.45pm   Dinner 7-9pm – £9
Ale – Bass   Access/AmEx/Barclaycard/Diners (but not in bars)
P – own car park

Newport, Gwent   map 2

R   ***THE CELTIC MANOR HOTEL*** – phone 413 000

Leave the M4 at junction 24 and look for 'hotels' sign.

The Celtic Manor looks good from the M4, standing high above the road with its huge conservatory, and even better close to – reminiscent of a French château if you ignore the modern bits. That conservatory is the Patio Restaurant, a beautiful place of glass, canopies and hanging baskets of plants where you can eat at reasonable prices looking out over hills and motorway (and Newport). The Patio serves sandwiches – plain and toasted – all day for 85p to £1.25. Its main courses at lunch and dinner are fish for about £4, poultry £4.50, charcoal grilled meats ranging from £3.75 to £8.35 (that for half a pound of Scottish fillet). The Hedley Restaurant is also beautiful, in a more sedate way, with ornate plaster ceilings and stained glass windows. Its menu is more sophisticated and more expensive: Fish – langoustine, shark steak, lobster; meat – suprême de volaille cordon vert, escalope de veau cordon bleu, coeur de filet Charlemagne, etc. You'd be lucky to get away with £14 à la carte. Jolly nice, but clearly the Patio is the place for parents with young children. Half portions are served to children at half price.

The manager who showed us round was born here in its hospital days. He assured us that help would be found for a mother who needed to attend to her infant. There are acres of grounds and some terraces.

The Cellar Bar, which serves a hot dish of the day and a cold table between 12 and 2.30, also serves real ale – Courage or Ansells.

Open all year   Lunch 12-2.30
Dinner – Patio 6.30-10.30pm,   Hedleys 7-10.30pm
Access/AmEx/Barclaycard/Diners   P – own car park

Newquay, Cornwall map 2

H   *TREVELGUE* – phone 2864

On the B3276 Newquay-Padstow road.

Related to the Bedruthan Steps Hotel at Mawgan Porth (q.v.). A spacious well-designed modern hotel with all you need for relaxation and entertainment (except total quiet). Under-6's can be abandoned to the crèche each morning Monday to Friday and over-6's are taken on various outings and offered Punch & Judy, magic shows, etc. Baby-sitting can be arranged with members of the staff. Slight air of holiday camp, but ideal for parents with very young children.

Indoor facilities include a swimming pool with separate children's pool, table tennis, pool, games machines and lots of space for the children to play. Outside is another swimming pool, tennis, squash, paddle tennis, jacuzzis, etc. Below the hotel are beautiful sandy beaches.

The hotel is well away from crowded, noisy Newquay and offers so much for the family that there's no need to venture into the town at all – unless you like that sort of thing.

Various reductions are available for children according to their age.

70 rooms, 42 family   Moderate   Closed Nov-Easter
No credit cards accepted   P – own car park

Newtown, Powys map 3

H R   *BEAR HOTEL* (Eagle) – phone 26964

In the town centre.

An ordinary, but comfortable, town hotel with a nice front and a

173

ratty extension. It makes an effort to look after families and is ideal for a stop-over or as a touring base.

At lunchtime you can eat in the bar, grill room or restaurant. The bar offers sandwiches, baked potatoes, and burgers at up to £1.50, and fish, scampi, chicken, and steak for £2 to £4. The grill room lunchtime à la carte menu offers a good selection of starters (smoked trout, snails, paté, garlic mushrooms) and fish (including Severn trout) and meat and poultry. Some dishes on the restaurant table d'hôte menu when we visited were beef with red pepper sauce, chicken chasseur, pork marsala. Evening meals are taken in the restaurant which offers dishes such as garlic mushrooms, smoked trout Clywedog, Anglesey eggs, Severn salmon, steaks, Welsh salted duck, etc.

Accommodation is free for children up to the age of 16 sharing with parents. Children can have a free plate (ie eat from their parents' plates), half portions or choose from the 'Menu for Young People'. This menu includes puréed vegetables and boiled egg and soldiers for babies as well as the usual fish fingers, burgers, sausages, beans and chips.

37 rooms, 18 family   Cheap   Open all year
Lunch 12.30-2pm – £5.50 (3 courses)
Dinner 7-9.30pm – £6.25   Ale – Sam Powell
Access/AmEx/Barclaycard/Diners   P – 60 spaces at rear of hotel

---

North Berwick, Lothian   map 5

H   ***THE MARINE HOTEL*** (THF) – phone 2406

Follow the sign from the main road.

We nearly didn't include this hotel – partly because of its forbidding exterior (they've done some ghastly things) and partly because of the unhelpful receptionist. The view over the West Links golf course and the facilities available changed our minds, however. It has two tennis courts, three squash courts, putting green, an outdoor heated swimming pool with a paddling pool. Indoors is a games room with table tennis and snooker and a playroom.

Accommodation is free for children aged up to 5 and a nominal £1 for children aged from 5 to 14. Children have their own menu or can choose half portions from the main menu.

85 rooms, 15 3-bedded, 6 4-bedded, 1 suite   Moderate   Open all year
Buffet lunches 12.30-2pm – £2.50   Dinner 7-9.30pm – £8
Access/AmEx/Barclaycard/Diners   P – own car park

Northallerton, N. Yorks map 5

P R   *THE GOLDEN LION* (THF), Market Place – phone 2404

In the centre of the town.

A typical town-centre Georgian coaching inn with a long regular white painted façade and square windows. It was one of the great coaching inns on the York to Scotland route. The pretty, well-decorated restaurant overlooks the market place which functions as exactly that, with a big street market every Wednesday and Saturday.

The bar lunches give wonderful value: shepherd's pie with three vegetables is a real bargain at £1.50; and there are meat salads at under £3, a daily hot dish at £2.50, etc. The restaurant also offers two-course set lunches or dinners, e.g. soup and rump steak at just under £8 as well as à la carte choice, mainly steaks, plaice, scampi, etc. They also have a table d'hôte menu at lunch and dinner.

We included this hotel as a restaurant because of the wide choice of meals available, and they include a children's menu and half portions from the adult menu. You could also stop here for a quick drink in one of the several lounges where you may sit with children.

Open all year   Lunch 12-2pm – £9.50 or bar meals
Dinner 7-9pm – £9.50   Ale – Tetley
Access/AmEx/Barclaycard/Diners   P – own car park

Northrepps, Norfolk map 4

R   *CHURCH BARN,* Church Road – phone Overstrand 588

Go into the village and watch out for a sign – the restaurant is, as you would expect, near the church.

A wonderful flint barn with rounded and eccentrically-framed windows. The interior is equally interesting, broken up as it is into three connected dining areas with French windows on to a small lawn at the side.

There is a very wide menu and the owner, who is also the chef, specialises in local fish and game. He also emphasises that his fresh vegetables are cooked individually for each order. As well as the restaurant menu there is a cold buffet and bar snacks at lunchtimes and half portions are available for children.

The 'Ladies' is spacious although without a table, but the owner will put a chair in there for mothers.

Open Tue-Sun   Lunch 12.15-2.15pm – £6
Dinner 7.15-10pm – £7.50 to £9.50   Ale – Adnams
Access/Barclaycard   P – limited

Norton Fitzwarren, Somerset   map 2

P   ***CROSS KEYS***

On the A361 at the junction with the A358.

A large and attractive stone pub with a roomy interior and separate eating area.

The children's room is small but inviting with bench tables, table football and a mechanical rocking horse, and overlooks a large grassy garden with swings and a climbing frame.

Hot and cold bar food is available all week except Sunday evening, and includes egg and chips, scampi, pasties, chicken and chips, salads, and there is always a dish of the day such as steak and kidney pie, lasagne, etc. You will not spend much more than £2 per dish.

Ale – Usher's   P – own car park

Norton St Philip, Somerset   map 2

P   ***GEORGE INN***

On the A366.

A magnificent old inn dating from the 14th century and possibly even earlier. Little has been done to spoil the oak-beamed and wood-panelled interior with its old tables and wooden settles. There is a small and appealing galleried courtyard in which to sit, the result of some modernisation which took place after a fire at about the turn of the 16th century.

The children's room is large with a good array of tables and chairs. Another children's room comes into play at the weekend when the 'Dungeon Bar', which once held a group of the rebel Duke of Monmouth's men prisoners, is open.

There is a wide range of hot and cold food available every day: turkey or ham and salad, sausages and pasties, smoked mackerel, plaice and chips and a hot dish of the day such as moussaka or lasagne. The prices go up to about £2.

Ale – Bass, Wadworth's   P – own car park

H   *BARNHAM BROOM HOTEL, GOLF & COUNTRY CLUB* (Best Western) – phone Barnham Broom 393

About eight miles west of Norwich between the B1108 and A47. In the depths of the country and very difficult to find; there is a complete absence of signposts. Why?

The hotel is composed of modern brick buildings which, with their deep tiled roofs, are reasonably attractive. The hotel has excellent facilities: an eighteen-hole golf course, three squash courts, three hard tennis courts, an outdoor heated swimming pool which is covered over for winter use. The Sports Bar, open from 9am to 11pm, has table tennis, a pool table and space invaders. It provides hot and cold snacks during that time. Trout fishing and horse riding can also be arranged by the hotel.

Accommodation is free for children up to 12, and the restaurant will serve half portions.

A good place to stay if you fancy a few days of low-key sporting relaxation in the Norfolk countryside.

34 rooms, 10 family   Moderate   Open all year
Lunch 12-2pm – £2.50   Dinner 7.30-9.30pm – £7.50
Ale – Adnam's, Tolly
Access/AmEx/Barclaycard/Diners   P – own car park

H   *SPROWSTON HALL* (Inter), Wroxham Road – phone 410 871

About three miles from the centre of Norwich on the A1151.

A recently renovated hotel in lovely spacious grounds with lots of trees and a terrace by the bar. The main building is quite pleasant – brick and Jacobean but has a slightly gloomy air. The extension is rather unfortunate but mercifully is not too big.

There are good facilities for adult guests' use albeit two miles away at the Oasis Leisure Centre: squash, tennis, a swimming pool, etc. Children are restricted to the hours of 10am to 12 noon from Monday to Saturday. (Sundays and bank holidays 10am to 4pm.) There is also a nine-hole, rather basic golf course adjoining the hotel but guests have to pay a green fee.

The accommodation charge for any baby or child sharing with parents is £8. Half portions are available in the restaurant for children.

22 rooms, 3 family   Moderate   Open all year
Lunch 12.30-2pm – £5.25   Dinner 7-9.30pm – £6.75
Access/AmEx/Barclaycard/Diners   P – own car park

Oakhill, Somerset

map 2

R **OAKHILL HOUSE**, Bath Road – phone 840 180

On the A367 north of Shepton Mallet.

The restaurant is in a fine classic two-storey stone Georgian country house approached through a large lawned and wooded garden and with a patio where one can eat during the summer months.

The three-course lunch is very good value at £5 and you will usually find a steak, a chicken dish and something like beef in Guinness amongst the main courses. The dinner menu ranges quite widely: moules marinières, hot mushrooms with bacon, celery and stilton crêpes or sweetbreads with a cream and mushroom sauce will start you off; and to follow there might be duck with cider and orange sauce, jugged hare, poached turbot, sole or chicken breasts in a creamy sauce. The children can have half portions and will be offered plainer food if required.

Mothers can tend their babies in the 'Ladies' which is spacious or in one of the upstairs rooms, if one is free.

Closed – Sunday dinner/26 December
Lunch 12-2pm – £5   Dinner 7-9.30pm – £10 alc   Licensed
Access/AmEx/Barclaycard/Diners   P – own car park

Oban, Strathclyde

map 5

R **SOROBA HOUSE HOTEL** – phone 62628

On the A85 about one mile south of Oban.

This white-painted hotel in which the owners clearly take great pride, stands above the road. It has lovely grounds where non-resident children are welcome to play and a putting green.

The bar and restaurant both have a children's menu with dishes all under £1. The bar menu offers plain hot meals – steak, gammon, chicken and various fish – for prices ranging from £1.80 to £4.25, and the restaurant offers a wider choice of dishes in the same price range, together with a 'business lunch' of two courses plus coffee at about £3. The dinner menu consists of good basic meat and fish dishes. Children can eat half portions from the adult menu.

The owners offer a private sitting room for breast-feeding and the whole place has a spotless look.

Open all year   Lunch 12-2.30pm   Dinner 7-11pm – £7.70
Licensed   Diners only   P – own car park

Oswestry, Shropshire map 3

H *WYNNSTAY HOTEL* (THF), Church Street – phone 655 261

In the town centre.

An elegant Georgian building in a pleasant market town. You can sit on the patio at the rear and, Beryl Cook-like, contemplate the bowlers on the 200-year-old green.

Accommodation is free for children up to 5 years with a nominal charge of £1 from 5 to 14. Special children's menu and half portions available in the restaurant. There are bar lunches only during the week – soups, paté, cold meat salad, lasagne and steak and kidney pie, at prices up to £2. The four-course dinner, if you can handle four courses, is quite good value at £7.50; the main courses might be a choice of sole fillets, post-roasted chicken or fisherman's pie.

31 rooms, 2 family Moderate Open all year
Bar lunch 12-2pm Dinner 7-9.30pm – £7.50
Access/AmEx/Barclaycard/Diners P – own car park

Ottery St Mary, Devon map 2

H *SALSTON HOTEL* (Best Western) – phone 2310

Off the B3180.

An impressive looking mansion surrounded by delightful countryside. There's plenty of garden, much of it lawned, and you can try your hand at croquet. There are some swings and a roundabout for children, plus a heated indoor swimming pool and two squash courts.

Accommodation is free for children, sharing their parents' room, up to the age of 15 and half portions are available in the two restaurants. The Cellar restaurant is open for lunch and dinner (à la carte only) and the hotel has the normal run of bar meals at lunchtime and a table d'hôte menu, also 'normal run', in the evenings.

32 rooms, 18 family Cheap Open all year
Bar lunch 12.30-1.45pm Dinner 7-8.30pm – £8.50
Cellar 7.30-10pm Ale – Eldridge Pope
Access/AmEx/Barclaycard/Diners P – own car park

Oundle, Northants map 4

H *TALBOT HOTEL* (Anchor) – phone 73621

In the centre of the town.

179

Fine example of a 16th century coaching inn built of stone. There is a courtyard with tables and chairs for clement days and on one side the bedrooms are formed from what might once have been a row of stone cottages. There is a quiet lawned garden at the back – if you can find it through a labrynth of twisting corridors.

Accommodation is free for children up to 2 years and thereafter up to 12 the charge is £6. There is a special children's menu and half portions are also available in the restaurant.

28 rooms, 1 family, 1 suite   Moderate   Open all year
Lunch 12-2pm – £5.50   Dinner 7-9.45pm – £7.95 or £10.50
Access/AmEx/Barclaycard/Diners   P – own car park

Oxenhope, West Yorks map 3

P **WAGGON & HORSES**

On the A6033.

This is a big busy pub – comfortable if a bit chintzy – with a room which families can use to the side of the bar. It is primarily intended as an eating area but is roomy and has a space invader machine. There is quite a range of food available including frogs' legs and rainbow trout; salads, curries, steak and kidney pie, chicken and chips, lasagne, chilli con carne and canneloni all at under £3; and steaks and mixed grills at just over £4.

There is a dearth of pubs to recommend in this area, and this is a useful one to know. We think it is in open countryside (foggy when we last visited it); we know it has a small grassy area with a swing; and for literary pilgrims it is very close to Haworth where the Bronte sisters wrote Jane Eyre and Wuthering Heights. You can have a 'Bronteburger' at the pub.

P – own car park

Oxford, Oxon map 1

H R **RANDOLPH HOTEL** (THF), Beaumont Street – phone 247 481

In the centre of the city.

A very stately hotel built in the middle of the 19th century in the characteristically florid, almost Gothic, style of that time. It has very large and well-proportioned public rooms and a particularly pretty restaurant with big windows on to Magdalen Street and the famous Ashmolean Museum.

Accommodation is free for children up to 5 with a nominal

charge of £1 for children up to 14. There is a special children's menu and half portions are available in the restaurant. Here the menu is standard British: at lunchtime there is a help-yourself cold buffet at £7.75 or a three-course menu (roast beef, sole, veal cutlets, etc) at £12.25. There are a number of different menus in the evening and the one at £12.25 offers such things as mousse of smokies and prawn, supreme of duck and salmon steak. You may think it wiser to patronise the Coffee Shop which is open from 10am to 7.30pm and serves a selection of snacks, grills, burgers and salads. It changes to a 'Fondue Bar' from 8pm to 11pm. Teas are also served from 3 o'clock to 5.30pm.

The hotel is central and obviously a good place to stay if you have a spot of spire-dreaming in mind. You could start just round the corner with Balliol College and try to discover why so many of our Prime Ministers went there.

109 rooms, 8 family   Expensive
Open all year   Lunch 12.30-2.15pm – £7.75 & £12.25
Dinner 7-10.15pm – £12.25
Access/AmEx/Barclaycard/Diners
P – limited, 100 yards away is a public car park

Paignton, Devon   map 2

H   *PALACE HOTEL* (THF), Esplanade Road – phone 555 121

On the sea front opposite the pier.

A handsome hotel in two acres of gardens and facing a large sandy beach. There are excellent facilities here for everyone. For children there is a playroom with table tennis, table football and space invaders. Along with the heated outdoor swimming pool is a paddling pool and a playground with a slide and a climbing frame.

A great bonus for parents is the nursery which is supervised from 9 to 5 every day during the summer season. You can then escape into the leisure centre to play squash, pump some iron in the gym, have a few sets of tennis on the outdoor hard court or simply doze over the latest health and fitness tome.

In any event you can work up an appetite for the comprehensive buffet lunch – paté, salads, hot dish of the day, scampi, salmon, chicken or lobster – the prices go up to £5 or so, except for the lobster (£12.50). The dinner menu offers a choice of such things as fillets of sole, loin of pork, braised silverside and so on.

Accommodation for children is free from 1-4 years and £1 from 5 to 14. Bar snacks only at lunchtimes, but a special children's menu and half portions are available.

54 rooms, 13 family   Expensive   Open all year
Lunch 12-2pm – £4 alc   Dinner 7-9pm – £7.50
Access/AmEx/Barclaycard/Diners   P – own car park

Pangbourne, Berks   map 1

H P R   *COPPER INN* – phone 2244

In the centre of the village, next to the church, on the A329 Reading-Oxford Road.

A roadside coaching inn which was built in the 19th century in this attractive village situated where the Thames is joined by the River Pang, a stretch of river which is always associated with The Wind in the Willows.

There is an elegant entrance hall with a welcoming log fire and for warmer days a large lawned garden at the rear.

Children sharing their parents' room are accommodated free up to the age of 12.

Bar lunches are served Monday to Saturday, from noon to 2.15, with a very wide range of plain, French bread and toasted sandwiches, salads, jacket potatoes and other hot dishes – all at reasonable prices. The restaurant, which overlooks the garden, serves lunch and dinner every day. It concentrates on English dishes cooked with fresh ingredients – sole, fillet of steak, duckling, beef casserole, etc. The kitchen will provide what you want for your children and charge accordingly.

21 rooms, 1 family   Moderate   Closed at Christmas
Lunch 12.30-2.15pm – £7   Dinner 7.30-9.30pm – £12 alc
Ale – Morland's, Brakspear's, Arkell's
Access/AmEx/Barclaycard/Diners   P – own car park

Parbold, Lancs   map 3

R   *WIGGIN TREE RESTAURANT,* Parbold Hill – phone 2318

On the A5209 west of junction 27 of the M6.

A bar and restaurant which is housed in a building which is partly 18th century stone cottage and partly modern brick – but it hangs together pretty well. Over the road you can gaze at stunning views of the countryside.

Bar meals are served at lunchtimes from Monday to Friday – soups, black pudding, burgers, jacket potatoes, steak and kidney pie, shepherd's pie, etc. – and nothing over £2. The full menu encompasses paté, prawn coquille, and a full range of meat and fish dishes: steaks, chicken, roast of the day, plaice, trout, gammon, duckling and scampi.

Children can have half portions of some of the dishes on the main menu, and also have their own menu of chicken, junior pizza, burgers, fish fingers, sausages, all with chips and beans and with ice cream to follow – at an all in price well under £2.

The 'Ladies' is spacious enough for a mother to attend to her baby.

Open all year   Bar lunch 12-2.15pm
Restaurant lunch Sat & Sun only, 12-2.15pm
Dinner 7-10pm – £10 alc (Sun 4.30-9pm)   Ale – Boddington's
Access/Barclaycard   P – own car park

Peebles, Borders   map 5

H   *PEEBLES HOTEL HYDRO* – phone 20602

On the main road.

A gigantic Victorian spa hotel with huge grounds and a multitude of facilities. They include an excellent fenced-in children's playground with swings, climbing frame and a roundabout, a mini-gym, two squash courts, three hard tennis courts, a volleyball court, a pitch and putt course, a putting green and a splendidly tiled, glass-roofed indoor heated pool.

There is a vast games room with three table tennis tables, billiards, table football and space invaders and in addition a bright and airy playroom which is supervised and has lots of toys. During the summer season the hotel has a number of full-time children's supervisors (nannies); and there are masses of events organised right through the day for children and for the adults. Plus dances and discotheques almost every night. So, this is very much a hotel for people who are interested in a busy and active holiday – a slight touch of the holiday camps but excellent facilities.

Children's accommodation costs from £1 to £7.25 depending on age. There is a children's menu at 6pm or dinner for a child is £4.50.

135 rooms, 29 family rooms of which 20 are family suites for 4
Moderate   Open all year   Lunch 12.45-2pm – £5.50
Dinner 7.30-9pm – £7.50   Ale – Greenmantle
Access/AmEx/Barclaycard   P – own car park

Pewsey, Wilts   map 2

R   *THE CLOSE* – phone 3226

Off the main street of the village.

At the end of a long tree-bedecked drive bordered by a stream stands this Edwardian house in a lovely large lawned garden.

Lunchtimes usually bring a shortish and tempting menu – spiced pork terrine or taramasalata followed by lamb baboushka or a prawn omelette with cheese sauce and a lovely pudding. The dinner menu, in turn, will offer a few interesting choices – crab mousse or herbed breast of duck terrine, stuffed loin of pork or guinea fowl. The menus are always changing according to what is seasonally available. The great feature on Sunday is the curry buffet – a choice of many and you can return for refills as often as you like.

Half portions are served for children, and there are no problems for mothers who wish to attend to babies: an upstairs room is offered and the 'Ladies' has plenty of room.

A lovely restaurant in the beautiful Vale of Pewsey, which features in many of Gerry Wright's evocative paintings of cricketers and cricket scenes.

Closed – Monday/Sunday dinner/31 December/1 January
Lunch 12.30-2pm – £8 alc   Dinner 7.30-9.30pm – £10 alc
Licensed   Access/AmEx/Barclaycard/Diners
P – own car park

Pimperne, Nr Blandford Forum, Dorset   map 2

H   *ANVIL – phone Blandford Forum 53431*

On the A354.

A marvellous 16th century thatched building (definitely a stray from a Hollywood movie about Olde England) two miles from Blandford Forum. It has a pretty garden at the front with lots of trees and flowers and a small lily pond. There are two tiled extensions, one of which (it houses a pool table next to the bar) is less successful than the other but neither is obtrusive. The owners are very helpful and attentive. Apart from lunch and dinner high teas are served and meals which appeal to children are always available. There is an outdoor heated swimming pool at the rear with a patio where barbecues are held in the summer. There's also an annexe here which houses four overflow rooms.

Accommodation for children costs £6 per night.

12 rooms, 2 family   Cheap   Open all year
Lunch 12-2.30pm – £7   Dinner 6.30-10pm – £7
Access/AmEx/Barclaycard/Diners   P – own car park

Pitlochry, Tayside

map 6

H   *ATHOLL PALACE HOTEL* (THF) – phone 2400

At the south-east end of the town on the main road the A9.

A massive and stately granite pile in the attractive town of Pitlochry. It stands in splendour atop a hill overlooking the town and is itself overlooked by gentle peaks. There is a wealth of facilities at this smart and impressively-managed hotel: its formal gardens sweep down to an outdoor heated circular pool; there are six tennis courts; par-three nine-hole golf course; a putting green; two nature trails; outdoor giant chess; a playroom for very young children with lots of toys and mini furniture and strategically placed near one of the bars; a large and airy games room with two table tennis tables, pool, space invaders and table hockey and this opens on to a side of the garden where there are swings and a slide.

Accommodation is free for children up to 5 and there is a nominal charge of £1 up to 14. There is a special menu for children and half portions can also be ordered from the restaurant menu.

83 rooms, 16 family   Moderate   Open all year
Hot and cold buffet 12.30-2pm – £3.50 alc
Dinner 6.30-9pm – £9
Access/AmEx/Barclaycard/Diners   P – own car park

Plumley, Cheshire

map 3

P R   *SMOKER INN* – phone Lower Peover 2405

On the A556 Chester-Nantwich road, about two and a half miles from junction 19 of the M6.

A very pretty white-painted thatched inn with a long history. It has an excellent – if a bit noisy – lawned garden with plenty of tables and chairs. Inside it's a smart, low-beamed, many-roomed pub.

There is a pretty children's room, with padded bench seats and tables, between the bar and the restaurant.

The restaurant itself serves the usual array of steak, chicken, avocado and prawn, roast beef, etc, and will divide one portion between two children and, at lunchtimes only, serve half portions to an individual child. The pub serves hot and cold food Monday to Saturday with sandwiches only on Sundays.

The 'Ladies' is very large — plenty of room for changing and feeding.

Restaurant closed Mon lunch   Lunch 12.30-2pm — £5.20
Dinner 7-10pm — £7.80   Ale — Robinson's
Access/AmEx/Barclaycard/Diners   P — own car park

Plush, Dorset
map 2

P   BRACE OF PHEASANTS

Signposted from the B3143 near Piddletrenthide — yes, Piddletrenthide.

A lovely low-slung thatched pub off the beaten track. There is a long beamed bar with an open fireplace at one end and an iron stove at the other. A room at the side is used mainly for meals but the children can be taken there. There is a pleasant, lawned garden at the back, and in the summer an alfresco steak bar comes into play.

Apart from that food is always available. There are various types of steak (fillet at just under £7), lamb chops (at around £4), cottage pie, lots of salads, plus sandwiches, soup and paté.

Ale — Usher's, Wadworth's   P — own car park

Pontargothi, Dyfed
map 2

P   CRESSELLY ARMS

On the A40 between Carmarthen and Llandeilo.

A smart black and white building nestling by the roadside. Inside there is a large bar with a beamed ceiling and a polished tiled floor, and to one side is a spacious room with bench seating where families may sit. It has the inevitable space invader machine (if they ever do invade they won't stand an 'earthly' against our trained-to-destroy youngsters).

There is good value bar food available all week from 12 to 2 and 7 to 10. Various ploughman's at around £1.50, sandwiches, salads, and plaice, chicken and scampi with chips at up to £2.50. There is also a dish of the day, normally a roast, and a good children's menu with dishes at under £1.

There is a separate restaurant, overlooking a fast-flowing stream, sadly without a high chair. For summer days there is a pretty lawned garden by the stream. The 'Ladies' is spacious and there is a handy shelf for changing a baby.

Ale — Bass   P — own car park

Porlock, Somerset

map 2

P   *SHIP INN*

On the A39.

At the foot of the precipitous Porlock Hill is this stone and white-washed thatched pub with flagged floors. It is in a very beautiful, very hilly tourist village overlooking Porlock Bay.

A separate small children's room is to the right of the main entrance and has tables and chairs, a piano, a fruit machine and space invaders. There is also a lounge where children may sit with their captive adults. There's a beer garden with plenty of seats.

A variety of hot and cold food is available all week with prices from 75p to £2 – pizzas, salads, fish mousse, patés, etc. The friendly landlady lets non-residents use the two bathrooms upstairs to attend to infants.

Ale — Courage   P – own car park

Portpatrick, Dumfries & Galloway

map 5

R   *OLD MILL HOUSE* – phone 358

On the A77 just as you come into Portpatrick.

We didn't want to include this restaurant owing to the difficulties of obtaining information. However we presume that the owners present a better face to customers than they do to researchers; and the rest of the staff were very pleasant. It's a wonderful spot if you're looking for a meal or snack – particularly in the warm weather as there's an outdoor pool with a shallow end roped off for children and non-swimmers. It's open all day, as is the restaurant, from 11am to 10pm. The restaurant serves half portions and both it and the bar have an under 12s menu of the fishfinger and pizza variety. The choice of food is very wide. There is a pub but we weren't allowed to view it.

The feeding and changing of babies might be a bit tricky and we didn't complete our tour of the place due to the aggro. The woman in the restaurant supposed 'they could do it in the restaurant' but somewhere more private could we suspect be found.

Closed end Oct to end Mar
Open 11am-10pm – £3.65 main course   Ale – Younger's
Barclaycard/Diners   P – own car park

Port William, Dumfries and Galloway map 5

H *CORSEMALZIE HOUSE HOTEL* – phone Mochrum 254

Not in Port William – on the B7005 west of Wigtown.

This 19th century country mansion (pronounced 'cawssmalyee' Sassenachs) offers a wonderful air of quiet within its forty acres of grounds, with spacious lawns, including a putting green, around the hotel. The hotel is a haven for fishermen with four and a half miles of salmon and trout fishing on the River Bladnoch and three miles on the Tarff. There is also trout fishing in the Malzie Burn and coarse fishing in the nearby lochs. Rough shooting and riding can also be arranged by the hotel.

Cots are charged at £1.50 and children's accommodation up to the age of 13 costs £2.50, with half portion meals at half price. High tea for children is served in the bar from 5-7.30pm.

The food is good, especially the local fish dishes, and the hotel is very useful to know in an area short of facilities for families.

15 rooms, 4 family   Cheap
Closed 8 weeks mid-Jan to mid-Mar
Lunch 12.30-2pm – £5.95   Dinner 7.30-9pm – £8.25
No credit cards accepted   P — own car park

Nr Postbridge, Devon map 2

P *WARREN HOUSE*

On the B3212 on Dartmoor.

It's a bit of a rough old pub – smoke-stained polystyrene between the beams, etc – but with a certain charm, and worth the stop anyway because of its magnificent situation mid-Dartmoor. There's a patio, but why use that when you have the spread of Dartmoor before you.

The children's room, though not pretty, has plenty of seating and tables, a couple of games machines and a rocking horse. It has a coffee bar which, during the morning, sells hot drinks and awful china horses.

Food – hot and cold seven days a week.

Ale – Ushers   Access/Barclaycard   P – own car park

Presteigne, Powys map 3

H R *RADNORSHIRE ARMS* (THF), High Street – phone 406

In the centre of town.

There isn't a great deal to do in this part of the world, but if you are in the area, this is a pleasant hotel at which to pause. It is a beautiful example of the Elizabethan style and was once the home of a favourite courtier of Elizabeth, Christopher Hatton (what did he find to do here?) There are some splendid rooms all with oak panelling and heavy beams. There is a pretty lawned garden with a rockery.

The bar snacks are inexpensive – bangers and mash for just over £1, a hot dish of the day for just over £2 (we had excellent chicken and ham pie with two vegetables), etc – and draught Bass is available. The dinner menu is basic roasts, pork chops, etc, and the special children's menu is available as are half portions from the main menu.

Accommodation is free for children up to 5 years and the charge is only £1 for children from 5 to 14 years.

16 rooms, 10 family   Moderate   Open all year
Lunch 12-2pm   Dinner 7.30-8.30pm – £7.50   Ale – Bass
Access/AmEx/Barclaycard/Diners   P – own car park

Redbourn, St Alban's, Herts   map 1

H   ***AUBREY PARK HOTEL*** (Best Western), Hemel Hempstead Road – phone 2105

On the B487 close to the pretty village of Redbourn.

This hotel is included because it is well placed to provide relief for M1 travellers (near Junction 9) and has several acres of lawns and woodland in which are set a heated outdoor swimming pool and a games room – also by the pool. The extensions are not too badly done in smallish blocks.

Accommodation is £5 for children up to the age of 12 sharing with their parents. There are two restaurants, both of which offer children's portions.

57 rooms, 1 family   Cheap   Open all year
Lunch 12.30-2pm – £10 alc   Dinner 7.30-9.45pm – £10 alc
Ostler's Room £5.50 for 2 courses
Access/AmEx/Barclaycard/Diners   P – own car park

Richmond, Surrey   map 1

R   ***REFECTORY, 6 Church Walk – phone 01-940 6264***   ¶¶

Consult your A-Z and park either in the Paradise Road multi-storey or in Sheen Road. Street parking is easy on a Sunday which is the favourite day for families.

The Refectory, right by the Parish Church, has a pretty and simple style which is immediately welcoming. The recipes are all English and freshly cooked with excellent and interesting meat and vegetable dishes and puddings. Some examples: starters – London Particular soup (pea souper – getit?), mushrooms in garlic mayonnaise, seafood flan, prawns in cream cheese; main courses – Shropshire fidget pie, fisherman's pie, Exmoor lamb casserole, honey orange chicken; puddings – treacle tart, apricot fool, coffee sponge tart. The wine list, too, is interesting with English and Antipodean wines.

Reduced prices are charged for children's portions and what they don't serve is cakes, lemonade, chips and the usual unhealthy muck that most restaurants serve for children. Two of the owners are young parents themselves and would 'always find a quiet corner' for a mother needing to tend her infant.

There's a little courtyard patio for warmer days. This is understandably a very popular restaurant and, for dinner, you must book. It is also open for coffee from 10am to noon from Tuesday to Sunday when scones, home-baked biscuits and the like are served.

The immediate appeal of this restaurant and the helpful and concerned outlook of its owners give it a place among the best three restaurants in the guide. The owners' attitude would have been delightful anywhere but was particularly refreshing in the context of the Greater London area, where the needs of parents with small children are generally ignored.

Closed Mondays, Christmas & New Year, 2 weeks in May and last week in Sept. Lunch Tue-Sat 12-2.15pm – £5 alc
Dinner Thur, Fri & Sat only £8.65 Licensed
No credit cards accepted P – street or public car park

Ripley, Surrey   map 1

P   *ANCHOR*, High Street

In the main street of the town.

A lovely ancient half-timbered coaching inn on what used to be the old A3. Inside are a number of charming interconnecting rooms with low-beamed ceilings. It used to be a favourite stopping place for cyclists at the end of the 19th century and the tradition continued. The pub is twenty-four miles or so from central London and made a good trip for cyclists before they all bought cars.

The children's room is fully in character and has tables, stools and benches. There is also an inner courtyard or patio where the children can play.

Snacks and meals are available at lunchtimes only, every day except Sunday and include ploughman's, sandwiches, steak and kidney and shepherd's pies, paté, plaice and chips, etc – all at under £2.

Ale – Ind Coope, Friary Meux   P – own car park

Rodborough Common, nr Stroud, Glos   map 2

H   *BEAR OF RODBOROUGH* (Anchor) – phone Amberley 3522

Off the A 46 south of Stroud.

Reminiscent of a small château the hotel is in Cotswold country near Minchinhampton Common and its golf course. It is a very odd looking building; the front is rather vulgar cream stucco with corner turrets which prompt the comparison with châteaux. At the rear the original Cotswold façade is beautifully intact and faces a delightful lawned and walled garden.

Cots are charged at £2.50 and children up to 12 are charged £6. The restaurant serves three set menus ranging from £8 through to £12 and half portions are available.

This is an alternative to the delightful Amberley Inn on the other side of the Common.

48 rooms, 2 sets of adjoining rooms   Moderate
Open all year   Lunch 12.30-2pm – £8-£12
Dinner 7.30-9.15pm – £8-£12   Ale – Bass, Courage
Access/AmEx/Barclaycard/Diners   P – own car park

Romsey, Hants   map 2

H   *WHITE HORSE HOTEL* (THF), Market Place – phone 512 431

In the centre of the town.

A very good looking hotel in an attractive town with a plethora of Georgian houses and an ancient abbey church. Nearby is the great Palladian house, Broadlands, which was re-designed in the 18th century by Capability Brown, was the home of the Palmerston family, and eventually of the Earl Mountbatten. The hotel itself acquired a Georgian façade although it is a great deal older as the very smart interior indicates. For example, there is a very fine oak-beamed lounge. The building rambles untidily but appealingly away at the back – part tiled, part old brick and part wooden and there is a patio here as well.

Children under 5 are accommodated free and from 5 to 14 there is a token charge of £1. The restaurant offers a special menu for children or half portions.

A good place for tourists to stop since it is more or less in the centre of the New Forest.

34 rooms, 7 family   Moderate   Open all year
Lunch 12.30-2pm – £5.75   Dinner 7-10pm – £8.95
Access/AmEx/Barclaycard/Diners   P – own car park

Rosedale Abbey, Nr Pickering, N. Yorks   map 4

R   *BLACKSMITHS ARMS HOTEL,* Hartoft End – phone Lastingham 331

Follow the Rosedale sign off the A170 at Wrelton – it's an unnumbered road.

A stone hotel in a moorland setting. The restaurant is made pretty by its delicate bamboo furniture. The table d'hôte menu offers a choice of plainish food and the à la carte offers a wider choice of steaks, duck, fish, beef, pork, etc. Chef will prepare for children pretty much what they want. There are also bar meals at about £2-3 – grilled fish and meat – as well as the usual soup and sandwiches. In the bar rather than half portions for their children, parents tend to be offered 'an extra plate', ie the children pinch ma's and pa's food or two children will share one meal between them.

There's a large grassy garden with picnic tables. The owner will provide some privacy and help should a baby need breastfeeding or changing.

Open all year   Lunch (bar only) 12-2pm   Restaurant opens for Sunday lunch 12-1.30pm – £5.50
Dinner 7-10pm – £7.50   Licensed
Barclaycard only   P – own car park

P   *WHITE HORSE FARM HOTEL*

Signposted off a minor road seven miles off the A170 north of Wrelton.

A stone hotel with stunning views over the North York Moors which on a fine day you can appreciate from the main bar and from the grass at the front where there are some bench tables – and ducks.

The children's room – which can be used up to 8.30pm – is the only ugly room in an otherwise cosy pub with stone walls, beams and all the right things hanging on the walls – horse tackle and brasses, animals' heads and the like.

A big range of bar snacks is available from 12 to 2pm Monday to

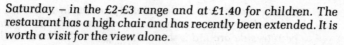

Saturday – in the £2-£3 range and at £1.40 for children. The restaurant has a high chair and has recently been extended. It is worth a visit for the view alone.

Ale – Tetley   P – own car park

Nr Ross-on-Wye, Hereford & Worcs map 2

H R   *PENGETHLEY HOTEL* (Best Western) – phone Harewood End 211

On the A49 four miles from Ross.

A fine looking Georgian country house, painted pale green and with shutttered windows in fifteen acres of lawns and gardens. You have wonderful views of the countryside, including an interesting array of animals in the fields below.

Inside is a pleasant bar, and a handsome library, a real one – its walls are lined with books, folks.

At the back of the coach house is the excellent and large heated outdoor swimming pool in a walled enclosure. Good news for fishermen too; the hotel has its own trout pond, and can also organise fishing on the Wye.

Children's accommodation is free up to 'a reasonable age' (around fourteen) and they are well looked after in the food line. There is a 'toddlers' menu' – eggs done in different ways – and a children's menu – mostly things and chips. Half portions can also be ordered from the main menu, and children below a certain age are not encouraged in the dining room at night – high teas are available. There are snacks at lunchtimes and an extensive restaurant menu which concentrates on local and fresh ingredients – vegetables from the garden whenever possible, Wye salmon, Herefordshire beef and lamb, venison, etc. There is a full vegetarian menu also – a facility rarely offered by hotels.

Altogether a peaceful and hospitable place in a beautiful part of the country.

20 rooms, 4 family   Expensive   Open all year
Lunch 12-2pm – £7.25 (3 courses)   Dinner 6.30-9pm – £12   Ale – Flowers
Access/AmEx/Barclaycard/Diners   P – own car park

H   *THE ROYAL HOTEL* (THF), Palace Pound – phone 65105

In the town centre, just off the A40.

A rather handsome white-painted building in a marvellous spot overlooking a swooping bend of the Wye river and the countryside around it. It's a fine sight, either from the lawned garden at the back of the hotel or from one of the comfortable hotel lounges and from here you might spot the great rugby player, Gerald Davies, training across the fields for a marathon – he lives nearby.

There is a fair range of snacks to be had at lunchtime (12-2pm) including hot pies, meat salads, fish and a roast of the day all at around £3, plus sandwiches, ploughman's, etc. In the restaurant there is plenty of fish available, eg fresh salmon, scampi and scallop pie and fresh trout, either kettled, baked or fried.

It's a pleasant town in which to pause and is a good base for exploring the Wye Valley. Children are well cared for with their own menu or half portions from the main menu. Their accommodation is free up to the age of 5; and costs £1 for children between 5 and 14.

35 rooms, 5 family   Moderate   Open all year
Lunch 12.30-2pm – alc and bar snacks
Dinner 7-9.30pm – £9.50   Ale – Usher's
Access/AmEx/Barclaycard/Diners   P – own car park

Rothes, Grampian

map 6

H   ***ROTHES GLEN HOTEL*** – phone 254

Stands on the A941 north of the town.

A splendidly handsome country mansion built in the late 19th century in the popular baronial castle mode. It stands proudly amidst its forty acres of grounds with rolling lawns and a burn which runs into a pond at the front of the building. There is a putting green, croquet lawn and at one side a small patio with a lily pond. The interior is beautifully furnished; there is a wealth of wood panelling and fine moulded ceilings; above the stair well is a striking ceiling of stained glass.

Accommodation for children is free (up to fourteen or so – the owner had no specific rules) and half portions are served in the restaurant.

A peaceful hotel which is well placed for fishermen and golfers.

20 rooms, 3 family   Moderate   Closed mid-Nov to 1st Mar
Lunch 12.30-2pm – £6   Dinner 7.30-9pm – £12.75
Access/AmEx/Barclaycard/Diners   P – own car park

Rothley, Leics

map 4

H **ROTHLEY COURT** (Best Western) – phone Leicester 374 141

On the B5328 – follow signs to Rothley from A6 and then signs to Cropston.

A fine medieval manor house built in stone with a lovely pink tinge. It is surrounded by open country – perhaps the Quorn will obligingly gallop past one's bedroom window in pursuit of their uneatable quarry – and has six acres of gardens of its own. These contain splendid lawns and a paved terrace in front of which a stone fountain plays. There is also a modern extension which is very well done in the same stone.

Attached to the house is a famous chapel of the Knights' Templars, who built it in 1240; and , to move on quickly, the historian Thomas Babington Macaulay was born here in 1800.

Accommodation is free for children up to the age of fourteen. Half portions are available in the restaurant, which serves a wide variety of dishes, though all of them come with rather rich sauces. There are no special facilities for children here (though horse riding and golf can be arranged nearby) but it is certainly an interesting and charming spot to stop and is very close to Junction 22 of the M1 if you are slogging from one end of the country to the other.

33 rooms, 1 set of adjoining rooms   Moderate
Closed on Christmas and Boxing Days
Lunch 12.30-1.45pm – £8.50   Dinner 7-9.30pm – £11.50
Access/AmEx/Barclaycard/Diners   P – own car park

Rusper, West Sussex

map 1

H **GHYLL MANOR** – phone 571

In the village which is a couple of miles west of Crawley.

An outstandingly handsome building, parts of which are Elizabethan, in a quiet and pretty village. It has a large and splendid garden with acres of lawn leading down to a large pond. There are large paved terraces at the back also where one might sit in peace. There is a hard tennis court, a croquet lawn, riding stables and an excellent heated pool secluded among arched walls – very Spanish – to one side of the grounds.

Children under 2 are accommodated free, and thereafter up to 12 are charged at 50% of the single room rate. A large family might rent the two suites in the 'Cottage'. Children's portions are served in the restaurant: for example the Sunday lunch is £8 for adults and £5 for children.

This is a most appealing place, and is only a few miles from Gatwick Airport should you have to catch an early plane – or a late one for that matter.

12 rooms, 7 family   Moderate   Open all year
Lunch 12.30-2pm – £6.50   Dinner 7.30-10pm – £13
Access/AmEx/Barclaycard/Diners   P – own car park

Ruthin, Clwyd
map 3

H R   *CASTLE HOTEL,* St Peter's Square – phone 2479

In the main square at the centre of town.

A good-looking brick three-storey town hotel in this pretty market square. The Myddleton Arms Hotel, an hotel of Elizabethan origins which crouches next door, is now part of the Castle. It has no special entertainment for children – or adults – but offers comfort for parents travelling with children. There's a minute enclosed garden and, each Wednesday during the summer, a medieval day in which many of the locals take part and the hotel roasts a whole pig.

The charge for a cot is £4 and £7 for an extra bed in parents' room. At lunch you can choose from the bar menu of soup, sandwiches, salads for under £1 and hot snacks – pizza, omelettes, grills, fish, scampi, etc – for up to around £3.50 or have the restaurant set menu of, for instance, soup, roast lamb and apple pie. The dinner menu is a wider choice which changes each day but has plenty of fish and plainish meat dishes on it.

There is a pretty Coffee Shop with an 'olde tea shoppe' air where hot drinks and sandwiches are available all day from 8am to 6pm.

35 rooms, 2 family   Cheap   Open all year
Lunch 12-2pm – £3.50 (bar lunches 11.30am-3pm)
Dinner 7-9pm – £6.95   Ale – Bass
Access/AmEx/Barclaycard/Diners   P – own car park

Rydal, Cumbria
map 5

H P R   *GLEN ROTHAY HOTEL* – phone Ambleside 2524

On the A591.

Excellent traditional country hotel, which dates from the 17th century, in a superb lakeland setting. Close to Rydal Mount where William Wordsworth lived; in Guide to the Lakes he refers to 'Ivy Cottage' which is now the Glen Rothay. The hotel

two and a half acres of grounds and is ideal as a tourist base and for walking, climbing and water sports. You can hire bikes, canoes and windsurfers from the hotel and golf is free for residents at nearby Threlkeld.

Non-residents wanting a drink in the Badger Bar can take children into the splendid panelled residents' lounge – lunchtimes only. There's a garden with tables and chairs faced by rocks (climbing forbidden). The Bar has a good menu, with special children's dishes, and prices range from 70p for soup and roll to £6.75 for a T-bone steak and includes salads, quiche, pies, fish and meat, open sandwiches.

Accommodation for children is half price and cots 'about £1'.

11 rooms, 2 family   Moderate   Open Feb-Dec
Lunch 12-2.30pm – £2-£6   Dinner 6-7.30pm – £8
Ale – Bass, Hartley's
Access/AmEx/Barclaycard/Diners   P — own car park

Rye, East Sussex
map 1

H   *GEORGE HOTEL* (THF), High Street – phone 2114

A pleasant enough building in the High Street with a Georgian façade hiding a beamed Elizabethan interior.

The charge for children sharing with their parents is £1 between the ages of 5 and 14 – free for younger children. The restaurant offers half portions and a special children's menu.

The food tends to be traditional British – roast turkey and beef, jellied ox tongue, rack of lamb, pot roasted chicken, etc. The hotel no longer offers the fifty-seven course banquet which was held for the Lord Mayor of London when the railway was opened in 1850. But you could ask.

22 rooms, 3 family   Moderate   Open all year
Lunch 12.30-1.45pm – £7.50   Dinner 7-9pm – £7.50
Ale – Bass, Shepherd Neame
Access/AmEx/Barclaycard/Diners   P – own car park

St Albans, Herts
map 1

P   *FIGHTING COCKS*

Off George Street down the hill from the Abbey.

Fine old inn which is nearly 400 years old and because of its octagonal shape was called the Round House for several centuries. It was indeed a centre for cock-fighting long ago, *hence the reversion to its present name. The interior has been extensively modernised and now has smart, dimly lit, bars on two levels.*

There is a separate, small but comfortable, children's room which was very busy when we visited one weekend lunchtime, and a spacious garden.

Pub food such as chicken and chips, scampi and a dish of the day – braised beef and vegetables for example – is available at prices up to £2 at lunchtimes from Monday to Friday. The menu is smaller on a Saturday and offers sandwiches only on Sundays.

Ale – Benskins, Ind Coope Burton   P – own car park

St Ann's Chapel, Devon   map 2

P   ***PICKWICK INN***

On the B3392 Kingsbridge to Plymouth road near Bigbury.

A pretty white-painted stone inn with a comfortable oak-beamed interior. There is a friendly and welcoming air about the place which extends to the large and comfortable children's room. There is a large lawned garden.

There is a very wide spread of hot food and snacks all week and this includes a special children's menu, of sausages or burgers and chips at just over 50p and jellies. The grown-ups can have jellies too, if they like, or can choose amongst scampi, pizzas, lamb chops (about £3), plaice, smoked mackerel or paté, or even prawn curry (just over £2), chicken suprême (about £4), or T-bone steaks (about £5).

Ale – Bass, Blacklawton   P – opposite pub

St Davids, Dyfed   map 2

They're close to each other, these two – follow the Fishguard road from the town centre and you'll find signs for them.

H   ***WARPOOL COURT HOTEL*** – phone 720 300

This is an odd-looking hotel in grey stone. Odd because a small and ugly extension has been tacked on to the front for very little apparent gain in space, whereas the extension at the back is just about passable although some ugly things have been done to the façade above. But we include the hotel because of its situation in this very popular and beautiful part of Wales. The hotel itself has stunning views of the sea and a lovely lawned garden with several pieces of statuary. There is an indoor pool housed in a large glass hangar, a pool table and children's videos are also run. You will sometimes spot that greatest of Welsh rugby players, Gareth Edwards, on a fishing trip here.

Children's accommodation is free up to one year old, and then on a sliding scale: 2-4 years £2.50, 5-10 years £4.50 and 11-16 years £8.50. But these prices include breakfast and high tea. A special children's menu is available at under £2.

25 rooms, 12 family   Moderate   Closed Jan
Brunch 11am-3pm   Dinner 7-9pm – £10.25   Ale – Bass
Access/AmEx/Barclaycard   P – own car park

R   *ST NON'S HOTEL* – phone 720 239

From the town centre follow the Fishguard road and you will find a sign.

A white painted stone building with a lawned garden to one side and a small patio. The dining room is a mite sombre with its heavily patterned wallpaper and dark furniture. But there are good value bar meals to be had – for example jacket potatoes with various fillings and salad at under £1; and quiches, scotch eggs, cottage pie, samosas all with salad and sauté potatoes at under £2.

There is plenty of local sea-food available – crab always, and oysters and lobster with a few hours notice. Children can order half portions and the friendly staff will find some space for a mother to feed or change a baby.

Closed Jan/Feb   Bar lunch 12-2pm   Dinner 7-9pm – £8.50
Ale – Bass
Access/AmEx/Barclaycard/Diners   P – own car park

St Ives, Cambs   map 1

R   *SLEPE HALL HOTEL*, Ramsey Road – phone 62824

Very difficult to find: you follow the signs for the Recreation Centre, but there is one badly positioned sign which points nowhere – obviously a legacy from World War II when all signs were re-arranged to deceive the potential invader – it would still fool Rommel.

The restaurant is housed in a Victorian mansion in mellow brick which looks Georgian, with its regularly spaced square windows and wooden shutters. It has a small but very pretty garden ringed by tall hedgerows. Try to avert your eyes from the ghastly Brunel Suite at one side.

The restaurant serves traditional English cuisine, and half portions for children. An interesting menu it is too. You will find Brie fritters with lemon and pear dip, Arnold Bennett turnover and eggs Tarama; a couple of vegetarian dishes; gamekeeper's pie, medallions of venison and quail. The bar snacks have plenty of choice too (at lunchtimes) – paté, jacket potatoes, ploughman's, quiche, pies, curries, burgers, etc, all at very reasonable prices – a rump steak is only just over £4 for instance.

Changing and feeding is possible in the 'Ladies', but staff will help with an upstairs room if one is free.

Closed Christmas & Boxing Day   Lunch 12-2pm – £9
Dinner 7-10pm – £9   Licensed
Access/AmEx/Barclaycard/Diners   P – own car park

St Ives, Cornwall   map 2

A famous resort on the 'Cornish Riviera', it is a town of steep twisting streets. It has always been popular with artists and some famous ones have lived here including Whistler, Sickert and Barbara Hepworth whose house is now a museum.

H   *PORTHMINSTER HOTEL* – phone Penzance 795 221

On the main road into the town.

An excellent traditional seaside hotel set high up above the town and with a commanding view of St Ives' bay. The gardens lead down to the sea and a lovely beach, to which there is a pathway for guests. There is a heated outdoor swimming pool.

Accommodation free for children up to 2, one-third price from 2 to 7 and half price from 7 to 12.

50 rooms, 4 suites   Moderate   Closed at Christmas
Access/AmEx/Barclaycard/Diners   P – own car park opposite

H   *TREGENNA CASTLE HOTEL* – phone Penzance 795 254

Off the main road into the town.

An 18th century castle in 100 acres, with a fine array of facilities: a heated outdoor swimming pool, a short golf course and a squash court, three grass and three hard tennis courts and a badminton court. Out of season, it had a forbidding air – with more signs telling visitors where not to park than any hints of a welcome – but it now has new owners.

The terms for children's accommodation are: £3 for cots, £7 for under-10s and £12 for over-10s.

200

85 rooms, 8 family   Cheap   Open all year
Buffet lunch 12.30-2pm   Dinner 7.30-9pm – £9
Access/AmEx/Barclaycard/Diners   P – own car park

St Mawgan, Cornwall

map 2

P   *FALCON*

The road numbering is a little confusing, but it's off the A3059 and the airport road is the best route.

Pretty stone village pub with patio and garden. It's well off the beaten track, but quite a nice pub in an area where we couldn't find much.

There's a spacious children's hut, well away from the pub, with a soft drinks bar, games and a covered patio.

Hot and cold snacks are available all week.

Ale – St Austell   P – own car park

Salisbury, Wilts

map 2

This city has a lot of car parking space available (although the two hotels both have car parks) and their traffic control system – to the casual visitor – really seems to work sensibly and seems actually designed to help not hinder. The City's Cathedral is magnificent (Pepys was guided 'all over the Plain by the sight of the steeple') and the town has many other fine buildings and is an excellent tourist centre.

H   *RED LION HOTEL* (Best Western), Milford Street – phone 23334

A fine city centre coaching inn dating back to the 14th century, with a splendid creeper-clad courtyard. It has a very attractive lounge, where children can go, and pleasantly decorated rooms overlooking the courtyard.

Accommodation is free for children under 14 who share their parents' room and small portions are served to them in the restaurant.

There's a good range of food here of the traditional British variety: smoked salmon and trout, braised oxtail, turkey, duck, venison and Wiltshire gammon.

55 rooms, 3 family   Moderate   Open all year
Lunch 12.30-1.45pm – £6 alc   Dinner 7-8.45pm – £7.50
Ale – Ushers, Bass, Wadworth's
Access/AmEx/Barclaycard/Diners   P – 24 spaces

H   ***WHITE HART HOTEL*** (THF), St John Street – phone 27476

An imposing pillared entrance marks out this Georgian stone building not far from the city centre. Look out for the hart sitting proudly atop the entrance.

There is no charge for accommodation for children up to 5 and a nominal £1 from 5 to 14. The restaurant has a special menu for children or will give them half portions.

The lunches are fairly conventional, with the occasional unusual dish, for example fillet of bream; so are the dinners, albeit there are interesting dishes such as sweet pear with tarragon mayonnaise as well as soups, trout and roasts. The buffet, available at lunchtime and in the evening offers good value: cold meat and salad or a hot pie and salad at just over £2 or lasagne at under £2.

72 rooms, 2 family   Moderate   Open all year
Lunch 12.30-2.15pm – £6.50
Dinner 6.30-9.30pm – £8.50   Ale – Courage
Access/AmEx/Barclaycard/Diners   P – own car park

Sampford Courtenay, Devon   map 2

P   ***NEW INN***

On the A3072.

Superb thatched pub dating from the 16th century. It has a low-beamed dining room and main bar with a lovely open fireplace with a baker's oven.

Children are welcome 'as long as they're on the lead'. The children's room has darts, pool and space invaders. It is off the main bar and leads to a huge grassy back garden.

Hot and cold food is offered every day except Sunday evenings and, apart from sandwiches and ploughman's, you can eat chilli con carne, lasagne and chicken or scampi and chips at under £2.50.

Ale – Whitbread   P – own car park

Sanderstead, South Croydon, Surrey   map 1

H   ***SELSDON PARK HOTEL*** (Best Western) – phone 01-657 8811

Little effort is made to signpost the hotel, apart from one sign, about postcard size and well hidden by foliage, within about 100 yards of the entrance. Not good enough.

A *striking and very grand country house, with a history traceable to the 9th century, in 200 acres of grounds. Fine leisure facilities include an excellent golf course, four tennis courts, an open air heated swimming pool and an adventure playground for children. The gardens are very splendid with velvet lawns and ancient cedar trees.*

Accommodation is free for children up to 2 with a charge of £15.00 for children from 3 to 13. There is a special children's menu at reduced, though not half, price; for example dinner is £8.50 for a child and lunch £6.50 for a child. Simple dishes of the chicken-and-chips variety can be prepared.

160 rooms, 30 family   Expensive   Open all year
Lunch 12.30-2pm – £9.75   Dinner 7-9pm – £11.25
Access/AmEx/Barclaycard/Diners   P – own car park

Saundersfoot, Dyfed   map 2

H   *ST BRIDES HOTEL* (Inter) – phone 812 304

On the A477.

Mock Tudor hotel with a nasty modern extension. Some of the interior, particularly the bar, is well furnished and decorated. Beautifully situated high over Carmarthen Bay, a view which can be appreciated from the restaurant and from the terrace of the outdoor heated swimming pool. There's little within the hotel to amuse children, but plenty roundabout in this wonderful stretch of coastline.

Accommodation is free for children up to 14 years sharing with their parents. Otherwise full rate is charged. In the restaurant they can have half portions or eat from a special children's menu for about £2. Dinner is served to them at 6pm in their rooms.

49 rooms, 6 quadruple, 18 triple   Moderate   Open all year
Lunch 12.30-1.30pm – £6   Dinner 7.30-8.45pm £8.45 3 courses
Access/AmEx/Barclaycard/Diners   P – own car park

Saunton, Nr Barnstaple, Devon   map 2

H   *SAUNTON SANDS HOTEL – phone Croyde 890 212*   ō

On the B3231.

Big modern hotel overlooking and with direct access to the breath-taking Saunton Sands and offering everything you could require for a totally relaxing stay. The excellent

facilities include an indoor heated swimming pool with children's pool, a tennis court, squash court and a mini-cinema. Horse-riding, sailing, wind-surfing, fishing, etc, can all be arranged by the hotel staff. Just down the road is Saunton Golf Club, a splendid links course which offers a stern enough test of golf to have been the setting for several English Amateur championships. Outside is a large grassy children's play area which has a bar, clock golf, climbing frame, etc, and inside a playroom where a nanny is available from 9am to 3pm (sometimes 5pm) Monday to Friday. The indoor swimming pool next to it is watched over by closed-circuit television.

Accommodation for children up to 5 is half the full rate; half portions and special children's menu are available in the restaurant as are high teas at 5.30pm.

This hotel has everything you would desire for a family holiday – everything and everyone is taken care of and it fully merits its commendation as one of the two runners-up for best family hotel.

90 rooms, 80 family   Moderate   Open all year
Lunch 12.30-2pm – £5.75   Dinner 7.30-9pm – £8.45
Ale – Bass
Access/AmEx/Barclaycard/Diners   P – plenty

Seend Cleeve, Wilts   map 2

P   *BREWERY INN*

Look for the sign off the A361 near Seend.

An attractive, white-washed and renovated one-bar village pub. Off to one side is a small but adequate children's room and the attraction on summer days is the large garden with slide, swing, etc, plus a goat, rabbits and hens.

Basic pub food – sandwiches, ploughman's, pies, chicken and chips, etc – is served in generous portions every day.

Ale – Usher's   P – own car park

Selkirk, Borders   map 5

H R   *PHILIPBURN HOUSE HOTEL – phone 20747*

Where the A707 joins the A708.

A pretty, welcoming hotel very much geared to keeping the children occupied while their parents 'who need a holiday as much, if not more' relax. While the children are knocking themselves out in an adventure playground which is more like a commando course, you can swim in the heated pool, ride, walk, fish, etc. The grounds are an adventure in themselves – large and rambling – there are several safer play areas for younger children as well as a games room, play room, trampoline, children's farm and a nanny to supervise them for the whole of your stay – you needn't set eyes on the little dears if you don't want to. What a find.

The prices for children sharing a room with their parents are: free under 2, £8 2-10 and £10 10-15, but enquire too about the suites and pine lodge.

The poolside restaurant offers a good choice of meals – a 'Quick Bite' menu with dishes in the £1.65 to £3.50 price range, a table d'hôte menu at £9 and an à la carte menu with main courses from £2.25 to £7.50 and which includes plenty of fresh fish dishes and an interesting selection of meat. Meals are taken outside by the pool when the weather allows. Dishes will be cooked as the children wish and they will probably like some of the 'Quick Bite' meals.

This hotel won the 1984 award as the best family hotel not just for its splendid and varied facilities, but above all for the obvious care and interest which the staff show for their guests. Their friendliness and their pride in their hotel was so impressive.

16 rooms, 4 family rooms, 7 suites, 2 poolside chalets
  Moderate
Open all year Lunch 12-2pm Dinner 8-10pm Licensed
Access/AmEx/Barclaycard/Diners P – own car park

Shaftesbury, Dorset   map 2

A nice old town in which we liked both these hotels:

H   *GROSVENOR HOTEL* (THF) – phone 2282

Near the Market Square.

Rambling old coaching inn with a pretty courtyard in which to sit. The slightly shabby exterior looks as if it needs a going-over with a large duster but this does not apply to the interior.

Children are accommodated free up to the age of 5 and a nominal charge of £1 is made for children of 5 to 14. A special menu is available in the restaurant as are half portions.

48 rooms, 3 family Moderate Open all year
Lunch 12.45-2pm – £3.75 Dinner 7-9pm – £7.50 Ale – Bass
Access/AmEx/Barclaycard/Diners P – public car park opposite

H   *ROYAL CHASE HOTEL* (Best Western), *Royal Chase Round-about – phone 3355*

On the A30 at Shaftesbury.

A Georgian country house, which was once a monastery. It has an attractive façade and acceptable brick extension (probably Georgian) to one side, but a rather ugly brick extension (probably Victorian) to the rear. A patch of lawn with tables and chairs is at the front but a much quieter and larger area of lawned garden with arrays of flowers to the rear. A good place for a stop-over in the heart of Wessex country.

Accommodation for children under 15 years sharing their parents' room is free and thereafter one-third of the adult rate. Half portions are served and high tea is available whenever requested.

There is plenty of choice in the Country Kitchen restaurant – perhaps snails, whitebait or prawns to begin, and then a steak, lamb cutlets, roast duckling Montmorence or Wessex beef.

20 rooms, 4 family   Moderate   Open all year
Lunch 12.30-2pm – £8 alc   Dinner 7-9pm – £8 alc
Ale – Wadworth's, Eldridge Pope, Hall & Woodhouse
Access/AmEx/Barclaycard/Diners   P – own car park

Shapwick, Nr Glastonbury, Somerset   map 2

H   *SHAPWICK HOUSE HOTEL* (Best Western) – *phone Ashcott 210 321*

Off the A39, west of Street.

There are no specific extra facilities for children, or for adults for that matter, at this hotel. But we include it because it is in holiday and sightseeing country – near Glastonbury and Wells and not too far from the Somerset coast. It is a beautiful country house built of grey stone in tranquil surroundings. Supposedly built for Charles I, it lies in wooded grounds with a lovely big lawn and a dovehouse. So you can repair here for a spot of relaxation and quiet.

Accommodation is free for children aged 12 and under. A 3-course dinner is served at £8.80 and half portions given to children.

12 rooms, 2 family   Moderate
Bar lunch   Dinner 7.30-9.30pm – £8.80
Access/AmEx/Barclaycard/Diners   P – own car park

Shedfield, Hants

map 1

H   *MEON VALLEY HOTEL*, Sandy Lane – phone Wickham 833
455

Just off the A334.

*A modern, quite pleasing, brick and timber building, and it has
a fine lay-out for the sporting set with its heated indoor pool,
three hard tennis courts, four squash courts and eighteen-hole
golf course.*

*Up to the age of 16 the accommodation charge for children is
£1.50 (for breakfast). Half portions are offered to children and
there is a special menu for them in the Clubroom.*

49 rooms, 5 family, the rest adjoining in pairs   Moderate
Open all year   Lunch 12.30-2pm – £6   Dinner 6.30-10.30 –
£7.50
Access/AmEx/Barclaycard/Diners   P – own car park

Sherborne St John, Hants

map 1

P   *SWAN*, Kiln Road

Off the A340.

*Superb thatched village pub with huge garden containing
swings and a slide.*

The large children's room has plenty of tables.

*Hot and cold food is served six lunchtimes per week (not on
Sundays) and includes scampi, plaice, lasagne, fishcakes,
cottage pie, sandwiches and ploughman's – and nothing will
cost you more than £2 or so. Sandwiches only are served in the
evenings.*

Ale – Wethered   P – own car park

Shocklach, Cheshire

map 3

P   *BULL INN*

Off the A41.

Pretty white-walled roadside pub with a large grassy garden.

*The landlord welcomes children in the clean pool room with
darts board and in the dining room.*

Hot and cold pub food is served all week and this includes steaks at just under £5, scampi, mixed grills, plaice, chicken, omelettes, as well as sandwiches and ploughman's.

Ale – McEwan's   P – own car park

Shrewsbury, Shropshire   map 3

'High the vanes of Shrewsbury gleam
Islanded in Severn stream'

wrote A. E. Housman, and whoever authorised the traffic regulations should be dropped in the Severn by the local Shropshire lads. Trying to park in the centre of the town is a nightmare; the system is designed to cause the utmost difficulty to any visitors – hardly the way to attract business and tourism to the town one would have thought. Arise, ye descendants of Clive of India and wreak your revenge.

H P R   *LION HOTEL* (THF), Wyle Cop – phone 53107

In the centre of the town.

The hotel is set on top of a hill in one of the oldest and best preserved parts of this lovely market town. Around it are narrow streets with Tudor houses and, as contrast, rows of elegant Georgian buildings. The main part of the hotel façade is Georgian, though older parts still remain, and there is a fine high-ceilinged lounge on the right as you enter.

There is a snack menu at lunchtime as well as a roast of the day (at under £4) in the restaurant, which in the evenings concentrates mainly on roast meats on the table d'hôte menu, with one or two interesting dishes on the à la carte, eg mushroom and cheese fritters and seafood pie.

Children's accommodation is free up to the age of 5, and costs only £1 from 5 to 15; and they have their own special menu and half portions from the main menu if requested. There are no other special facilities and this is primarily an hotel for a stopover if you fancy a look at this appealing and historic town or are en route for the North or mid-Wales tourist beat. The hotel is not far from one of the nicest pubs in a town noted for its pubs – 'The Old Bush' – which is between the Abbey and Lord Hill's Column.

69 rooms, 4 family, 1 suite   Moderate   Open all year
Lunch 12.30-2pm – £3.75   Dinner 7-10pm – £8.50
Ale – Wilson's
Access/AmEx/Barclaycard/Diners   P – own car park

Sidford, Devon
map 2

P *BLUE BALL*

On the A3052.

A thatched pub with a history going back to the 14th century, it is now a big, busy and well-run roadside pub.

There is a large and cared-for children's room which is separate from the pub – it's called 'The Stable' and has plenty of tables and chairs. A terrace looks out over a pretty flower garden, and there is a bigger lawned garden at the back.

A very good range of food is available from Monday to Saturday, and on Sunday the menu is limited to ploughman's, sandwiches, pasties and one hot dish of the day. On the other days you can have a T-bone steak for under £6 or a rump steak for about £4.50; there is an array of salads at £2 to £3 and several dishes of the day at about £2 – steak and kidney pie, chilli con carne, etc. The children can have smaller portions, or their own choice from sausage and chips, pasties, etc.

Ale – Devenish   P – own car park

Southam, Nr Cheltenham, Glos
map 2

H R *HOTEL DE LA BERE* (Best Western) – phone Cheltenham 37771

On the A46 north of Cheltenham.

You must dip into your list of superlatives to describe this magnificent manor house built mainly in the time of the Wars of the Roses. Its honey-coloured stone gives it a warm look as it sprawls with beautiful windows and eccentric roofs through lawned grounds. There is a small formal garden at the front as well. Inside the panelled walls, black beams, intricately carved fireplaces and stone walls are preserved and the only disappointment is the 'bistro' – it looks out of place in this environment.

There are fine facilities too: an excellent outdoor heated swimming pool with a garden to lounge in; four hard tennis courts; five squash courts; a pitch and putt course; and croquet lawn. There is lots more to come – a gymnasium has been built and it is hoped that work will start on badminton courts and an indoor tennis court.

Accommodation is free for children up to 3 and a charge of £6 is made from 3 to 14 years. High teas for children are served at 5.30pm and half portions are available in the restaurant. The *lunches here are rather good value; for example the table d'hôte meal of cream of cauliflower soup, lamb cutlets, fresh fruit salad and coffee will cost you £4.75 including VAT and service. A lovely place to stay for those seeking either quiet relaxation or a busy time.*

25 rooms, 4 family   Moderate   Open all year
Lunch 12.30-2pm – £4.75   Dinner 7.30-10.30pm – £7.25
Ale – Hook Norton
Access/AmEx/Barclaycard/Diners   P – own car park

Sparsholt, Nr Winchester, Hants   map 1

H   *LAINSTON HOUSE HOTEL* (Prestige) – phone Winchester 63588

Off the A272 Winchester to Stockbridge road. Look for hotel sign.

Half a mile up a winding drive through lime trees is this very attractive early 17th century building. It has been restored over the last few years with great style and sits elegantly amid its sixty or so peaceful acres of grounds – lovely lawns and trees. The interior is elegant too: the rooms are beautifully proportioned with oak cedar panelling and the dining room is delightfully done in pale green.

The great attractions of the hotel are its spacious grounds – there are no special facilities apart from a croquet lawn, a 'short' tennis court, a swing and a see-saw – its peaceful situation and of course its proximity to the interesting old town of Winchester two and a half miles away with its village school where Tim Brooke-Taylor was educated.

Cots and beds for children cost £5 a night and the restaurant will provide half portions or any food which children may request.

28 rooms, 1 family   Expensive   Open all year
Lunch 12-2.30pm – £12 alc   Dinner 7-10.30pm – £12 alc
Access/AmEx/Barclaycard/Diners   P – own car park

Stamford, Lincs   map 4

H R   *THE GEORGE OF STAMFORD* – phone 55171

In the centre of the town.

A glorious stone coaching inn the main part of which was built by Lord Burghley in 1597. Only half a mile from one of the most magnificent examples of Elizabethan building, Burghley

House, begun in 1552 by William Cecil and completed over thirty years later.

The hotel has a lovely cobbled courtyard in which you can sit surrounded by ivy-clad walls, and to the side a superb walled garden with a sunken lawn. The hotel has a splendid interior of stone walls and heavy beams; and one of the lounges is particularly notable for its dark oak panelling.

There is sustenance available most of the day here. The cold buffet is available at lunchtime and in the evening: open sandwiches and triple decker sandwiches sound good, as does Bouillabaise with garlic bread at just over £3. There is also paté, pies, trout, etc. You could then try a traditional English tea, and gourmands can then attack a substantial and interesting dinner: start with Ardeche ham with fresh peaches and strawberries or smoked eel; then try poached salmon or rack of lamb or seafood pot. A couple of pints of Ruddles, and so to bed! The hotel specialises in trout (from Rutland water) and will offer eight variations on this fishy theme.

Cots are free, and extra beds are charged at £8.50. The menu is à la carte only, but half portions can be ordered for children.

A fine and historic town – a good place to stay or at which to pause if you are sight-seeing.

38 rooms, 2 family   Moderate   Open all year
Lunch 12.30-2.30pm – £12-£15 alc
Dinner 7.30-10pm – £12-£15 alc   Ale — Ruddles
Access/AmEx/Barclaycard/Diners   P – own car park

Stinchcombe, Nr Dursley, Glos   map 2

H R   *STINCHCOMBE MANOR HOUSE* – phone Dursley 2538/2577

In a lane which joins the B4066 and B4060 not far from the M5. Close to the church.

Absolutely delightful 19th century manor house (with a Georgian look) with quiet extensive and shady gardens where there is a croquet lawn, patio, tennis court and outdoor heated swimming pool. An extension has been added on with great skill and fits very well with the original building.

You can choose a full lunch at £7 or a two-course lunch at under £5, and that is very good value. Salade Niçoise and braised steak would be a typical choice – but would you have the self-control to reject treacle and walnut pie with hot custard? The dinner menu has some interesting touches: mixed Chinese salad, pork kebabs with savoury rice, etc.

*Cots are charged at £2 per night; children up to 4 have a
reduction of two thirds and up to 10 of one half.*

*A special children's menu is available and the restaurant serves
high teas between 5 and 6pm.*

16 rooms, 4 family   Moderate   Open all year
Lunch 12-2pm – £7   Dinner 7.30-9.30 – £9.50
Ale – Butcombe
Access/AmEx/Barclaycard/Diners   P – own car park

Stoke Gabriel, Nr Totnes, Devon map 2

H   *GABRIEL COURT HOTEL* – phone 206

Go to the village and, glory be, there's a signpost to the hotel.

*A pretty 16th century manor house, white-painted, with an
ornamental balustrade and a square tower, and set in three
acres of tranquil, sloping gardens in this quiet village situated
between Paignton and Totnes. There is a heated outdoor
swimming pool, a grass tennis court and an outdoor play area
with swings and slides.*

*The menus include a lot of local produce – fruit and vegetables
from the garden (and you can't get more local than that), salmon
and trout from the Dart, and poultry and venison from nearby
farms and woods.*

*Half-board rates for children are £10 per day up to the age of 12.
There are separate meal times for younger children and high tea
at 5.30 which is included in the accommodation price.*

25 rooms, 5 family   Moderate   Open all year
Access/Barclaycard/Diners   P – own car park

Stoke Mandeville, Bucks map 1

P   *WOOLPACK*, Risborough Road

On the A4010.

*A lovely part-thatched and part-tiled pub smartly painted in
white. Inside is a very large bar, and children can frequent the
hallway with its few chairs. It is a small area, but just about
adequate.*

*The great appeal of the pub is its large back garden, with a patio
and plenty of lawn on which are several swings and a climbing
frame. The front garden, with its smooth lawn and array of
flowers, is particularly pretty.*

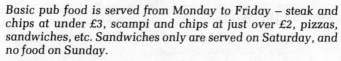

Basic pub food is served from Monday to Friday – steak and chips at under £3, scampi and chips at just over £2, pizzas, sandwiches, etc. Sandwiches only are served on Saturday, and no food on Sunday.

Ale – Aylesbury, Bass   P – own car park

Stoke-sub-Hamdon, Somerset   map 2

P   *PRINCE OF WALES*

To find this old stone pub look out for the sign on the A3088 (the main street of Stoke-sub-Hamdon) to Ham Hill. It is perched on top of a hill in Ham Country Park and there are wonderful views of the Somerset countryside to be seen.

There is a small but adequate children's room and a garden, but it is worth a visit for the view alone.

You will always find food here and that includes a children's dish of sausages, beans and chips at £1. The grown-ups can have a steak, grilled gammon, scampi, chicken, a curry or just a sandwich.

Ale – Usher's   P – own car park

Stone, Nr Kidderminster, Hereford & Worcs   map 3

H R   *STONE MANOR HOTEL* – phone Chaddesley Corbett 555

On the A448 south east of Kidderminster.

In an odd way this is an appealing building. It is a mock-Tudor, stockbroker-belt mansion taken to its ultimate expression and very well done too. The style is carried right through the spacious interior with beams and panelling. There are twenty-five acres of grounds. From the terrace you look out over huge and lovely rolling lawns, and to one side there is another garden, enclosed by walls, with a lily pond, a rockery with a willow tree in its middle and another terrace to sit upon with a drink or a book or both. There is one hard tennis court and an outdoor pool sheltered by sculptured hedges. It's for enthusiasts only – it's unheated.

The set lunches give a choice of three main courses, e.g. lamb cutlets or sole or beef and salad; and the dinner menu is very comprehensive. Half portions can be served up for children. Cots cost £5 per night and an extra bed £10 per night.

22 rooms, 6 family, 3 sets adjoining   Moderate
Open all year   Lunch 12.30-2.30pm – £5.10
Dinner 7.30-10.30pm – £12 alc
Access/AmEx/Barclaycard/Diners   P – own car park

Stow-on-the-Wold, Glos   map 2

An attractive Cotswold town which is packed with lovely stone cottages and antique shops.

P   *UNICORN HOTEL,* Sheep Street

In the town on the A436.

A very appealing 17th century stone coaching inn on the main road through the town and where it meets the Fosse Way. As you enter there is a sizeable and comfortable lounge with low beams and children may sit here with their adults. There are plenty of easy chairs.

Bar food is available every lunchtime except Sunday and on Thursday, Friday and Saturday evenings. Prices range from £1.50 to £3.50 — salads, toasted sandwiches, paté, smoked mackerel, steak and Guinness pie, country chicken pie, etc. A nice place to relax after hunting antiques.

Ale – Bass   P – own car park

R   *RAFTERS,* Park Street – phone 30200

In the main street through the town, the A436.

An unexceptional looking restaurant of cotswold stone with bow windows and an attractive interior of plain walls, beamed ceilings and good wooden furniture.

There is a very enterprising menu based upon a series of set meals. It is rare to find such choices as frogs' legs, marinated breast of chicken, graved lax, sea bass and pigeon on the same menu. The owners also run evenings of French provincial cooking.

Half portions are served and the 'Ladies' is sizeable and well-appointed enough to deal with a baby's needs.

Closed Sun, Mon and Christmas   Lunch 12.30-2pm – £5.50
Dinner 7.15-9.30pm (Sat 7-10pm) – £7.50
Ale – Wadworth's, Hook Norton
Access/AmEx/Barclaycard/Diners   P – on street

Strachur, Strathclyde   map 5

H P R   *CREGGANS INN* – phone 279

On the A815.

On the 'Eastern Approach' of Loch Fyne is Sir Fitzroy McLean's famous inn, a lovely long white building with terrace and lawned garden with lots of flowers. Contemplate the loch and the hills from here and decide on walking, swimming, drendology or contemplation. The interior lives up to the promise of the exterior with a number of attractive rooms: a good bar and lounge, a very pretty dining room, and a conservatory just off the hallway.

Cots are charged at £3 per night, and an extra bed in parents' rooms costs £5.

There is a good selection of bar snacks for lunch, including the local trout and prawns, plain meat dishes at around £2.50-£4 and lighter snacks such as toasted sandwiches or bacon and egg roll for under £1. The interesting dinner menu also emphasises local dishes – Argyll smoked salmon, Loch Fyne langoustines, oysters and sea trout, as well as charcoal grills, salads, venison and duckling. Some more unusual dishes when we visited were green almond soup, iced curry vichyssoise, haggis Creggans and polpettini (beef patties with cordon bleu sauce). Children may order half portions or from the bar snack menu at both lunch and dinner. Teas are served from 3pm to 6pm, and high teas for children from 5.30-6pm if ordered in advance.

23 rooms, 6 family   Moderate   Open all year
Bar lunches   Dinner 7.30-8.45pm – £9   Ale – McEwan's
Access/AmEx/Barclaycard   P – own car park

Stratford upon Avon, Warwickshire   map 3

H   *ALVESTON MANOR HOTEL* (THF), Clopton Bridge – phone
       204 581

On the roundabout as you enter the town on A422 from Banbury.

The original building is a magnificent Elizabethan creation of dark brick and timber, with wonderful carved doors and panelling inside. It is said that the first production of A Midsummer Night's Dream took place in the grounds.

There are later additions tacked on to the original building, and at the back is a number of new rooms – built in that dire modern 'Wimpey estate' style around a large, but rather scruffy, garden. But a small pitch and putt course is being laid out here for 1984. The front garden is much more elegant, and has a small patio by the entrance, but is rather noisy, as it is adjacent to a major roundabout. Beware, real ale fans, the Flowers was off 'because of the summer'.

A good spot for tourists since the centre of the town is a short walk across the bridge.

Accommodation is free for children up to 5, a nominal charge up to 14 – special children's menu and half price portions are served in the restaurant and teas are served from 2.30-5.30pm.

120 rooms, 4 family   Moderate   Open all year
Lunch 12.15-2pm – £7.95   Dinner 6.15-9.30pm – £8.50
Ale – Flowers (sometimes)
Access/AmEx/Barclaycard/Diners   P – own car park

H   **WELCOMBE HOTEL,** Warwick Road – phone 295 252

On the A46 road to Warwick.

This is a tremendously grand hotel built in 1869 in a florid but appealing Jacobean style. It was once owned by the popular historian G M Trevelyan (so there is money in books after all) and was bought by the LMS in 1929. It is very much in the style of the great railway hotels – but here without a railway.

The grounds are formal and delightful and from the long terrace you can look out at the spreading countryside and the hotel's eighteen-hole golf course. There is also a games room attached to the 'Welcombe Pub' and it has table tennis and snooker.

Cots are free of charge; an extra bed costs £10; and 2 children sharing a room cost half the adult rate.

The lunch is fairly standard hotel fare, as is the dinner. A useful facility is the pre-theatre dinner from 6 to 7pm, and afternoon teas are also available.

A relaxing place to stay, especially if you are intent on tourist raids to Stratford and other spots.

84 rooms, 7 family   Expensive   Open all year
Lunch 12.30-2pm – £8.50   Dinner 7-9.15pm – £9.95
Access/AmEx/Barclaycard/Diners   P – own car park

Strathcarron, Highland   map 6

R   **CARRON RESTAURANT** – phone Lochcarron 488

On the A890.

This charming restaurant overlooks Loch Carron and is loomed over by the West Highland ranges. It is a very attractive cream building next to a similar small cottage and with a pottery and gift shop also attached. Inside, the restaurant is smartly and brightly furnished in pine, and there is a good range of food available: cakes and pastries, soups, toasted sandwiches and salads. Steaks, venison and salmon are cooked on the charcoal grill. Prices from £1 to £6.

Children's portions can be made available and there is a secluded corner of the restaurant where a mother might deal, quite modestly, with a hungry baby.

Closed 2 weeks Jan; open Wed, Fri and Sat only from mid Oct to end Mar 10.30am-9.15pm   Licensed
Access/Barclaycard   P – own car park

Sudbury, Suffolk

map 1

H   ***MILL HOTEL,*** Walnut Tree Lane – phone 75544

In the centre of the town.

This is quite an attractive hotel: the old stone mill forms part of it and the modern extension is married reasonably skilfully to it. The old mill wheel is on show in the restaurant, which offers half portions for children. There is standard hotel restaurant food here.

For anglers the hotel has coarse fishing rights on the River Stour.

Accommodation for children up to 14 is half price; or probably a better offer is an extra bed in the parents' room at £10.

46 rooms, 2 family   Moderate   Open all year
Lunch 12.30-1.45pm – £6   Dinner 7.30-9.15pm – £8
Ale – Greene King, Mauldon's
Access/AmEx/Barclaycard/Diners   P – own car park

R   ***FRIAR'S RESTAURANT,*** 17 Friar's Street – phone 72940

In one of the main streets.

Spacious attractively beamed tea rooms where the cakes, scones and bread are all home made. There is a good range of omelettes and other snacks and the two- or three-course lunches at under £4 give you exceptional value. Apart from cold meats and salads, there are roast beef and Yorkshire pudding, stuffed hearts, plaice and halibut, and to finish steamed golden sponge and custard. Lovely.

Children's portions are also served.

There is a small patio to one side.

The 'Ladies' is 'big enough to cope with a dozen babies'.

Closed Sunday & bank holidays   Open 10am-5.30pm (except Wednesday when they close at 2pm)   Licensed
No credit cards accepted
P – some street parking, but difficult; car park in Station Road

Sunninghill, Ascot, Berks   map 1

H R   *BERYSTEDE HOTEL* (THF), Bagshot Road – phone Ascot 23311

On the B3020 at junction with the A330 just south of Ascot.

A very large rambling hotel with a rather florid, and typically Victorian, look to it, (it was mainly built in the 1880s) with its rounded towers with minarets at the corners. There are various extensions which give the place an untidy air, but it is a well-situated hotel, especially for racing fans and golfers (Sunningdale is just up the road) and has reasonably good facilities. These include an outdoor swimming pool, which is overlooked by a long terrace and has a sizeable patio around it; a putting green; and a croquet lawn in the extensive tree-laden grounds. There is also a big, airy games room with a pool table, table tennis and space invaders.

Children under 5 are accommodated free with a nominal charge of £1 for 5s to 14s. The THF special children's menu is available, as are half portions from the main menu.

The lunch menu is short but interesting – for example leek au gratin, pheasant, salmon trout and, on loan from the Dragon Hotel, Swansea 'medallions of beef Dylan Thomas' – no doubt the beef is bought from Butcher Beynon who will stroll for ever down the streets of memory 'with a finger, not his own, in his mouth'. There are good things on the dinner list too – gazpacho, Elizabethan plank steak and a touch of nouvelle cuisine (two dishes available).

90 rooms, 6 family   Moderate   Open all year
Lunch (hot and cold buffet) 12.30-2pm – £7.95   Dinner 7-10pm – £10.25
Access/AmEx/Barclaycard/Diners   P – own car park

Sutton Coldfield, West Midlands   map 3

H   *MOOR HALL* (Best Western), Four Oaks – phone 021 308 3751

Off the A453 north of Sutton Coldfield.

The original Tudor brick building is seen to its best advantage from the garden or the adjoining golf course. The house was built in 1521 by Bishop Vesey and was undoubtedly visited by Henry VIII. They would not be pleased by the various modern accretions which mostly hide the front façade. It is quite a mess.

However, we have included it as an alternative to staying in Birmingham, which is not far away. It is in the countryside and looks out over a golf course, at which unfortunately there are no concessions for guests of the hotel.

There is both a restaurant (standard hotel fare) and burgers to be had in 'Jake's'. Half portions are available. Both cots and extra beds cost £5 per night.

52 rooms, 6 family   Moderate   Open all year
Lunch 12.30-2pm – £6.25 (als. bar snacks, sandwiches, etc).
Dinner 7.30-10pm – £8.25
Access/AmEx/Barclaycard/Diners   P – own car park

Swyre, Nr Bridport, Dorset   map 2
P   *BULL INN*

On the B3157.

Nice-looking brick pub with deep roofs and set in rolling countryside above the sea. In the summer there are tables and chairs on the patio (with its wishing well) and in the garden at the rear.

There is a separate, spacious children's room, 'The Hayloft', and food can be served in there.

Bar meals and snacks are available all week, mornings and evenings, and range through ploughman's, quiches, steak and kidney pie, chicken, scampi, plaice, etc, at prices up to £2.75.

Ale – Devenish   P – own car park

Tan-y-Bwlch, Maentwrog, Gwynedd   map 3
P   *OAKELEY ARMS HOTEL*

On the A487.

This hotel is in a great spot – standing back from the road and overlooking beautiful countryside. It's an 18th century stone coaching inn and they haven't mucked about with the exterior (rare). There are three rooms where you can take the children – two rather cafeteria like and one a reasonably comfortable lounge. It has a nice atmosphere and, although it's a bit scruffy, it is gradually being done up.

There's a good choice of food – sandwiches under £1, lots of salads for £2 or less, fried dishes with chips at about £1.50 and hot 'specials' – chicken curry, kidneys thermidor, steak and kidney pie all around the £2 mark. There are a few children's dishes – things and chips and spaghetti bolognese at less than £1. Food is served Monday to Saturday 11.15am to 2.15pm and 6.15-9.15pm.

Closed on Sundays   Ale – Bass   P – own car park

219

Tarrant Monkton, Dorset
map 2

P *LANGTON ARMS*

Just off the A354. The pub is by the lovely church.

The local thatcher must be kept very busy in this delightful village. A very pretty brick and flint thatched pub with a façade festooned in climbing plants and flowers. The long lawned garden, with bench tables, looks away to open country.

Children are welcome in the large skittle alley at the rear; it obviously doubles as a function room – there's a piano, plenty of tables and chairs, space invaders, darts and an old stove.

A good and interesting choice of food is served every day – salmon mousse, curry, moussaka, pasta, etc.

Ale — Bass   P — own car park

Taunton, Somerset
map 2

H *CASTLE HOTEL* (Prestige), Castle Green – phone 72671

A marvellous stone building with battlements on top and covered in ivy, this hotel was once part of a Norman fortress, some of the ruins of which can be seen in the Norman garden to one side. It is situated in a quiet close behind the main street and in there also is the Somerset County Museum.

£9 per night is charged for children occupying an extra bed and £7 for a cot. Half portions can be ordered from the restaurant menu. The dinner menu is rather expensive, but lunch not so stretching if you stick to the two courses at £5.90 – leek and onion soup followed by Lancashire hot pot might be sufficient for many appetites. There is also a range of bar snacks, flans, pancakes, chicken curry, and a chef's special dish – all at around £2.

An elegant hotel in a convenient place if you are exploring the West Country.

40 rooms, 3 family   Expensive   Open all year
Lunch 12.30-2pm – £5.90 (2 courses) £7.50 (3 courses)
Dinner 7.30-9pm – £12.90   Ale – Bass, Whitbread
Access/AmEx/Barclaycard/Diners   P – own car park

H *COUNTY HOTEL* (THF), East Street – phone 87651

An attractive hotel with a long white-painted Georgian façade in the centre of town. An alternative hotel at which to stop in this popular West Country town.

Accommodation is free for children under 5 and £1 for ages 5 to 14. Half portions and a special menu are available for children in the restaurant. Here the food is pretty standard British – beef sirloin, pork escalopes, saddle of lamb, sole Veronique, etc. The lunchtime snacks are good value – cold meats and salad or a hot dish at between £2 and £3.

76 rooms, 3 family   Moderate   Open all year
Lunch 12.30-2pm – £5.50   Dinner 7-9.30pm – £7.95
Ale – Ushers
Access/AmEx/ Barclaycard/Diners   P – own car park

P   **WINCHESTER ARMS,** Castle Green

Opposite the Castle Hotel.

The people of this famous West Country town were in the past noted for their rebellious spirit. They were daft enough to proclaim Perkin Warbeck as King ('King Perkin') and Judge Jeffreys hanged a few hundred of the local populace after the Duke of Monmouth's rebellion. Well, they should rise up again in rebellion against the horribly loud music that was ruining this splendid pub when we last visited it. It is a lovely stone pub with pointed arched windows and it mirrors the style of the elegant Castle Hotel across the Green.

Children can use a plushly decorated lounge off the main bar and there is a good-sized patio outside for summer days. The music is a little less deafening in both places. Food is served at lunchtime except Sunday and includes sandwiches, salads at under £2 and a few hot dishes such as cottage pie, chilli con carne, etc, also at under £2.

Upstairs is a restaurant – Troupers – which is not all that exciting because it concentrates on the usual pub grills of steak and veal, scampi, paté and a dish of the day. But they do serve half portions for children and there was no loud music. Troupers serves lunch from 12 to 2pm and dinner from 6.30-10pm – an à la carte meal costing about £7.

Ale – Whitbread   P – public car park opposite

Tavistock, Devon   map 2

H P   **THE BEDFORD HOTEL** (THF) – phone 3221

In the centre of the town.

This elegant town is ideal as a touring centre, close to Dartmoor. The hotel is a stone, crenellated building with lovely public rooms pleasingly decorated and furnished and the staff are *pleasant and helpful. Next door is the hotel's pub, the Bedford Bar, which has a glass fronted veranda for the children and where snacks are served all week. It overlooks a small garden.*

There is no accommodation charge for children from 1 to 4 years, and from 5 to 14 the extremely modest price of £1 is asked.

32 rooms, 3 family   Moderate   Open all year
Lunch 12.30-2pm – £5.95   Dinner 7-9.15pm – £7.95
Ale – Ushers, Bass   Access/AmEx/Barclaycard/Diners
P – limited space in garage at the back

Tempsford, Beds   map 1

P R   *ANCHOR INN* – phone Biggleswade 40233

On the A1.

A big and welcoming pub which affords relief from the rigours of the A1. There is a big bar area and an equally big restaurant which has a special children's menu. Hot and cold food is served in the bar at lunchtime and cold snacks in the evening.

There is a large and airy children's room with slot machines and table football, and a soft drinks bar. Outside are acres of grassy garden alongside the River Ouse. Swings, climbing frames, etc, are also provided, and the cheerful and efficient owners even run a children's club.

The ladies' room has space and facilities to change and feed a baby.

Lunch 12-2.30pm – £5.50   Dinner 6.30-10pm – £5.50
Ale – Greene King, Everard's
Access/AmEx/Barclaycard/Diners   P – own car park

Tetbury, Glos   map 2

H   *THE CLOSE HOTEL* (Prestige), 8 Long Street – phone 52272

In the centre of the town.

A lovely 16th century building of warm Cotswold stone. A Cistercian monastery once stood on this site and you can imbibe a suitable air of tranquility in the walled garden at the rear. Here there is a long paved terrace overlooking a sunken croquet lawn, a lily pond and lime trees – useful for the vodka and tonics. It is a well maintained hotel with an elegant dining room which overlooks the garden.

The hotel's brochure states that accommodation is free for children up to 3 years; with a charge of £6 from 3 to 14. The under-manager, however, stated that £6 was charged for both a cot and an extra bed. We are sorry but we could not break through his studied off-handedness to clear up the confusion. Please check. Half portions are served in the restaurant and there's a tea time menu for children at 5.30pm. A good place to stay for tourists – and we'd like to hear how you fare.

11 rooms, 2 family   Moderate   Open all year
Lunch 12.30-1.45pm £5.50 or £8.50
Dinner 7.30-9.45pm – £12.50
Access/AmEx/Barclaycard/Diners   P – there is a car park but no clear signs at the front of the hotel to indicate how to reach it

Tewkesbury, Glos   map 2

H   ***ROYAL HOP POLE CREST HOTEL,*** Church Street – phone 293 236

In a main street in the centre of the town (on A38).

A town centre hotel, with a half-timbered façade, which we include as a stopping-off point either for a meal (The Buttery is open all day) or a night. Behind the hotel it is reasonably and unexpectedly quiet in the long narrow lawned garden which stops at the River Severn, full here of small craft and barges. Quite peaceful especially if you secure one of the garden rooms. There is a patio too.

Accommodation is free for children up to 14; there is a special children's menu and half portions can also be provided. The Buttery serves pastries, snacks, grills, dish of the day, etc.

29 rooms, 2 family   Expensive   Open all year
The Buttery 10am-5.30pm   Lunch 12.30-1.30pm – £5.95
Dinner 7.30-9.30pm – £8.25   Ale – Bass, Fussell's
Access/AmEx/Barclaycard/Diners   P – own car park

H   ***TEWKESBURY PARK HOTEL GOLF & COUNTRY CLUB*** (Country Club Hotels), Lincoln Green Lane – phone 295 405

Off the A38 south of Tewkesbury.

This hotel is included because of its excellent sporting facilities. The main building itself is passable – average Georgian – but the new extension is very ugly: a two-storey motel block in mud brown. The club area – with its good and large heated pool, sauna and snooker tables is ugly to look at too. But there are four squash courts and an eighteen-hole golf course, which, incidentally, is not free to guests although green fees are reduced.

Accommodation is free for children under 14 and there is a children's menu in the Buttery in the Club house. Half portions are also served in the restaurant.

52 rooms, 12 family   Moderate   Closed 4 days from Boxing Day
Buttery 10am-9pm   Lunch (not Sat) 12.30-1.45pm – £5.50
Dinner 7-9.30pm – £7.50   Ale – Flowers
Access/AmEx/Barclaycard/Diners   P – own car park

Thaxted, Essex   map 1

R   **RECORDER'S HOUSE,** 17 Town Street – phone 830 438

Right in the centre of the village.

This is an attractive bow-fronted building of 15th century vintage in that rarity in Essex – a pretty village. The dining room, with lovely panelling, a beamed ceiling and an inglenook fireplace is very appealing.

Half portions are served for children, and the owners make a great effort to welcome children: as well as the high chair, there are bibs, children's drinking cups, etc. The restaurant is open too for morning coffee and afternoon tea.

The ladies' cloakroom is adequate for changing and feeding a baby – and you will find the owners very helpful.

Closed Sunday dinner/Monday/28-31st Dec
Lunch 12.15-2.15pm – £4.50   Dinner 7-9.30pm – £9 alc
Licensed   Access/AmEx/Diners   P – on street, but not difficult

---

Thetford, Norfolk   map 4

H   **THE BELL** (THF), King Street – phone 4455

Part of this hotel dates from the late 15th century, and its original wooden gallery is still there above a cobbled courtyard. Opposite is a statue of Tom Paine, born here and author of 'The Rights of Man'. He might not have approved of the hotel's extension, which is just-about-bearable modern.

Accommodation is free for children up to 5, and there is a standard charge of £1 from 5 to 14 years. They have their own special menu or can choose half portions from the main menus, which are British in emphasis: soups, patés, roast meats, lamb cutlets Reform, plaice, etc.

A useful place to stop if you intend to explore this ancient town.

42 rooms, 1 family   Expensive   Open all year

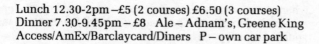

Lunch 12.30-2pm —£5 (2 courses) £6.50 (3 courses)
Dinner 7.30-9.45pm — £8   Ale — Adnam's, Greene King
Access/AmEx/Barclaycard/Diners   P — own car park

Thirsk, N. Yorks

map 3

H R   *THE GOLDEN FLEECE* (THF) – phone 23108

A smashing looking brick hotel, with lovely windows and a hanging golden fleece, in the attractive Market Place. You can't see the full beauty of its front on Mondays and Saturdays – they're market days. It has a good interior with antique furniture and, as befits a racing centre, some interesting horse paintings.

There is no accommodation charge for children up to 5 years and from 5 to 14 years only a token charge of £1. There is no entertainment for them within the hotel, but it's a good touring base with lots of interesting things to do and see in the area – racing at Thirsk, fishing, golfing, pony trekking and the glorious Yorkshire moors.

The Paddock Bar offers a good range of snacks and the restaurant has the usual Hungry Bear menu for children. The restaurant offers plain fare with the emphasis on English dishes – roast beef and Yorkshire pud, Wensleydale and mushroom flan, steak and kidney pie.

22 rooms, 5 family   Moderate   Open all year
Lunch 12-2.15pm – £4.50   Dinner 7-9.15 – £8.50   Ale – Tetley
Access/AmEx/Barclaycard/Diners   P – own car park

Three Cocks, Brecon

map 2

H   *THREE COCKS HOTEL* – phone Glasbury 215

On the A438, south of Hay-on-Wye.

This is a lovely-looking stone hotel, smothered in Virginia creeper. Its rooms are delightfully furnished and decorated. There's a huge stone fireplace open to the restaurant and one of the lounges and there is a further lounge which is beautifully panelled.

Lunch is not served in the hotel and if you don't wish to go far afield you can lunch at the Old Barn pub across the road (which belongs to the hotel) where there is a good variety of pub food (steak, gammon, cottage pie £1.50-£5) and a 'Kiddies Korner' menu at 40p. The hotel will provide food for young children

225

whenever it's required. They are accommodated in cots for £4 or in extra bed for £7.50. The restaurant has a fixed price à la carte gourmet dinner each evening.

Behind the hotel is a nice grassy garden and a field where the children can play and at the Old Barn is a fenced play area with swings, slide, see-saw, etc.

7 rooms, 2 family   Moderate   Closed mid-Dec to mid-Feb
Dinner 7.30-9.30pm – £11.75
Access/AmEx/Barclaycard/Diners   P – own car park

Thurlestone, Devon   map 2

H   *THURLESTONE HOTEL* (Best Western) – phone 382

In the centre of the village.

Run by the same family for ninety years, the hotel is situated in one of South Devon's loveliest coastal villages. Within the splendid gardens there are lots of leisure facilities including hard tennis courts, squash courts, and indoor and outdoor swimming pools. There is a paddling pool for very young children with the indoor pool, and in the garden a climbing frame, swings and a slide. There is golf at Thurlestone Golf Club, and a par-three course at the hotel.

Accommodation is free for children aged 12 and under sharing their parents' room. A special children's menu is offered at tea and dinner and smaller portions are also available. Good news – the listening service extends to the pub next door.

It's wonderful to find an hotel which offers so much for families without being 'touristy'.

74 rooms, 36 family   Moderate   Open all year
Lunch 12.30-2pm – £3.25   Dinner 7.30-9pm – £8.50
Ale – Palmer's
Access/AmEx/Barclaycard/Diners   P – own car park

Tiverton, Devon   map 2

R   *THE LOWMAN,* 45 Gold Street – phone 257 311

A small very attractive restaurant by the Great Western Canal (a mucky stretch in 1983 but a clean-up promised for this year).

The new owners welcome children and will prepare pretty well anything that is asked for: from fish fingers and sausages with plenty of tomato ketchup to vegetarian dishes. Half portions are *also available from the large à la carte menu and there is a meal of the day each lunchtime.*

No facilities are available for changing or feeding an infant.

Closed on Wednesday   Lunch 12-2pm – £5   Tea 3-4pm, summer only
Dinner 7-9.30pm – £7.50   Licensed   Access/Barclaycard
P – on street or in nearby public car park

Tomintoul, Grampian
map 6

R **GLENMULLIACH RESTAURANT** – phone 356

On the A939 east of Tomintoul.

A purpose-built small restaurant in beautiful surroundings in skiing and sheep country on the mountainous A939 road. It was built and is run by a family who offer a wide range of dishes of excellent value: for example roast lamb and vegetables at £2.45, mutton pie and vegetables at £1.50, a host of snacks and pastries and a few children's dishes.

There is a small lawned garden at the front and swings for the children at the side. From November to mid-March the restaurant is open only at weekends, except 'when the road is closed by snow'. Make sure you check (the phone goes through to the owners' house) before making a winter visit.

Sorry, absolutely no space or facilities for baby-feeding or changing.

Open 10am-7pm (or later if the custom's there)
No credit cards accepted   P – own car park

Tonbridge, Kent
map 1

H **ROSE & CROWN HOTEL** (THF), High Street – phone 357 966

In the town centre.

A traditional THF town centre hotel. It is an old coaching inn, with an 18th century brick façade and modern additions at the rear, and an oak-beamed and panelled interior.

Accommodation for children is free up to the age of 5 and £1 from 5 to 14. A special children's menu and half portions are offered in the dining room.

52 rooms, 1 family, 1 suite   Moderate   Open all year
Lunch 12.30-2pm – £5.25
Dinner 7-10pm Mon-Sat – £6.50   Ale – Fremlins
Access/AmEx/Barclaycard/Diners   P – own car park

Tormarton, Avon   map 2

P   *COMPASS INN*

---

*Half a mile from junction 18 of the M4 – a right turn off the A46
going towards Stroud.*

*A fine old creeper-covered pub which is only a minute or so
from the motorway. It has a number of bars including a food bar,
which leads into a huge glass-roofed orangery which even in the
depths of winter is pleasantly warm. There is a big garden with
plenty of tables.*

*Children are welcome in the food bar or the orangery, but at
lunchtimes only.*

*The food display, with many types of salads, is very tempting,
and children's portions are available. A beef salad costs around
£3.50 and, apart from soups and sandwiches, there are usually
several hot dishes (at about £3) each day: for example, coq au
vin, seafood pancake, fisherman's pancake and a meat pie.
Food seven days a week.*

Ale — Bass, Wadworth's   P – own car park

Torquay, Devon   map 2

H   *PALACE HOTEL* – phone 22271

---

*On the coast road to the north-east of the town centre. Take the
Babbacombe road from the harbour.*

*An imposing hotel in the grand seaside tradition with
twenty-five acres of magnificent gardens, a terrace, sauna and
excellent swimming pools both indoors and out. There is also a
nine-hole pitch and putt, billiards and table tennis. There are
squash courts and, rarely for Britain, indoor tennis courts where
Sue Barker learned her craft.*

*Children are accommodated free up to 3 and from 3 to 12 are
charged £4.50 including breakfast. There is a special menu for
children and half portions are served. A resident nanny is on
call and baby-sitting can be arranged. This is a fine place to go
for a few days' relaxation – you need never leave its portals –
and there would be no need to brave the terrors of the Torquay
seafront.*

138 rooms, 26 family   Expensive
Closed for a trade fair in January
Access/AmEx/Barclaycard/Diners   P – own car park

Trefriw, Gwynedd map 3

R **WELSH KITCHEN** – phone Llanrwst 640991

On the B5106 north of Betws-y-Coed.

A pretty little café which is open Monday to Saturday all day but whose owner didn't wish to go in the guide unless she could vet the entry. Well, it was a busy time for her and she's probably very pleasant to customers, so she's in anyway – though not unfortunately with full details as she wouldn't answer our questions.

We did discover from a helpful waitress that they do have a high chair, but don't know what her policy is regarding small portions for small appetites nor if there would be any help should a mother need to change or feed an infant.

Our notes, necessarily brief in the face of such hostility, mentioned salads at up to £2.50, steaks at about £4, trout at about £2, pastries and cakes.

Closed Sundays and Mon-Thur from Nov to Easter and for 2 weeks in Nov
Lunch 12-2pm   Teas 3-5pm   Dinner 7.30-8.45pm
Licensed   P – own car park

Tregrehan, Par, Cornwall map 2

P **THE BRITANNIA INN**

On the A390 west of Par.

Good-looking pub with a thoughtful landlord (he's newish – let's hope it lasts). There are lovely large lawned gardens with lots of tables and seating, a play area with swings (some especially for under-5s) and climbing frame well away from, but in sight of, the main lawn.

There is an area for children in the foyer with electronic games and more room above where they can sit.

The extensive cold buffet is available 7 days a week and a restaurant serves meals 'to suit the children'.

Ale – Bass, Devenish   P – own large car park

Troon, Strathclyde map 5

H **SUN COURT HOTEL** – phone 312 727

The road runs along the coast to the east of Troon – look for the Marine Hotel which is at the start of the road.

It's odd that in an area of such natural beauty, there is so little on offer in the way of hotels: this hotel is remarkable in that it's the only one in the area we could find for possible inclusion. It has a shabby exterior, but is quiet as it's at the end of a cul de sac and overlooking Troon golf course and the Firth of Clyde. All you can hear is the sound of the sea, and a short walk will take you to the sand dunes and beach with good swimming. The hotel has a Real tennis court, a hard tennis court and four squash courts.

The accommodation charge for a child sharing with its parents is £14 and the dining room serves half portions. Bar lunches are available from £1.80 and high teas are served to residents' children from 6 o'clock on. Vegetables are supplied from the hotel's walled kitchen garden and there is a spacious garden where children can play – though not much else immediately on offer for them.

21 rooms, 3 family Moderate Open all year
Lunch 1-2pm – £6.50
Dinner 7.30-9.30pm – £9.50 (children £7)
Access/AmEx P – own car park

Trumpington, Cambs   map 1

P   ***COACH AND HORSES,*** High Street

On the A10.

This is a charming white-washed pub on the main road near Cambridge.

The staff are also helpful and charming and, as one of them emphasised when we called in, will 'always plant cushions under the children and lay on sausage and chips'. Or chicken and chips for that matter. There is an excellent choice of food here: you can start with the twenty or so salads which go to make up the cold buffet. Then proceed to a dish of the day at just over £3 – chicken chasseur, roast lamb or steak and kidney pie. There are grills – gammon, steaks, etc – and lasagne, moussaka or curries at around £2.

It's an excellent pub and well worth travelling the short distance from Cambridge – but you will not find any food on Sunday evenings.

Ale – Adnam's, Greene King P – own car park

Turnberry, Strathclyde   map 5

H   ***TURNBERRY HOTEL*** (Distinguished Hotels) – phone 202

Follow the sign to Turnberry off the A77 at Turnberry. The hotel stands above the road overlooking the golf course – you can't miss it.

This very famous and very grand hotel sits in its Edwardian elegance above one of the greatest golf links in the world – the Ailsa course, home of the Open Golf Championship on many occasions and known as one of the sternest and most compelling of golfing tests. There are many other excellent facilities: two full size snooker tables (not for children), table tennis, a mini-gymnasium with excellent equipment, an indoor swimming pool with French windows on to the garden, two tennis courts and a pitch and putt course to rebuild one's confidence after the rigours of the Ailsa. Riding, shooting and fishing can be arranged. Various entertainments are provided for children as well as baby-sitting on request.

The many public rooms are very attractive, especially the restaurant which overlooks the golf course.

Accommodation for children up to 16 years is £10 per night including breakfast, and as well as half portions there is a special children's menu. The Dormy House coffee shop (the club house) is open all day and provides hot and cold snacks and buffet.

126 rooms, 3 family   Expensive   Open all year
Lunch 1-2.30pm – £7   Dinner 8-9.30pm – £14.50
Dormy House 11am-8pm (Apr-Oct) – from £2
Access/AmEx/Barclaycard/Diners   P – own car park

Tyndrum, Central   map 5

R   *CLIFTON COFFEE HOUSE* – phone 271

On the A82.

It looks like a shack from the outside and the restaurant is like a motorway café – a good one. It's part of a wool/tweed shopping complex of which there are quite a few in this area. There's a good variety of dishes – soups, salads and interesting hot dishes from 75p to £2.25 – salmon crumble, lasagne, mutton pie. Very popular so a good idea to miss the rush hours if you can. Huge no smoking area.

There are two lavatories for the disabled with shelves ideal for nappy-changing, and the owner will allow a mother to breast-feed in the house which is a few yards from the restaurant.

A busy, friendly place, providing good food and facilities for a family on the road – at very reasonable prices.

Closed end Oct to end Mar   Open every day 8.30am-5.30pm
Licensed   Access/AmEx/Barclaycard/Diners   P – own car park

Uphall, Lothian
map 5

H R   *HOUSTOUN HOUSE* – phone Broxburn 853 831

On the A899, west of Edinburgh.

A superb 16th century manor house which comes as an amazing sight after driving through the nearby industrial wastes of Edinburgh and its attendant motorways. An extension has been added with such care that you can hardly see the join, and the gardens too are stunning with Cypress trees and yew hedges (some of which are like a children's playground in themselves). The interior matches up to expectations with flag floors, stone walls, huge fireplaces and lovely rooms with drapes and four-posters.

Surrounding the hotel is the Uphall golf course.

There is a charge of £7.50 for a child using a cot or a Z-bed in its parents' room. At lunchtimes children will be served half portions, but are encouraged to eat supper in their rooms not in the restaurant where the adults are at play. There are some interesting dishes including chachouka, poached trout Czarina, coulibiac of spiced salmon, and so on. (Has anyone got a Larousse handy?)

30 rooms, 1 triple   Expensive   Closed 1 and 2 Jan
Lunch 12.30-2pm – £8   Dinner 7.30-9.30pm – £12.50
Access/AmEx/Barclaycard/Diners   P – own car park

Upper Slaughter, Glos
map 2

H R   *LORDS OF THE MANOR HOTEL* – phone Bourton-on-the-Water 20243

The village is off the A436 west of Stow-on-the-Wold; look for the sign to the Slaughters.

An absolutely superb 17th century stone manor house in a small classic English village in the heart of the Cotswolds.

There is a lovely walled garden at the rear, with lawns and climbing flowers and a small fountain – next to a large kitchen garden which bodes encouragingly for the food here. The front garden is immaculately lawned, and surrounded by fine trees. It looks down over the ears of ruminating resident donkeys to a stream where guests can tickle a trout or two.

There is a good value lunch on offer at under £6 for three courses: ham mousse to start, for example; and a choice of trout, loin of pork, or sauté of lambs kidneys to follow; and to finish lemon and ginger cheesecake perhaps. The bar lunches are equally good value – mostly at under £2 – for example smoked mackerel salad or turkey fricassé with rice. At dinner there are some interesting items: fish chaudrée (a bowl of prawns, scallops, sole, halibut and tarragon with garlic croutons), locally smoked salmon, etc.

A cot costs £6.50, and an extra bed for a child is £12.50. Half portions are available in the restaurant.

15 rooms, Moderate Open all year
Lunch 12.30-2pm – £5.80 Dinner 7.30-9.30pm – £10 alc
Ale – Wadworth's
Access/AmEx/Barclaycard/Diners P – own car park

Uppingham, Leicestershire   map 4

H P   *THE FALCON HOTEL,* High Street East – phone 823 535

In the centre of the town.

A pleasant enough old coaching inn of mellow stone in the main square. It has a very attractive courtyard, with several rooms, at the back and here also is a delightful quiet walled garden with apple trees, remarkably fecund when we looked at it early in September.

Apart from a rather scruffy games room with a pool table and space invaders there is little here for children, but it might be okay for a stop-over and the lobby is comfortable – you could sit here with your offspring and get gently ruddled.

The restaurants serves half portions for children and there is no charge for cots or extra beds.

26 rooms, 2 family Moderate Open all year
Lunch bar snacks only Dinner 7-10pm – £6.25
Ale – Ruddles
Access/AmEx/Barclaycard/Diners P – own car park

Walberton, Nr Arundel, West Sussex   map 1

H   *AVISFORD PARK HOTEL* – phone Yapton 551 215

On the B2132 just off the A27.

Quite an attractive hotel – a large, long and low Georgian building set amid forty acres of parkland. There is a lovely *sprawling garden with some fine trees and a patio at the rear. There are good facilities including an outdoor heated swimming pool, tennis court and two squash courts. The games room has snooker and table tennis. A nine-hole golf course is promised for some time this year.*

Accommodation is free for children up to the age of 12; children's portions are available in the restaurant and high teas are also provided from 6pm.

80 rooms, 2 family, 1 set adjoining   Moderate   Open all year
Lunch 12.30-1.45pm – £5.75   Dinner 7.30-9.30pm – £8.75
Access/AmEx/Barclaycard   P – own car park

Water Oakley, Nr Windsor, Berks   map 1

H   *OAKLEY COURT HOTEL*, Windsor Road – phone Maidenhead 74141

From Junction 6 of the M4 take the Windsor road and then the A308 to Maidenhead.

An extremely interesting old Gothic-type manor house built in the mid-19th century with turrets and tall chimneys. It really has style. So has the garden which spreads, tree-laden and so peaceful, down to a wide sweep of the Thames. The extensions are modern, but in mellow brick with stone bow windows which tone in pretty well. A good place for visitors to Windsor and not too far from Heathrow. Unexpected and peaceful.

Accommodation is free for children occupying cots; and thereafter £15 is charged for an extra bed. The restaurant will serve smaller portions for children.

90 rooms, 11 suites, 8 sets of adjoining rooms   Expensive
Open all year   Lunch 12.30-2pm – £9.50
Dinner 7.30-10pm – £15
Access/AmEx/Barclaycard   P – own car park

Watermillock, Cumbria   map 5

H   *OLD CHURCH HOTEL* – phone Pooley Bridge 204

On the A592.

We include this hotel because it is a handsome country house, built in the mid-18th century, set in lovely lawned gardens in a stunning position on the shores of Ullswater and loomed over by Cumbrian hills.

We were however surprised by the off-handedness of the 'resident proprietor'. We managed to drag a few facts out of him: Children under 11 are accommodated at half the single rate and the hotel is closed from November sometime to April sometime. We think there is no official lunch, but residents may order what they wish and high teas are also available.

Good luck! Perhaps he flogs himself into a gentle walk for guests. More reports please.

12 rooms, 1 family   Moderate   Closed? Nov-? April
Dinner 7.30-8.30pm – £9.50
No credit cards accepted   P – own car park

Welford-on-Avon, Warwicks   map 3

P   *BELL*

Just off the A439 a few miles from Stratford-upon-Avon.

This is a busy pub in a pretty village. It has a very inviting low-beamed lounge, crowded with tables, and with an open fireplace. At one end of the pub is a spacious children's room, also with a beamed ceiling, and with plenty of seats.

There is a lawn at the back, ringed with flower beds.

You will pay no more than £2 for the food, which is available every day – the standard pub range of salads with various meats, plaice, cod, chicken and steak and kidney pie.

Ale – Whitbread, Flowers   P – own ample car park

West Runton, Nr Cromer, Norfolk   map 4

H   *LINKS COUNTRY PARK HOTEL* (Best Western) – phone 691

On the A149, west of Cromer.

We could not find many places to include in this part of the world, and this hotel has its own nine-hole golf course for guests and, we were told, is close to a safe, sandy beach. It is an angular Victorian hotel, which has recently been modernised, but its exterior still looks a bit shabby and run-down. We had visions of Norman Bates appearing at the top of the stairs. But along with the golf course, there is a pleasant and shady garden, and we thought it good value for the price.

Accommodation is free for children aged 12 and under. A children's menu is available from 5-6pm. The bar lunches are fairly basic – toasted sandwiches and cold meat salads.

235

34 rooms, 9 family   Cheap   Open all year
Bar lunch   Dinner 7.30-9.30 – £8.25   Ale – Adnam's
Access/AmEx/Barclaycard/Diners   P – own car park

Wester Howgate, Nr Penicuik, Lothian   map 5

P R   *OLD HOWGATE INN* – phone Penicuik 74244

On the B7026 by the A6094 turning.

Halleluyah – a pretty Scottish pub. It has a business-like wood panelled bar and two delightful little low-ceilinged family rooms. A small back garden with fields beyond leads off the stone floored and walled restaurant.

An amazing choice of smorgasbord – forty to be exact – must have something for even the fussiest child. The prices range from £1.10 to £4.50. You can also have a selection of 'finger' versions for eating in the pub. There are a few soup and meat dishes. There's an uninspiring little wine-cum-craft shop next door.

The restaurant 'Ladies' has table and stool – okay for changing and feeding a baby at a push.

Open all year   Lunch 12-2pm (Sun 12.30-2.30pm)
Dinner 6.30-10pm   Ale – Belhaven
Access/AmEx/Barclaycard   P – own car park

Weston, Nr Honiton, Devon   map 2

H   *DEER PARK HOTEL* – phone Honiton 2064

Follow the signs for Buckerell from the A30 and you'll pick up the hotel sign.

A delightful Georgian mansion a couple of miles from Honiton standing in twenty-six acres of beautiful wooded grounds. It has three miles of fishing on the River Otter. The excellent facilities include a heated outdoor swimming pool, and tennis and squash courts. There is a very well furnished games room with table tennis, table football, space invaders, etc, and a conservatory with grape vines, tables and chairs.

Cots are charged at £5 per night; from 2 to 4 years accommodation has a 75% discount; from 5 to 8 a 50% discount and from 9 to 12 25% discount.

Half portions are served in the restaurant, but children must take high tea instead of dinner to qualify for the reductions.

There is a reasonable choice in the restaurant, if of a rather conventional stamp (avocado prawn, pork chops, steak, plaice, etc) – and served in a friendly and charming way by the youthful staff.

31 rooms, 2 family, 3 sets of adjoining rooms   Moderate
Open all year   Lunch 12.30-2pm – £5.25
Dinner 7-10pm – £9.50   Ale – Devenish
Access/AmEx/Barclaycard/Diners   P – own car park

Weston-on-the-Green, Oxon map 1

H   *WESTON MANOR* (Best Western) – Bletchington 50621

North of Oxford on the A 43 near its junction with the A 421.

A very fine 16th century stone manor house in ten acres of grounds with a good spread of lawns and an orchard. A putting green winds between the trees on one side; there is a sunken, partly paved, garden; and a topiarist was obviously once at work in the grounds. There is a squash court and an outdoor heated swimming pool.

Accommodation is free for children who share a room with their parents and half portions are served in the restaurant.

23 rooms, 2 family   Moderate   Open all year
Lunch 12.30-2pm – buffet £3.50, carvery £5.75
Dinner 7.30-9pm – £8.75   Ale – Hook Norton
Access/AmEx/Barclaycard/Diners   P – own car park

P   *CHEQUERS*

North of Oxford on the A 43 near its junction with the A 421.

A busy pub which is housed in an attractive long low stone building with a thatched roof. There is a good-sized lawn at the back with plenty of tables and chairs.

Inside there is a large room off the bar and children may use this. It is well stocked with tables and is primarily intended for customers to eat their food. There is another smaller room which children may use and which has a pool table and darts.

A good array of food is served seven days a week – pizzas, burgers, steaks, salads, ploughman's, etc – all at very reasonable prices (eg pizza at £1.50, rump steak, chips and peas at £3.75).

Ale – Hall's, Ind Coope, Burton   P – own car park

Weston-under-Redcastle, Shropshire　　　　map 3

H R　　*HAWKSTONE PARK* (Best Western) – phone Lee Brockhurst 611

Off the A 49 south of Whitchurch.

A sprawling white-painted hotel which forms a hollow square around the croquet lawn. It started life as an inn in the early 18th century and has the 'Red Castle' (13th century) in its grounds as well as a lake – made by an 18th century eccentric.

There are very good facilities here including a good-sized outdoor heated swimming pool, a grass tennis court, a games room with snooker and pool, and a small exercise room with a rowing machine, static bike and a few weights. But its real raison d'être is the golf – two excellent courses – and a playing professional of some note in Sandy Lyle, who, despite being born in Shropshire's broad acres, elected to play golf for Scotland – shame on you, Sandy.

The hotel therefore tends to be full of golfing societies on days or weekends out, and both the courses and the hotel are usually busy.

The accommodation is free for children up to 2, and there is a reduction of 75% for older children sharing a room with their parents. Lunch is served in the restaurant and in the bar, which serves food from 12.30 to 9.30pm, and where you can get club sandwiches, burgers, seafood platter, paté, etc, from £1 to £3. The restaurant will provide children's meals and half portions from the adult menu. This tends to concentrate on English roasts, trout, smoked salmon, dover sole, etc, with the flambé pan much in evidence.

59 rooms, 10 family　Cheap　Open all year
Lunch 12.30-2pm – £4.95　Bar food 12.30-9.30pm
Dinner 7.30-9.30pm – £6.95　Ale – Wilson's
Access/AmEx/Barclaycard/Diners　P – own car park

Westonbirt, Tetbury, Glos　　　　map 2

H　　*HARE AND HOUNDS HOTEL* (Best Western) – phone 233

On the A 433 south of Tetbury.

An attractive Cotswold stone building, part of which began life as an inn in the early 19th century, and the hotel part of which was added in this century and tones in very skilfully. There are spacious grounds, with lots of lawn, beautiful flower beds and mature trees and hedgerows.

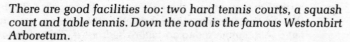

There are good facilities too: two hard tennis courts, a squash court and table tennis. Down the road is the famous Westonbirt Arboretum.

Accommodation is free for children up to 13; a children's menu is available in the early evening; and half portions are also available in the restaurant.

28 rooms, 15 family   Moderate   Open all year
Lunch 12.30-2pm – £5 alc   Dinner 7.30-9pm – £7.75
Ale – Wadworth's, Whitbread, Archer's
Access/AmEx/Barclaycard   P – own car park

Wetheral, Nr Carlisle, Cumbria   map 5

H P R   ***THE CROWN HOTEL*** (Best Western) – phone Carlisle 61888

Near Junction 43 of the M6. Go to the village and ask – we had to.

A truly successful mix of ancient and modern. The three-storey 18th century farmhouse has been married to a good-looking modern wing and a leisure centre, and the whole is a model of successful design. There are excellent facilities including three squash courts and a games room with two pool tables, snooker table, table squash and space invaders.

The pretty conservatory restaurant, which looks out to a patio and the lawns of the garden, is decorated with taste and is a pleasure to sit in. The menu depends mainly on roasts, and there are bar snacks as well at lunchtimes: sandwiches, two dishes of the day, etc.

Children are accommodated free up to 12; and there is a children's menu in the restaurant – things and chips for around £2.

A super place to break a journey or for a longer stay.

50 rooms, 3 sets of adjoining rooms, 1 triple   Expensive
Open all year   Bar lunch 12.15-2.15pm
Restaurant lunch 12.30-2.15pm (exc Sat) – £9
Dinner 7-9.30pm – £9   Ale – Thwaites
Access/AmEx/Barclaycard/Diners   P – own car park

Weybourne, Norfolk   map 4

H R   ***MALTINGS HOTEL*** – phone 275

On the A149.

A delightful 17th century building of flint walls about half a mile from the sea, and three miles from Sheringham. To the rear the old outbuildings and attached cottages ramble away and have been converted to add more bedrooms. There is a lawned garden here too, and the hotel has its own pub which serves Bass, and hot and cold snacks.

Accommodation is free for children up to 16; and half portions are served in the restaurant, where they are notable for their emphasis on fresh ingredients and insistence on being as self-sufficient as possible. They make their own rolls, pies and pastries and smoke their own fish. You have an excellent choice of dishes in the restaurant: frogs' legs, salmon mousse or paté or artichokes to start; then best end of lamb, Norfolk duckling, halibut, trout or steak.

This is a lovely spot to stop and the owner offers a warm welcome to families.

23 rooms, 5 family   Moderate   Open all year
Lunch 12.30-2pm – £7.30
Dinner 7.30-9pm – £9.60   Ale – Bass
Access/AmEx/Barclaycard/Diners   P – own car park

R   *GASCHE'S* – phone 220

On the A149.

A small and pretty building (very close to the Maltings Hotel) made of brick and flint and with a thatched roof. The restaurant is long-established and has a lovely interior with beamed ceilings and scrubbed wooden tables. You can choose one to three courses from the set price lunch menu (£5-£7) and two to four courses at dinner (£10-£14); simple starters – minestrone, melon, dressed crab; main courses like chicken chasseur, sole meunière, grilled steak; and fresh fruit dishes as well as puddings of the creme caramel, peach melba variety. The helpful owner will provide special dishes for children – 'whatever they want' – and mothers are welcome to use the rooms upstairs to feed and change their babies.

Closed Mon all day and Sun evenings
Lunch 12.30-2pm – £7 (3 courses)
Dinner 7-9pm – £12 (3 courses)   Licensed
AmEx/Barclaycard/Diners   P – own car park

Wickham, Hants   map 1

H   *OLD HOUSE HOTEL* – phone 833 049

In the main square of the village.

A classic early Georgian house by the side of a lovely Georgian square. This small hotel has a very pleasant garden at the rear.

The attractive restaurant concentrates on French provincial cooking and has a short but tempting menu. You can start with fresh carrot soup or mousseline of sole, and go on to loin of pork in a wine and prune sauce, or fresh skate in an orange and anchovy sauce.

Half portions are served for children and late teas can also be taken. Accommodation for children up to 2 years costs £2, up to 5 £3 and up to 12 £5. There is a baby-listening system, but the friendly staff will also 'keep an eye on' the children.

10 rooms, 1 family, 2 sets of adjoining rooms   Moderate
Closed Christmas and end July/early August
Lunch 12-2pm – £12   Dinner 7.30-9.30pm – £12
Access/AmEx/Barclaycard   P – 12 spaces

Wimborne Minster, Dorset   map 2

H   **KING'S HEAD HOTEL** (THF), The Square – phone Wimborne 880 101

Off the A35.

This is a smart ivy-covered building which overlooks the town's main square. It was re-built in the late 19th century and is a good town centre hotel – well-placed for holidaymakers.

The cooking is British in emphasis with quite a few 'Taste of England' dishes. The three-course lunch at £5.50 looks good value: bacon and cheese flan followed by baked whole plaice and pudding for example. So is the choice in the evening.

Accommodation is free for children under 5 and from 5 to 14 a charge of £1 is made. The restaurant offers a special menu or half portions for children.

The Minster is worth a look and has a Grenadier figure which appears and bangs the ancient clock every quarter hour.

'How smartly the quarters of the hour march by
That the jack-o-clock never forgets;
Ding-dong; and before I have traced a cusp's eye
Or got the true twist of the ogee over
A double ding-dong richohetts.'

Thomas Hardy wrote that: he must have been at the Wadworth's all day.

28 rooms, 3 family   Moderate   Open all year
Lunch 12.30-1.45pm – £5.50   Dinner 7-9.30pm – £8.50

Ale – Ringwood, Wadworth's
Access/AmEx/Barclaycard/Diners   P – own car park

Winchcombe, Glos   map 2

R   ***OLD WHITE LION,*** 37 North Street – phone 603 300

In a main street off the High Street.

The owners have stamina – this restaurant is open 364 days a year from 9am to 10.30 pm. Apart from lunchtimes and dinner times, you can eat a huge range of hot and cold snacks all day at very reasonable prices – lots under £1. At lunch or dinner venison costs £5, lamb £3, sole under £5 and pizza and salad just over £2.

It is a nice stone building with plenty of room in the stone dining room with overhead beams. A flower-festooned yard leads to a pretty little garden with tables and benches.

Mothers who need to tend their babies can do so in comfort in the bathroom upstairs. This is a real find.

Closed Christmas Day   Open every day 9am-10.30pm
Lunch 12-2.30pm – £5 alc   Dinner 7-30-10pm – £7 alc
Licensed   No credit cards accepted   P – on street

Wincle, Cheshire   map 3

P   ***WILD BOAR***

On the A54.

White-walled pub in splendid moorland isolation and quite a haven for local sportsmen who go shooting on the moors.

There are two rooms where you can take the children – one with games machines, chairs, tables and bench seating and the other a dining room.

Except on Monday evenings you will always find something to eat here, including rump steaks at just over £4. Spare ribs, scampi, chicken, various fish dishes and steak pies are around £2, and lasagne is £1.50. There are plenty of salads and children can have half portions if they wish.

Ale – Robinsons   P – own car park

Windermere, Cumbria   map 5

H   ***LANGDALE CHASE HOTEL*** – phone Ambleside 2201

On the A591 north of Windermere.

A very fine Victorian mansion with extensive gardens down to the Lake where guests can swim, if they have a tough constitution, or make use of the hotel's rowing boat. There is a balustraded terrace on two sides, with superb views of the water and the countryside, and stone steps lead down to the two tennis courts and the Lake. There is also a putting green and table tennis table. The entrance hall is a wonderful sight with panelled walls, gallery, stained glass ceiling, ornate carved fireplace and its collection of antique furniture and oil paintings.

Cots cost £2; children up to 12 are accommodated for £8 and from 12 to 14 or thereabouts for £12. High teas can be arranged for them at 6pm and served either in the restaurant or their rooms, and they can also choose half portions from the menu.

A lovely place to stay and peacefully situated away from the main resort of Windermere.

35 rooms, 6 family   Moderate   Open all year
Lunch 12.45-2pm – £6.25   Dinner 7-8.30pm – £10.95
Access/AmEx/Barclaycard/Diners   P – own car park

Windsor, Berks

map 1

H R   *CASTLE HOTEL* (THF), High Street – phone 51011

A classic Georgian building in the centre of town and right opposite the royal castle – a great spot to stay for the paparazzi and other royalty hunters.

Accommodation is free for children aged 1 to 4 and £1 is charged from 5 to 14. The restaurant offers half portions and a special menu for children. The coffee shop is open from 7.30am to 10.30pm, and has the usual array of grills, club sandwiches, burgers, salads, etc. The restaurant brings you a shortish menu with some interesting dishes: chicken with prunes and lemon sauce, Peking style duck, poached bream, pork fillets in pineapple juice, etc, as well as chargrilled steaks and chops.

85 rooms, 18 family   Expensive   Open all year
Lunch 12.30-2pm – £6.50   Dinner 7.30-10pm – £8.25
Access/AmEx/Barclaycard/Diners   P – own car park

Woburn, Milton Keynes, Beds

map 1

H   *BEDFORD ARMS HOTEL* (Kingsmead), George Street – phone 441

In the main street.

A very handsome Georgian building which has been renovated

with care and modern additions blend in very well and form a courtyard at the back of the hotel. It's not far from the stately home of Woburn and its famous wildlife park.

The interior is elegantly done, and the dining room with its splendid ceiling is particularly striking.

Bar snacks are available at lunchtimes and include salads with meat, chicken and prawns at £3 to £4, plus sandwiches, ploughman's and a hot dish of the day. There is plenty of choice on the table d'hôte menu – mostly roast and grills but also venison pie, baked smoked haddock with cheese, suprême of chicken Bombay, etc.

The accommodation charge for children up to 5 is £4 and from 5 to 16 £7. There is a special children's menu and half portions are also available.

60 rooms, 4 family   Moderate   Open all year
Lunch 12.15-2.15pm – £7.50   Dinner 7-10.30pm – £7.50
Ale – Benskins, Courage
Access/AmEx/Barclaycard/Diners   P – own car park

Wolf's Castle, Dyfed   map 2

R   **THE WOLFE INN** – phone Treffgarne 662

On the A40 south of Fishguard.

A delightful stone pub on this busy main route. It has a small lawned garden to one side, and a snug interior with, in all, three bars.

There is no food available on Mondays and at lunchtimes on Sunday bar meals only. These include local smoked trout at under £2, and meals such as scampi, plaice and chips, salads, etc, at up to £3.50. The restaurant itself, again housed in a pleasant room off the main bar, serves plain food; various fish dishes, steaks, chicken, gammon, etc, up to around £5.50. Reduced portions are served to children.

The very helpful owners will always make facilities available to mothers who need to change or feed a baby.

Closed Mondays   Lunch 12-2pm   Dinner 7-10pm – £7 alc
Ale – Felinfoel
No credit cards accepted   P – own car park

Woodbridge, Suffolk   map 1

H   **SECKFORD HALL HOTEL** – phone 5678

Look for sign on A12 close to Woodbridge sign.

If you need accommodation this is a far sounder bet than the town itself, which owing to the idiocies of the Woodbridge 'planners', is impossible to penetrate – although somewhere therein is a THF hotel, The Crown. Perhaps it has a helicopter pad?

This hotel is a magnificent example of Tudor architecture set in thirty acres of peaceful lawns and woodland with a lake where you can fish for trout and, monk-like, for carp. There are also swings and slides for children.

Cots are charged at £2.50 per night (but are negotiable items for longer periods) and extra beds cost half the single rate. Half portions can be served in the restaurant.

24 rooms, 1 set of adjoining   Moderate
Closed Christmas Day   Lunch 12.30-2pm – £6.50
Dinner 7.30-9pm – £10 alc   Ale – Tolly
Access/AmEx/Barclaycard/Diners   P – own car park

Woodstock, Oxon   map 1

The town of Woodstock is perhaps considered a side-show to the main event of Blenheim Palace but, if so, is an interesting and attractive one.

H   **BEAR HOTEL** (Prestige), Park Street – phone 811 511

In the main street.

A charming ivy-clad building of beautiful Cotswold stone. It was first licensed as an inn in 1232. Close to Blenheim Palace, the home of the Marlborough family and birthplace of Sir Winston Churchill.

There is no charge made for the accommodation of children up to 12 years who share their parents' room. The restaurant serves children half portions at half price.

43 rooms, 4 family   Expensive   Open all year
Lunch 12-2.30pm – £6.25 & £8.25
Dinner 7-10.30pm – £8.50 & £10.50
Access/AmEx/Barclaycard/Diners   P – own car park

R   **BROTHERTONS,** 1 High Street – phone 811 114

In the town centre across the road from the Bear.

A wine bar and brasserie in a pretty, creeper-clad stone house. You'll find sustenance throughout the day with morning coffee, hot meals and afternoon teas available. It is nicely furnished with wooden tables and chairs.

There is standard fare on the menu – smoked salmon, spare ribs, cannelloni, steaks and salads and a daily vegetarian dish. Prices from £1 to £7. A handy place to rest weary tourists' feet.

The 'Ladies' is just about big enough to change a baby. There is no chair but the staff could 'drag a chair in'.

Closed – Christmas week Open 10.30am-10.30pm Licensed
Access/AmEx/Barclaycard/Diners
P – restricted parking in market square

Woolhampton, Berks

map 1

P   *ROWBARGE INN,* Station Road

Just off the A4 east of Newbury.

A tiled and white-painted pub by the River Kennet. It has an inviting air, low-ceilinged and rambling, with alcoves here and there.

A small wood-panelled children's room with wooden settles opens on to a quiet and pretty garden with a few tables.

Hot dishes are available every day except Sunday, when at lunchtimes (but not in the evenings) sandwiches and ploughman's can be had. There is a good range of salads with cold meats, mackerel, or trout at up to £3 and three or four hot dishes of the day – rissoles, braised steak, steak and kidney pie – at the same sort of prices.

Ale – Courage, Bass, Arkell's P – own car park

Woolverton, Somerset

map 2

P   *RED LION*

On the A36 at the junction with the B3110.

A large stone pub which is set back from the road, and which has recently been extended.

The children's room with wooden tables and padded seats is just off the main bar. There is a large lawned garden with spreading trees and plenty of tables and benches – an inviting prospect for summer days.

Food is available every day, and is the usual pub selection: salads from £2 to £5, jacket potatoes, steak and mushroom pie at around £2.50, sandwiches and ploughman's.

Ale – Wadworth's, Bass P – own car park

246

Wotton, Surrey map 1

R **WOTTON HATCH** – phone Dorking **885 665**

On the A25 near Dorking.

Large ivy-clad pub with a plush, well-furnished restaurant and lounge. As well as a reasonably conventional range of grills, roasts, fowl and fish dishes, there are some imaginative touches such as rabbit, faggot and mussel pie, rabbit and venison pie, jellied ham with pickled walnuts, etc. There is a small patio and a large garden.

Half portions are served to children.

The 'Ladies' is adequate for feeding and changing a baby.

Closed Monday, Sunday dinner and 27th-31st December
Lunch 12.15-2pm – £7 Dinner 7.15-9.30pm – £9.50
Ale – Fuller's
Access/AmEx/Barclaycard/Diners P – own car park

Wrelton, Nr Pickering, N. Yorks map 4

R **THE HUNTSMAN RESTAURANT** – Pickering 72530

Turn on to the Rosedale road from the village – it's a few yards.

A smallish low-slung stone building but inside the dining room is spacious enough, and there is a bar as you enter. You will encounter a very comprehensive menu, and the lunch menu in particular offers enterprising dishes at very good prices. The farmhouse flan, with egg, mushrooms, onions and cheese plus salad and chips is a copious meal at under £2; chicken Dansak with vegetables is under £3 and the local trout with salad and potatoes is under £2.50. The dinner menu offers such dishes as grilled salmon steak, chicken Annette, duckling, lamb cutlets chasseur.

Children's portions are available, and the owners will always help a mother wishing to feed or change a baby – sometimes, for example, a room is available upstairs.

Closed Mon, Sun dinner, Christmas, 1st week Oct, last 2 weeks Feb Lunch 12-2pm – £2.50 alc
Dinner 7-9.30pm – £8.50 alc Licensed
No credit cards accepted P – own car park

Wroxton St Mary, Oxon map 1

H **WROXTON HOUSE HOTEL** (Prestige) – phone 482

On the A422 three miles from Banbury.

A fine old building of mellow Cotswold stone. It is low and rambling, partly thatched, with a balustrade round the middle. A small lawned garden at the side has some tables and chairs.

The food is fairly conventional but with plenty of choice from paté, herrings, mackerel, lamb, turkey, pork, beef, etc. It's good value at lunchtime too with three courses for £5.50, or one main course for £3.55.

Accommodation is free for children up to 12 years and half portions are served in the restaurant – the staff's attitude is to serve up whatever children want and to charge accordingly. Close to the well-known Wroxton Abbey, a 17th-century building which incorporates the remains of a 13th-century priory.

15 rooms, 2 family Moderate Open all year
Lunch 12-2.30pm – £5.50
Dinner 7-9.30pm – £7.25 Ale – Phillips
Access/AmEx/Barclaycard/Diners P – own car park

Yelverton, Nr Plymouth, Devon   map 2

H   *MOORLAND LINKS HOTEL* (Forestdale) – phone 852 245

Look for the hotel sign on the A386 south of Yelverton.

A long low white hotel in nine acres of grounds on the edge of Dartmoor. The hotel has its own tennis court, putting green and outdoor swimming pool (unheated) and can also make special arrangements for golf at nearby Yelverton Golf Club and for horse-riding at Crossways Stables two miles away.

There is no charge for children up to 15 sharing their parents' room. The restaurant will serve half portions and more or less whatever the children want. Children's tea is served each afternoon.

Nothing special for children here, unless they're horse-mad, but a comfortable base in an area of great beauty.

23 rooms, 3 family Moderate Open all year
Lunch 12.30-2pm – £7.95 Dinner 7.30-10pm – £7.95
Access/AmEx/Barclaycard/Diners P – own car park

York, North Yorks   map 4

H R *DEAN COURT HOTEL* (Best Western), Duncombe Place – phone 25082 (or 01-940 9766)

A bit difficult – head for the west side of the Minster.

This is a good city hotel run by helpful efficient staff and bang next door to the splendid York Minster; a good place to stay if you wish to have a good look at this lovely city.

The Coffee Lounge, which is open from 10am-8pm all week – serves toasted snacks and open sandwiches at £1. And there are lots of little rooms where you can eat, drink and relax.

The chef will prepare anything required for children eating in the restaurant and they can also have half portions from the adult menu. Both the lunch and dinner menus include grilled and roasted meats together with richer dishes like Duckling Judge Henry Bean (with black cherries and rum and orange sauce) and sauté of venison in Burgundy, and various fish dishes.

Accommodation for children is £5 per night up to the age of 14.

35 rooms, 2 quadruple, 2 triple   Expensive
Open all year   Lunch 12-2pm – £6.50   Dinner 6.30-9pm – £10
Access/AmEx/Barclaycard/Diners
P – porter will take car to hotel car park for you

P   *JUDGE'S LODGING,* Lendal

You'll have to ask – sorry.

A nicely furnished – red velvet and oak – comfortable pub in the brick cellar of the hotel. A slightly dreary dining room is offered for children but better is the little lounge, next to the bar, where they can also sit.

From 12-2.15pm sandwiches (around 75p) and hot dishes (around £2) are served.

Upstairs is a restaurant with high chair but the only member of staff we could find in the hotel would not allow us to see it – ah well, next year perhaps?

P – park in a public car park and walk – it's a beautiful city to walk in.

STATELY HOMES, ZOOS, MUSEUMS, etc

Since visits to these places are likely to be lengthy, we thought that they should provide, at the very least, changing tables and a place where a mother could feed her baby in privacy.

We contacted over 500 of these establishments and had a reply from about 200 of them. The great majority of these (about three-quarters) had none of the basic facilities, let alone high chairs in their cafés.

Our favourite quote during this phase of our research was from someone who claimed to be in 'public relations' for the National Trust: 'Families normally visit in cars and they "do it" there.' He did not have any future plans to help families with small children 'unless we receive any complaints'. Go to it!

However, we found a few places which could provide absolutely basic help to a parent with a small child. For example a table or chair or both in the Ladies' lavatory. Many of them professed a willingness to help mothers if requested.

We'd like to mention these places with exceptional facilities:

Beaulieu Abbey National Motor Museum, and House, Beaulieu, Hants

Chatsworth House, Chatsworth, Bakewell, Derbys

Shire Horse Centre, Yealmpton, Nr Plymouth, Devon

Conwy Valley Railway Museum, Betws-y-Coed, Gwynedd

Fritton Lake and Country Park, Fritton, Gt Yarmouth, Norfolk

London Zoo, Regents Park, London, N W 1

Lake District National Park Visitor Centre, Windermere, Cumbria

Kilverstone Wild Life Park, Thetford, Norfolk

And these, with reasonable facilities:

Museum of British Road Transport, Cook Street, Coventry

Model Village, Torquay, Devon

Bentley Wild Fowl and Motor Museum, Harveys Lane, Halland, Sussex

Edinburgh Zoo, Murrayfield, Edinburgh

Gwydir Castle, Llanrwst, Gwynedd

Clevedon Craft Centre, Newhouse Farm, Moor Lane East, Clevedon, Avon

Chessington Zoo, Leatherhead Road, Chessington, Surrey

Sheldon Manor, Chippenham, Wilts

Chester Zoo, Upton by Chester, Chester, Cheshire

Cornwall Aero Park, Helston, Cornwall

Cotswold Wildlife Park, Burford, Oxon

Museum of Mankind, 6 Burlington Gardens, London W1

A mere handful of places with facilities for parents with small children is not much of a testimony for a sector of the 'leisure industry' which very much aims to attract the family through its doors. Many owners and administrators could not be bothered to answer our queries and we intend to research this sector in more detail for the next edition of the Guide. We hope you will write to us and give us the benefit of your experiences at these places – good or bad.

STORES AND SUPERMARKETS

Very few of the large stores and supermarkets are in any way interested in providing basic facilities for parents out and about with small children. After all, most of them do not even provide lavatories for their customers let alone changing tables or feeding areas for mothers with babies.

The exceptions are some large department stores which often provide 'mothers' rooms' within or attached to their ladies' lavatories. For example in London, Harrods, Peter Jones and nearly all the Oxford Street stores have reasonable facilities. John Lewis in their other branches (Peterborough, Bristol, Liverpool, Reading, Sheffield, Nottingham and Milton Keynes) also have facilities of various kinds.

The major supermarket chains whose customers are primarily women, and particularly mothers with small children, and who spend quite a long time in these shops, have no interest in providing changing or feeding areas. The usual explanations for this lack of interest in their customers' comfort and well-being are clap-trap:

> 'We would have to reduce our selling space and the cost would inevitably be passed on to all our customers.'

> 'Shops simply do not have space to set aside appropriate areas ensuring adequate privacy.'

> 'As the average length of stay in supermarkets is relatively short, the need to provide special facilities has not been considered a priority.'

Not much consolation for a mother with an armful of groceries and a wet, smelly baby.

It is noticeable that even Mothercare, who describe themselves as 'the acknowledged specialist and market leaders in the mother-to-be and baby business', have no special facilities for mothers with small babies.

The executives of store groups pay cursory lip-service to their customers' needs by saying that their staff will always help 'in an emergency'. This is simply not true. We have tested this willingness to help in a random way and, although a manageress in a Marks and Spencer store passed the examination with credit, the staff at other supermarkets and stores were uncomprehending and unhelpful. So, our advice is to ask for such help without any hesitation when you need it: if you do not get help complain loudly and long until it is provided; and follow this up with a written complaint to Big Brother (head office).

TRAVEL

Motorway Service Areas

The forty or so service areas on the motorway system are traditionally denigrated, but their standards are improving in some ways. Many of them have been smartened up and, instead of offering just egg, sausage and chips (cold, usually) or steak and kidney pie (congealed and cold), they are actually displaying good selections of salads, fresh fruit and, very occasionally, wholemeal bread, alongside the usual fare. The main operators – THF, Granada, Motoross, Rank and Roadchef – almost invariably offer well-equipped mother and baby rooms, high chairs, children's menus and/or half portions and their staff will heat baby food and bottles if customers ask them.

The exceptions to this rule are:

Bothwell Service Area – M74 Southbound Bothwell, Lanarks – Baby room and children's menu, but no high chairs.

Harthill Service Area – M8, Harthill, Shotts, Lanarks – Baby room and children's menu, but no high chairs.

Killington Lake Service Area – M6 southbound, near Kendal, Cumbria – no facilities.

Scotch Corner Service Area – A1/M south of Darlington – no facilities.

Railway Stations

We questioned about 100 of the station masters at main railway stations. Some of these have well-equipped changing rooms or 'Nursing Mothers' Rooms' within the ladies' lavatories. In London they are: CHARING CROSS, KINGS CROSS, LIVERPOOL STREET and WATERLOO. And in the rest of the country: BLACKPOOL NORTH, BRIGHTON, BIRMINGHAM NEW STREET, EDINBURGH, GLASGOW CENTRAL and GLASGOW QUEEN STREET, LEEDS and SHEFFIELD.

Apart from these small offerings, mothers have to fend for themselves, but one of the advantages of British Rail is the existence of Ladies' Waiting Rooms. These are usually warm in winter and have tables and chairs. A baby can therefore be changed with ease, and breast-feeding accomplished in semi-privacy.

Airports
LONDON HEATHROW

Terminal 3 has basic facilities which, by most travel standards are pretty good: a quiet, private room for feeding; changing shelves, cooking facilities, potties and lavatories and enough space for older children to sit and play.

A new mother and baby room with the same facilities has recently been installed in Terminal 2.

The Terminal 1 facilities make all others pale into insignificance – if ever you are held up at Heathrow, make for this haven. It is beautifully decorated throughout and offers:

> excellent changing tables
>
> quiet room with two cots and baby alarm
>
> fully-equipped kitchen
>
> comfortable nursing room
>
> washing machine and drier
>
> child-size lavatories and pots
>
> prams and high chairs
>
> playpen
>
> many games and toys, paper and colouring pens
>
> special tables and chairs for children (including a 'Lego' table)
>
> nappy dispenser

It should be emphasised that these excellent facilities are for 'departure' babies only.

LONDON GATWICK

There are three nursery rooms: on the third floor of Arrivals – it is accessible to men as well as women and has changing tables, wash basins and partitioned feeding areas with comfortable chairs.

The other two rooms are within the Ladies' lavatories in Departures – one on the 3rd floor and the other on the ground floor. Both have changing tables, partitioned feeding areas, a small cooker and a playpen.

MANCHESTER

Manchester Airport has a nursery in the international departures area with facilities for changing and feeding a baby. It is not accessible to people arriving.

LUTON

There is a nursing mothers' room at the terminal.

EDINBURGH

The nursing mothers' room is on the main concourse with wash basin, changing table, lavatory, couch and playpen.

PRESTWICK

Nursing mothers' rooms in both arrivals and departures.

NEWCASTLE

Nursing mothers' room in ladies' lavatories.

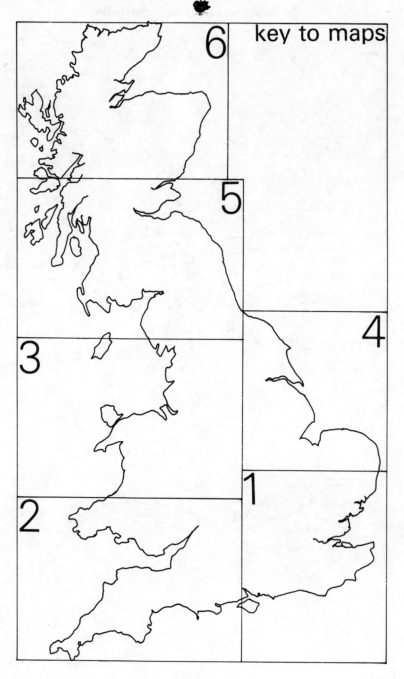

key to maps

6

5

4

3

1

2

WARWICK
• Brandon HR

NORTHAMPTON

Huntingdon HR   Needingworth P
Buckden H   • St Ives R
• Bar Hill H
• Cambridge HR
• Trumpington P

CAMBRIDGE

Long
Melford
HP

Tempsford PR

BEDFORD

Castle
Hedingham P

Wroxton St Mary H
Banbury H •

Thaxted R •   Great Bardfield H

Buckingham HPR   Woburn H   HERTFORD

Great Dunmow H

BUCKINGHAM

• Chesterton R

Aston
Clinton H
Weston-on-the-Green HP • Aylesbury HR •   Redbourn H
Woodstock HR
Stoke Mandeville P
St Albans P
• Oxford HR
Fyfield P •   Clifton Hampden P   • Chipperfield H
Abingdon HR •   Bledlow P •   Amersham
HR

OXFORD

Fingest P
Marlow H
Fawley R •   Cookham
Henley HR R • Bray HR
East Ilsley P •   Water Oakley H •   Windsor HR

GREATER
LONDON

Heathrow H

• Richmond R

Pangbourne HPR •

BERKSHIRE
Binfield P •
Newbury H •   • Woolhampton P
Bagshot HR
Chobham P
Sherborne St John P •   Ripley P •   • East Horsley H
Wotton R •   • Dorking H

Sunninghill HR •
Cobham H
• Sanderstead H

Tonbridge H •

Box Hill HR

SURREY   Charlwood H •
HAMPSHIRE   Chiddingfold PR   Gatwick H •
Rusper H •   Crawley HR E A S T
Haslemere H •

SUSSEX

Sparsholt H

Adversane R   Bolney R •   Cuckfield P   Blackboys P
Midhurst HR   WEST   Chailey P •   Framfield R
Byworth P   SUSSEX   Isfield P
Horton Heath P   • Bramber R   • Magham Down
Hedge End HR   Shedfield H   Walberton H   Berwick Station P
• Botley R   • Chichester HPR   Alfriston HR •   Milton Street P
Wickham H   Brighton H •   • Eastbourne H
Hamble R   East
Preston R

Isle of Wight

SUFFOLK

Woodbridge H

●Lavenham HPR

Ipswich H

udbury HR

Dedham P ● Harwich R

Maldon H

● Canterbury H

K E N T

● Dover H
Folkestone H
● Biddenden P
Hythe H

Rye H

astings HR

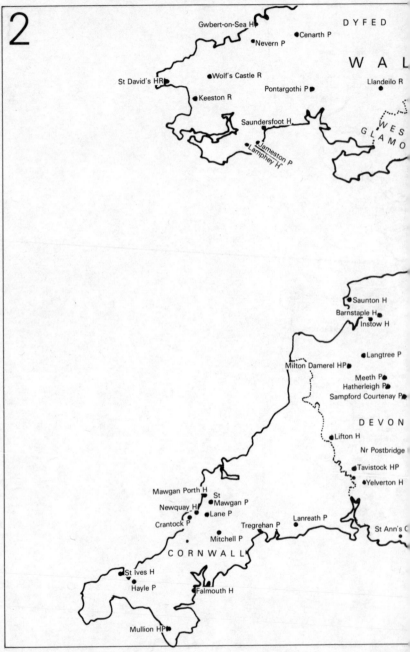

2

Gwbert-on-Sea H
Nevern P
Cenarth P
DYFED
WAL
Wolf's Castle R
Llandeilo R
St David's HR
Pontargothi P
Keeston R
WES
GLAMO
Saundersfoot H
Jameston P
Lamphey H

Saunton H
Barnstaple H
Instow H
Langtree P
Milton Damerel HP
Meeth P
Hatherleigh P
Sampford Courtenay P
DEVON
Lifton H
Nr Postbridge
Tavistock HP
Yelverton H
Mawgan Porth H
St
Mawgan P
Newquay H
Lane P
Lanreath P
Crantock P
Tregrehan P
St Ann's C
Mitchell P
CORNWALL
St Ives H
Hayle P
Falmouth H
Mullion HP

Hay-on-Wye R

Three Cocks H
Llangammarch Wells H

S

P O W Y S

Abergavenny HPR

M I D

GLAMORGAN

Newport R

Bretforton P
Broadway HR

Hereford HR

H E R E F O R D A N D
W O R C E S T E R

Corse Lawn R   Winchcombe R

Nr Ross-on-Wye HR

Southam HR

WARWICK

Moreton-in-Marsh H

Tewkesbury H

Stow-on-
the-Wold
PR

Chipping
Norton HP

Upper Slaughter HR

G L O U C E S T E R

O X F O R D

G W E N T

Rodborough
Common H

Stinchcombe
HR

Westonbirt H

Aust P

Dunkirk H

Tormarton P

Amberley
HPR

Nailsworth P
Kingscote P

Tetbury H

Malmesbury H

Castle Combe HP

Cirencester H

Lechlade P

Clanfield P

Hungerford
HPR

A V O N

Bath HPR

Compton
Martin P

Hinton Charterhouse R

Norton
St Philip P

Litton P

Woolverton P

Beanacre R

Seend
Cleeve P

Marlborough
HR

Pewsey R

Everleigh P

Porlock P

Dunster HR

Bilbrook HR

Monksilver P

S O M E R S E T

Shapwick H

Oakhill R

W I L T S H I R E

Amesbury HPR

Bishops Lydeard P

Norton Fitzwarren P

wear P

Taunton HP

Barrington P

Tiverton R   Dinnington P

Lapford P

Weston H

Cheriton
Bishop P

Exeter H

hagford H   Sidford P

Moretonhampstead H

East
Lambrook
P

Stoke-
sub-Hamdon P

Chedington P

Ottery St Mary H   Charmouth H

Swyre P

Abbotsbury P

Moonfleet H

Hindon HR

Fonthill
Bishop P

Shaftesbury H

D O R S E T

Plush P

Ansty P

Salisbury H

Romsey H

Tarrant
Monkton
P

Ibsley
P

Linwood P

Pimperne H

Horton PR

Wimbourne
Minster H

Ferndown
H

Dorchester HP

Burley
HPR

Brockenhurst
HPR

Mudeford H

Bournemouth H

olne P

Ipplepen P

Torquay H
Paignton H
Stoke Gabriel H
Dartington R

Thurlestone H

Exmouth H

Dawlish H

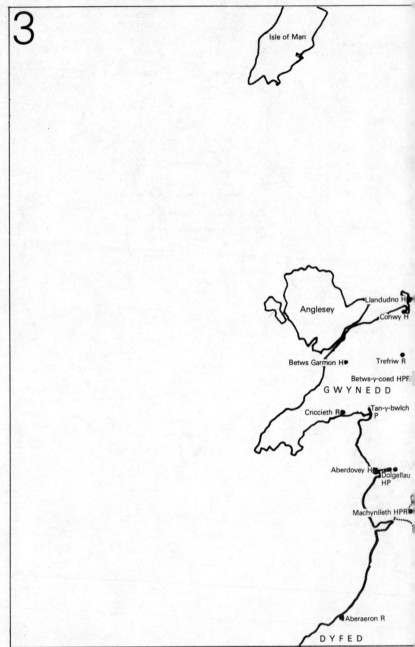

3

Isle of Man

Anglesey

Llandudno H
Conwy H

Trefriw R

Betws Garmon H

Betws-y-coed HPF.

G W Y N E D D

Criccieth R
Tan-y-bwlch
P

Aberdovey H
Dolgellau
HP

Machynlleth HPR

Aberaeron R

D Y F E D

Newby Bridge HPR●

Cartmel Fell P

C U M B R I A

Thirsk HR●

Cartmel
P

●Chapel-le-Dale P

NORTH YORKSHIRE

Melling HPR●

●Forton P

Gisburn H

Gargrave P●

Harrogate H●

Addingham P●

Oxenhope P●

W E S T   Y O R K S H I R E

Clifton P

L A N C A S H I R E

Parbold R

Bromley Cross HR

G R E A T E R   M A N C H E S T E R

S O U T H
Y O R K S H I R E

MERSEYSIDE

Knutsford R●
Plumley PR

D E R B Y

●Hurdlow P

●Baslow HR

Bodfari P◄

C H E S H I R E
●Chester HR

Wincle P●

Beeley P●

Congleton R●

Llanrhaeadr HR●

◄Ruthin HR

C L W Y D

Shocklach P

Nantwich
R
●

Dovedale HR●

Matlock
Bath H

Llangollen HPR●

Glyn Ceiriog HPR●

Llanarmon D.C.●
PR

◄Oswestry H

Llanyblodwel
P

Weston under
Redcastle HR

E N G L A N D

STAFFORDSHIRE

W A L E S

Shrewsbury HPR●

●Newtown
HR

Caersws HR●

S A L O P

W E S T
M I D L A N D S

Sutton Coldfield H

Kinver P●

●Birmingham H

P O W Y S

Hopton
Wafers P

Stone HR●

Ludlow HR●

Presteigne HR●

Leominster HPR●

◄Abberley HR

Hallow P●

W A R W I C K

Billesley H●

Llandrindod
Wells HPR●

H E R E F O R D
A N D   W O R C E S T E R

●Claines P

Stratford
upon Avon H

Welford-on-Avon P

L E I C E S T E R

261

CLEVELAND
● Hackness H
● Wrelton R
Rosedale Abbey PR●

NORTH YORKSHIRE
● Helmsley HPR

● York HPR   HUMBERSIDE

Beverley HPR●

SOUTH
YORKSHIRE

● Bawtry R

E N G L A N D
● Barnby Moor HPR   ● Lincoln HR

LINCOLN

N O T T I N G H A M

Blakeney H ●

● Grantham HPR

Cottesmore P●
Rothley H●   ●Stamford HR

Uppingham HP●

LEICESTER   CAMBRIDGE   Thetford H ●
●Oundle H
N O R T H A M P T O N

4

N O R T H   S E A

FIFE

North Berwick H
Gullane HR

LOTHIAN
Wester Howgate PR

Eddleston R

BORDERS

Peebles H

Selkirk HR   Kelso H

Jedburgh R

Longframlington R

Longhorsley HPR

NORTHUMBERLAND

Chollerford H   Gosforth H

TYNE AND WEAR

Wetheral HPR

Blanchland H

CUMBRIA   DURHAM

CLEVELAND

Bassenthwaite H

Coatham Mundeville H

Loweswater P   Watermillock H

ENGLAND

Borrowdale H

Eskdale   Grasmere HPR   Rydal HPR
Green P   Elterwater P   Ambleside R
Hawkshead P   Windermere H   NORTH YORKSHIRE
Near Sawrey P   Bowness H   Northallerton PR

6

HIGHLAND

• Strathcarron R

S C O T

• Kentallen R

S T R A T H C L Y D E

C E N T R A L

Nairn H · · Brodie R

· Rothes H

GRAMPIAN

ichity PR

· Tomintoul R   · Kildrummy HR

L A N D

· Pitlochry H

Kinloch Rannoch H

TAYSIDE   · Auchterhouse HR

Kinclaven H

READERS' COMMENTS

Please use this sheet to recommend hotels, pubs and restaurants which you think should be considered for the next edition of the Guide. The basic facilities we look for are:

> Hotels – cots, high chairs, baby-listening service
> Pubs – separate children's or family room
> Restaurants – high chairs and children's menus and/or reduced portions

Comments, adverse or otherwise, are welcome about any of the current Guide's entries.

To: The Editors, The Peaudouce Family Welcome Guide, c/o Hamer Books Ltd, 35 Brompton Road, London SW3 1DE

Full name and address of establishment:

....

....

....

....

Phone number:

....

Recommendation/Complaint ....

....

....

....

....

....

....

....

....

....

Name and address of sender: ....

....

....

....

We regret that we cannot acknowledge these forms, but they will be properly considered.

READERS' COMMENTS

Please use this sheet to recommend hotels, pubs and restaurants which you think should be considered for the next edition of the Guide. The basic facilities we look for are:

> Hotels – cots, high chairs, baby-listening service
> Pubs – separate children's or family room
> Restaurants – high chairs and children's menus and/or reduced portions

Comments, adverse or otherwise, are welcome about any of the current Guide's entries.

To: The Editors, The Peaudouce Family Welcome Guide, c/o Hamer Books Ltd, 35 Brompton Road, London SW3 1DE

Full name and address of establishment:

....

....

....

....

Phone number:

....

Recommendation/Complaint ....

....

....

....

....

....

....

....

....

Name and address of sender: ....

....

....

....

We regret that we cannot acknowledge these forms, but they will be properly considered.

READERS' COMMENTS

*Please use this sheet to recommend hotels, pubs and restaurants which
you think should be considered for the next edition of the Guide. The
basic facilities we look for are:*

> Hotels – cots, high chairs, baby-listening service
> Pubs – separate children's or family room
> Restaurants – high chairs and children's menus and/or reduced
> portions

*Comments, adverse or otherwise, are welcome about any of the current
Guide's entries.*

*To: The Editors, The Peaudouce Family Welcome Guide, c/o Hamer
Books Ltd, 35 Brompton Road, London SW3 1DE*

Full name and address of establishment:

....

....

....

....

Phone number:

....

Recommendation/Complaint ....

....

....

....

....

....

....

....

....

....

Name and address of sender: ....

....

....

....

*We regret that we cannot acknowledge these forms, but they will be
properly considered.*

READERS' COMMENTS

Please use this sheet to recommend hotels, pubs and restaurants which you think should be considered for the next edition of the Guide. The basic facilities we look for are:

> Hotels – cots, high chairs, baby-listening service
> Pubs – separate children's or family room
> Restaurants – high chairs and children's menus and/or reduced portions

Comments, adverse or otherwise, are welcome about any of the current Guide's entries.

To: The Editors, The Peaudouce Family Welcome Guide, c/o Hamer Books Ltd, 35 Brompton Road, London SW3 1DE

Full name and address of establishment:

....

....

....

....

Phone number:

....

Recommendation/Complaint ....

....

....

....

....

....

....

....

....

....

Name and address of sender: ....

....

....

....

We regret that we cannot acknowledge these forms, but they will be properly considered.

READERS' COMMENTS

Please use this sheet to recommend hotels, pubs and restaurants which you think should be considered for the next edition of the Guide. The basic facilities we look for are:

> Hotels – cots, high chairs, baby-listening service
> Pubs – separate children's or family room
> Restaurants – high chairs and children's menus and/or reduced portions

Comments, adverse or otherwise, are welcome about any of the current Guide's entries.

To: The Editors, The Peaudouce Family Welcome Guide, c/o Hamer Books Ltd, 35 Brompton Road, London SW3 1DE

Full name and address of establishment:

....

....

....

....

Phone number:

....

Recommendation/Complaint ....

....

....

....

....

....

....

....

....

....

Name and address of sender: ....

....

....

....

We regret that we cannot acknowledge these forms, but they will be properly considered.

READERS' COMMENTS

Please use this sheet to recommend hotels, pubs and restaurants which you think should be considered for the next edition of the Guide. The basic facilities we look for are:

> Hotels – cots, high chairs, baby-listening service
> Pubs – separate children's or family room
> Restaurants – high chairs and children's menus and/or reduced portions

Comments, adverse or otherwise, are welcome about any of the current Guide's entries.

To: The Editors, The Peaudouce Family Welcome Guide, c/o Hamer Books Ltd, 35 Brompton Road, London SW3 1DE

Full name and address of establishment:

....

....

....

....

Phone number:

....

Recommendation/Complaint ....

....

....

....

....

....

....

....

....

....

Name and address of sender: ....

....

....

....

We regret that we cannot acknowledge these forms, but they will be properly considered.